SECOND DEGREE

From Med School to Murder:
The Story Behind the Shocking
Will Sandeson Trials

KAYLA HOUNSELL

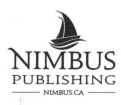

NIMBUS
PUBLISHING
— NIMBUS.CA —

Nimbus Publishing Limited
3660 Strawberry Hill Street, Halifax, NS, B3K 5A9
(902) 455-4286 nimbus.ca

Printed and bound in Canada

NB1739

Editor, *Second Degree*: Angela Mombourquette
Editor, *First Degree*: Elaine McCluskey
Design: Jenn Embree

Nimbus Publishing is based in Kjipuktuk, Mi'kma'ki, the traditional territory of the Mi'kmaq People.

Library and Archives Canada Cataloguing in Publication

Title: Second degree : from med school to murder, the story behind the shocking Will Sandeson trials / Kayla Hounsell.
Other titles: First degree
Names: Hounsell, Kayla, author.
Description: Expanded & updated edition. | Revision of: First degree.
Identifiers: Canadiana (print) 20240393198 | Canadiana (ebook) 2024039321X | ISBN 9781774712771 (softcover) | ISBN 9781774712924 (ePUB)
Subjects: LCSH: Sandeson, Will, 1992- | LCSH: Samson, Taylor (Taylor Dean James), 1993-2015. | LCSH: Murder—Nova Scotia—Halifax. | LCSH: Trials (Murder)—Nova Scotia—Halifax. | LCSH: Murder victims—Nova Scotia—Halifax.
Classification: LCC HV6535.C3 H68 2024 | DDC 364.152/309716225—dc23

Nimbus Publishing acknowledges the financial support for its publishing activities from the Government of Canada, the Canada Council for the Arts, and from the Province of Nova Scotia. We are pleased to work in partnership with the Province of Nova Scotia to develop and promote our creative industries for the benefit of all Nova Scotians.

For Kyrah.

With so much tragedy and heartache around us, you are a constant reminder of all that is good in this world.

CONTENTS

Introduction   7

CHAPTER 1   Interrogation   9
CHAPTER 2   Who Was Taylor Samson?   33
CHAPTER 3   Who Is William Sandeson?   51
CHAPTER 4   A Voluntary Witness   61
CHAPTER 5   Preparing for Trial   75
CHAPTER 6   The Crown's Case: Family First   89
CHAPTER 7   The Crown's Case: Police Work   101
CHAPTER 8   The Crown's Case: Witness to Murder   126
CHAPTER 9   Application for Mistrial   147
CHAPTER 10   The Crown's Case: Friend or Foe   167
CHAPTER 11   The Crown's Case: Searching the Farm   173
CHAPTER 12   The Crown's Case: Forensics   179
CHAPTER 13   The Crown's Case: Motive for Murder   188
CHAPTER 14   In His Own Defence   194
CHAPTER 15   Verdict   203
CHAPTER 16   The Appeal...And Other Legal Matters   208
CHAPTER 17   The Bitcoin Factor   230
CHAPTER 18   New Lawyer in Town   241
CHAPTER 19   In His Own Words   250
CHAPTER 20   Convicted...Again   279
CHAPTER 21   Where Are They Now?   291

Epilogue   312
Note About Sources   318
Acknowledgements   319

INTRODUCTION

In January 2023, as William Sandeson's retrial in the death of Taylor Samson was getting underway in Halifax, I was in Africa. I had made the difficult decision not to be in court after following this case very closely for nearly eight years. Instead, I was in Kenya, working with Journalists for Human Rights—a Canadian media-development organization near and dear to my heart. I was working alongside local journalists in human rights reporting, helping them work to hold governments to account and to include the voices of those most affected. It's a great passion of mine—one I've had since my first trip to Africa, when I was still a journalism student visiting Rwanda in 2006.

While the work and the stories could not have been more different than covering a court case in Nova Scotia, my motivation was similar. At home in Nova Scotia, I had always wanted to give voice to the victims of crime, including Taylor Samson. I felt those who loved him deserved a chance to tell their story—the whole story.

As January turned to February, I was finally settling into my new role in Nairobi, when I got the news Sandeson was taking the stand in his own defence. I was immediately torn between the deeply meaningful work I had committed to in Africa for several months and the drama unfolding back home.

I was able to follow the developments in real time online. Nova Scotians began reaching out to me, asking if there would be another book. I told several of them no.

But soon the verdict was in—William Sandeson had been convicted again, but this time of second-degree murder, not first-degree. The jury didn't believe he'd *planned* to kill Samson—a significant change.

I began to think I had a responsibility to update this book, to ensure that the most complete version of the facts was the one I put out into the world. I had also been in touch with Samson's mother, Linda Boutilier, at various points throughout the trial. I didn't want to ask her to do this again. She had already given me so much—so much time, so much trust. Then one day, she asked me if I was considering another book. I asked her if she'd be willing to do another interview. She said she would.

At that moment, I knew there would be another book. I reached out to my publisher, Nimbus Publishing, and they readily agreed. What you are about to read is the result.

It is not a play-by-play of the second trial. I was not there. Besides, most of what occurred was similar to the first trial, about which I have already written. Rather, this is a work of original journalism based partially on audio tapes from the retrial and on my own observations from the years in between, from the months of bail hearings and pretrial negotiations that I did attend, as well as from court documents I've unearthed, fresh research, and nineteen new in-depth interviews.

This is my best effort to capture the most complete version of events. It includes William Sandeson's version—now told to a court of law in his own words—and Linda Boutilier's. Her truth is that she still longs for the return of her son's remains and for people to know he was not "just another drug dealer."

Kayla Hounsell, October 2024

CHAPTER 1
INTERROGATION

Constable Jody Allison of the RCMP major crime unit was in Ottawa arresting someone for a bank robbery when he received a call asking him to come home to Halifax to interview a twenty-two-year-old man in relation to a missing persons case.

After landing at the airport outside Halifax, a coastal capital with a population of just over four hundred thousand, Allison drove straight to police headquarters on Gottingen Street, arriving at roughly 11:30 P.M. on August 18, 2015. Another officer was interviewing William Sandeson. Allison had a brief meeting with the lead investigators and then went home to catch a few hours of sleep before returning to the police station at 6:00 A.M.

One of the first things investigators learned about Sandeson was that he was interested in medicine. Allison knew he had been accepted to Dalhousie University's medical school and was about to start classes any day. He also knew Sandeson had spent some time at a med school in the Caribbean. He decided to use this information as a strategy.

William Sandeson, who often goes by Will, was already waiting for Constable Allison in an interview room, but he had no idea what was about to occur. The five-foot-ten, 150-pound blond-haired, blue-eyed varsity athlete worked at a group home for adults who live with disabilities. He had no criminal record.

Jody Allison, clean-shaven with salt-and-pepper short hair, enters the twelve-by-twelve interrogation room in plain clothes—pants and a collared shirt with a sport jacket, no tie. He's not a big guy. The room contains two chairs; cameras are mounted on the walls. Sandeson's chair is bolted down, the other chair is on wheels. There is one door into the room, which is usually locked.

"How's it going there, Will?" Allison introduces himself as an officer with the RCMP in Halifax and tells Sandeson he's looking a little bit scared or nervous. He asks Sandeson if he knows why he's been arrested. Sandeson, wearing sneakers, beige pants, and a blue-green T-shirt, says he does. At this point, he's being questioned for kidnapping, trafficking, and misleading police.

"You were in your first year of being a medical doctor, right? So I take it that you're somewhat educated," Allison begins. Sandeson says he's completed five years of post-secondary school.

The officer asks him if he's ever watched *CSI*. Sandeson says he doesn't have a TV, but Allison continues his point.

"Okay, but you would be familiar, I mean, *CSI*, a lot of what you see on that program is true; it's just that some of the stuff takes a little longer, you know? They get it done in a half an hour in the show, where it takes, in real life, a lot longer than that."

Allison explains to Sandeson that officers have already entered his apartment. He describes how police use DNA samples and fingerprints.

"There's nobody else that has the same fingerprint as me," Allison says. "Nobody else." He tells Sandeson that fingerprints used to be the "gold standard," that no matter what you do to your finger, your fingerprint will grow back the same. "But you know all this," he tells the promising young man seated before him.

Then Allison moves on to DNA, explaining that one of the first times it was used in Canada was in the case of Allan Legere, a New Brunswick serial killer. Legere killed five people between 1986 and 1989, when he was finally arrested. Due to the brutality of his crimes, he became known as "the Monster of the Miramichi."

"I know the guy," Allison tells Sandeson, explaining that DNA was used to convict Legere. "There's always something that the suspect leaves behind," he goes on, "and there's always something that the suspect takes with them."

Sandeson just sort of nods in agreement.

Allison also tells Sandeson that experts can do calculations to figure out what happened, based on how much blood there is and where it landed. Sandeson seems to be following along, chiming in that he knows they can determine things based on the velocity of the spatter. Allison adds that even if people try to clean up, blood may still be there years later.

It seems to be a warning of some kind, but the officer also seems to be trying to bond with Sandeson, telling him he has an aunt who lives with a disability and that he knows it takes a special kind of person to work with people who have disabilities, as Sandeson does.

"I give props to anybody that can go in there and have the patience, and basically a good heart. I think you've got a good heart," Allison tells Sandeson. "I think that sometimes people, for whatever reason, they make some mistakes."

By all accounts, William Sandeson comes from a good family. His parents own a farm in Truro, his mother works for the Nova Scotia government in the agriculture department and was the president of the local Rotary Club. He is the eldest of four boys. Unlike Allan Legere, he has never been in trouble with the law.

"There's times for whatever reason that things don't go quite as planned," Allison continues. "Actually, if you think about it, things never go quite as planned, right, Will? They never go quite as planned."

Then it comes back to the medicine. It always comes back to the medicine. Allison asks Sandeson what specifically his aspirations are, whether he wants to be a GP, a surgeon, or something else. Sandeson responds with two words only: "sports medicine."

Allison acknowledges that that will take a long time, nearly a decade of Sandeson's life, while his buddies are all out making money. "So why does anyone want to become a doctor?" Allison asks. "Because they genuinely want to help people." That's when he produces the Hippocratic oath, a pledge taken by doctors in which they swear to uphold certain ethical standards. "You must have read it before, right?"

Sandeson says he knows the synopsis.

"The thing about it is that this whole thing is based around helping other people," the officer tells Sandeson, going on to draw out certain points from the lengthy script. "When you're looking after the patient, you don't do them any harm."

Then for the first time, Allison mentions the man who is missing—six-foot-five, 220-pound Taylor Samson, a physics student at Dalhousie.

"Do you know Taylor's brother?"

"I didn't really know Taylor."

"Taylor's brother has an intellectual disability. He's missing his brother and he's a mess. Somebody's got to explain to him what happened, what happened to Taylor."

Sandeson stares in silence.

Allison continues, telling Sandeson he knows things aren't always as they appear. He uses an analogy, trying to compare a doctor's work to that of a police officer. "It's sort of like when somebody comes into the emergency room and presents with a chest pain. You're the attending physician, and you're trying to figure out their symptoms...you're doing an investigation. You're trying to get a picture of what's going on with this person, and that's the same thing we do," he says.

Silence.

"Do I think that you're one of these guys who goes around doing this stuff all the time? No. Unless I'm wrong."

Silence.

"I know you're a good guy because you were going to swear that oath. You work in a home for people with intellectual disabilities. You're a good guy."

There's a knock at the door.

It's breakfast.

Allison continues, pulling out some photos of Taylor Samson and his brother, Connor. He proceeds to read Sandeson a post taken from Connor's Facebook page.

"'There was a little boy inside the man who is my brother. Oh, how I hated that little boy when I was one also, and how I loved him too at the same time. If anyone has seen or heard from my brother, Taylor, please let me or my mother know.'"

Then Allison tries to turn the tables, asking Sandeson to imagine how he would feel if his girlfriend went missing.

"Is she okay now?" Sandeson asks. "I know they picked her up."

"Yes, she's fine," Allison responds, before returning to his narrative.

"You're a good person. Do you maybe buy some weed once in a while and sell some weed? Yeah."

Allison explains that he knows about weed, he used to be in the Guns and Gangs unit. He says lots of people sell weed for whatever reason. "But Will, the difference here is that when most people meet up, one person doesn't go missing."

Silence.

"Will, you're at a crossroads right now. One way is going to take you in a certain direction, the other way is going to take you in a direction you don't want to go."

Still nothing.

"You're a mess. Did you sleep last night?"

Sandeson shakes his head.

"Not a wink," reiterates Allison.

He tells Sandeson that he had trouble sleeping because he's a good guy. "The bad guys—the monsters, Will—they have no trouble sleeping."

Allison is trying to be his friend. "Will, you know I'm not lying to you. I'm not trying to trick you." No matter the tactic, nothing gets Sandeson talking.

"I want to help, but I just want to talk to the lawyer first," Sandeson says.

Allison explains that he's already had that opportunity.

"Twenty pounds of weed, that's a lot of money, right?" Allison asks, although he already knows the answer. (Police later estimated its worth at $90,000.)

"But for what happened, do you think twenty pounds of weed is worth that? What's your heart tell you? Your heart tells you, William, that two million pounds of weed is not worth that, right?"

Sandeson again says he just wants a lawyer to help him articulate what he needs to say.

"Something you've got to remember is that if you tell the truth, you don't have to remember. Ever."

Sandeson agrees, pointing out that his dad says there's no such thing as a good liar because no one has a perfect memory.

Allison reminds him that the interview is being recorded, so if he can't remember his story two months from now, police will still have the tape.

"Saturday morning, did you wake up saying that you were going to be involved in a big racket? You know what I'm saying? Did you wake up—*boom!* 'I think I'm going to do some crazy stuff tonight'?"

Sandeson is silent. Allison notes he's crying.

"Are you concerned about the trafficking?"

"Not as much as I'm concerned about finding Taylor."

"Well then, why don't you tell us what happened?"

"I don't know how much help I can be, and how much it's going to hurt me."

"What the police see, what we think happened, that may not be the way it happened and, Will, you need to speak up and say what the heck happened."

Sandeson is showing his intelligence, asking why he can't speak to a lawyer. Allison tells him again that he already has. Sandeson says the lawyer told him not to say anything and he continues asking questions about what will happen if he remains silent and how long he can be held, but Allison is undeterred. This will later become a problem for the police.

"Will, what happened to Taylor? Is he alive?"

Sandeson just stares ahead. Allison is speaking calmly, almost sympathetically. It's as though he thinks he's about to make a breakthrough.

"Tell me what happened. Was there other people involved?"

But Sandeson still isn't talking.

"Is Taylor alive? You know the answer to that."

Sandeson shakes his head. "I don't know."

It's now 11:15 A.M. on Wednesday. The interrogation has been under way for just over an hour and nothing has been achieved.

"Will, you're telling me you want to help him. Well, what's holding you back right now? We need to find out—"

Sandeson interrupts him, "As soon as possible, I know." He's crying harder now.

Allison presses on. "Was it just you and him, William? These are questions that are not difficult to answer."

Sandeson is looking at the floor.

"Did somebody force you to do this?"

There's a knock on the door, and someone passes in Kleenex. Will Sandeson is hunched over with his head in his hands.

"William, if you were in my shoes—" Allison starts.

Sandeson interrupts him again. "I'd be so mad at me for not talking."

Allison says he's not mad.

"I'd be so mad and frustrated," says Sandeson. "I wouldn't understand."

Allison becomes firm. "You know that something happened Saturday night, Will. Is there a chance he's still alive?"

"I think so."

"You're telling me you think he's still alive? Well, then, you better start talking. Doctors are logical people. Do you not see the logic in this whole thing?"

Sandeson blows his nose.

"What happened, Will? Who are you trying to protect?"

"Me, I guess," he sobs.

Now Allison reaches out to put his hand on the accused's shoulder. Whatever the intent, it seems to work. Sandeson starts talking.

"Someone came in my house," he begins. He is still sobbing when he starts his story—one that becomes, in the telling, more elaborate and implausible.

"When Taylor was there?" Allison asks.

Sandeson nods, but he won't say who came into his house.

"Okay, what happened when they came in?"

"They were wearing masks. One of them had a gun, just one of them. We were sitting at the kitchen table. We were counting the money."

Allison pulls his hand away. Sandeson is talking. This is what he wants.

"The door wasn't locked, so they just came in. I tried to run to my room 'cause I was on the far side of the table. I got hit on the back of the head. I heard more fighting. They were telling me to stay down, and I knew they had a gun." He looks up at the officer, before continuing, "I just stayed down. They all left at the same time, I think. There was a lot of blood."

Sandeson stops to blow his nose. He is sobbing hard and appears to be struggling to breathe.

Allison takes the opportunity to continue questioning.

"What did you say he hit you with?"

"I don't know, it felt, like, lumpy."

"Did you go down right away?"

"No, like, I turtled and crouched, and they just kept screaming, 'Get down,' and I tried to flatten out and then I got kicked in the head. And he was fighting, I'm sure he was fighting, and it was just this scuffle."

"How long were they there at your apartment?"

Sandeson cries and shakes his head, as though he's trying to figure out the answer. He eventually tells the officer he doesn't know. "They didn't even take all the money," he says. "What was bloody they just left in blood, so I put it in a bag and cleaned it, and I cleaned the blood."

"Cleaned the blood off the money?"

"No, no," says Sandeson, almost hysterical. "The bloody money's in that bag."

Allison tells Sandeson he hasn't been in his apartment and asks him about the layout. Sandeson offers to draw it. "There's a long hallway," he says as he begins drawing on the back of a file folder. "There's two doors here." He continues for a couple of minutes, drawing and mumbling to himself. Then, "The weed's in a sack over by Taylor."

Allison jumps in: "The weed's in a sack? Like what do you mean?"

"Huge, like the biggest bag I've ever seen. I don't know if it was a hockey bag, but the biggest thing I've ever seen."

He insists he doesn't know the people who were in his apartment.

"The guy with the gun was probably six feet. They were all in black, like black jeans. I only counted—it was three when I went down—I don't know if there were more," he says, sounding exasperated.

Allison wants to know how much money was on the table. Sandeson tells him there was $40,000 that the two planned to exchange for the twenty pounds of weed in the bag.

"Who knew that you and Taylor were meeting up?"

"No one should have."

"You know what I'm saying, for someone to randomly come into your place—"

"Right in the middle," says Sandeson, filling in the blank.

"Right in the middle of something like this," agrees Allison, the first sign he's not really buying Sandeson's story.

"How long were they there with Taylor?"

"It felt like forever, and I didn't get up until it was quiet."

"Which way did they go?"

"They went through the door. I don't know if he chased them or if they took him, but there was blood on the floor and money in the blood."

"So they just went right back out this way?" Allison says, referring to the drawing again.

"They had to," Sandeson replies, although he would later declare that the door wasn't the only entrance to his apartment.

"Do you have surveillance in here? Video surveillance?"

"I put cameras in, but they don't record."

"They don't record, hey?"

Sandeson shakes his head. "They're shitty," he says, explaining that he put them in after his friend was robbed. He goes on to say that he's already put in complaints about the system not working; that it's supposed to record for two days without interruption, but it's been recording over itself every twenty minutes.

"The thing about it—those things are like a computer hard

drive," Allison explains. "Chances are it's probably on there. They're actually checking it out, maybe even right now. So is that video going to show us pretty much what you told me?"

"Who goes up the hallway and who goes down the hallway," says Sandeson.

"Would there be blood anywhere else?"

"From me walking around probably—I don't know—I tried to clean it."

"Where else did you try and clean?"

"I walked into my room. I walked into the bathroom to wash my hands. I took a shower. I didn't go into my roommate's room."

"Did you buy a new curtain for your bathroom?"

"Yes."

"What'd you do with the old one?"

"Threw it out." The reason Sandeson threw out the shower curtain would become a point of interest during his trial.

"Will, are you being truthful with me about everything?"

Sandeson nods.

"'Cause in everything that you say there's a certain element of truth, but sometimes there's some things that are left out."

"I admitted everything. Ask more questions if I don't have enough detail."

At this point, Allison reminds Sandeson that as part of the investigation, officers will be speaking with a lot of other people.

Sandeson bows his head, gaze to the floor.

"Look at him," Allison says, reaching for a photo of Samson and his brother, previously discarded on the floor of the interrogation room.

Sandeson looks away, crying.

"William." Allison points to the image of Samson now placed on Sandeson's knees.

"Don't make me think you're a monster, bud. Tell me the truth."

The two become engaged in a silent standoff until the officer finally speaks. "You know where Taylor is."

"I don't know where he is!" Sandeson exclaims.

"Your body language is telling me something totally different."

Allison makes contact again, placing a hand on Sandeson's shoulder.

"Don't overthink it. Where do you think he is?"

"I'm trying. I've been trying to think, okay!"

"In your heart, where do you think he's at?"

"I think someone took him."

"Where did they take him?"

"I don't know where they took him. I don't know who took him. I don't know who came in. I don't know. I tried to find out where he got his stuff from."

"Here's the thing, Will; listen to me for a second. I want you to think about something here. How long was he at your apartment before this happened?"

"Not long."

"Around two o'clock in the morning, you started sending him texts—'Hey man this isn't cool'—right?"

The officer is suggesting Sandeson sent the texts to cover his tracks, to make it look like Samson was still alive, when he knew full well the texts would never be answered.

"So you start trying to cover up what happened. Just listen to me," Allison says.

"I'm listening. I'm listening. I'm listening," Sandeson replies.

"So within a few hours, you're trying to cover up what happened. You go, you buy a new shower curtain, you clean up, right?"

"'Cause I'm scared."

"What I'm saying to you is that your story is missing some pieces, some big pieces."

Sandeson's body is heaving with emotion, but he says nothing.

"What happened to the dope?"

"I dunno—same thing that happened to the money."

"Which was what?"

"It's gone."

"Here's a very simple question for you—when he left your apartment, was he alive? Yes or no."

"I don't know."

"Okay, well what do you know, Will? Do you know who these three people were?"

"No," he barely whispers.

"There wasn't three people was there?"

"Yes! There were."

Allison is adamant that if there were three people Sandeson had to know who they were, but Sandeson insists he does not know. Sandeson mentions an interview he had done the day before with a different investigator, RCMP sergeant Charla Keddy. At that time, he was a witness, not a suspect.

"Why'd you give a version of events then that's totally different?" Allison asks.

Sandeson had told the first officer he was supposed to meet up with Taylor Samson that night to buy a small amount of marijuana, but that Samson didn't show up.

"I was scared," he says in response to Allison's question.

Sandeson is now rocking in his chair with his hands clasped behind his head.

"You're a very intelligent man trying to make a version of events fit with what you think we have found. That's not how it works," Allison says.

But the officer still appears to have faith in Sandeson. He explains there are different kinds of people—some calculated and cunning, others just scared because they made a mistake and got tangled up in something that wasn't supposed to go that way.

"Did you not have enough money?" he asks. "What really happened? I don't see any bumps on your head."

Nothing is working.

Allison pulls out the Hippocratic oath again. He begins reciting, "'...the joy of healing those who seek my help.'"

"Did Taylor cry out for help? Did you hear him?" Allison's head is only inches from Sandeson's at this point. "Because if there was a big man, six-foot-five, 220 pounds, being taken somewhere he doesn't want to go, he'd be doing some screaming, right?"

He pauses again.

"Unless of course he couldn't scream."

The silence stretches on.

Allison tries to appeal to Sandeson's humanity, saying he knows he wants to help Samson's family and asking him to imagine what his own family would be going through if he were the one missing.

"The worst part for the families, Will, is the not knowing. I'm sure they have no idea what we found in that apartment, or what we found in your knapsack," he explains, pointing out Samson has now been missing for three and a half days.

Sandeson is not moving, bent over, his face shielded.

After three hours of interrogation, Constable Jody Allison is not getting the confession he's seeking.

Allison leaves the room.

When Sandeson is alone, he tucks the photos of Taylor Samson and his brother, Connor, inside the file folder. Then he sits quietly, picking at his fingers. Eventually, he begins to pace in the tiny room. He rubs a shoulder injury, which the police would also question him about, then lies on the floor for more than thirty minutes.

When Allison returns, he confronts Sandeson with photos from his apartment, telling him what the forensic identification team (also known as "Ident") has found doesn't match his story.

"I'm not sure what the plan was at the beginning of it, but I don't think it turned out quite the way that it was supposed to. If you're the ringleader in this, Will, if you're the master planner, that's one thing. If your part in this was something different, then that's quite another."

Then Allison starts questioning Sandeson about the others involved, explaining that, whoever they are, they'll drag him down with them. "It's a race to the finish line, so I think it's time that you reassessed what you told me."

But he doesn't.

"Are you the mastermind in this?"

Sandeson shakes his head.

"Did you know that your phone pings off cellphone towers even when you're not making and receiving calls?" Allison asks.

"When you said you cleaned up, how good a job do you think you did?" Allison asks, flipping through a stack of photos he's holding.

"Probably awful."

"Awful, yeah, I would say."

"You have a firearm registered to you, right?"

Sandeson said that he did, and that he'd used it to shoot targets.

"Do you know where your firearm is right now?"

"I don't know if you have it in your possession or not."

"Would we have it in our possession if we searched your apartment?"

"Yeah, it's stored in my safe."

Allison resumes flipping through photos of Sandeson's apartment. "What'd they find in the bathroom?" He points to an image showing what looks like blood spatter. "What happened in there?"

Allison flips through more photos. "Look at this. There's still blood on the money, for God's sake, Will, there's blood on the money. That's blood money."

Sandeson sobs. He's shaking.

"If you were used in this to set this thing up then you gotta say, 'cause I'm having a hard time making the leap between somebody who wants to be a doctor, who helps out at group homes, to this happening."

Allison is now clearly playing "good cop," in the typical good cop/bad cop scenario, telling Sandeson that he's trying to explain to the other officers that he doesn't believe Sandeson is the ringleader. "'This guy is a good guy, he's going to be a doctor, for Christ's sake,'" he says, begging Sandeson to help him make the others understand.

The sobbing is intensifying rapidly.

Allison tells Sandeson he will feel so much better once he talks. "You've got so much weight on you right now, so much weight."

Allison pulls his chair even closer to Sandeson.

"Get a grip on yourself, okay. Listen to me, listen to my voice. Calm down, okay. Take a couple of deep breaths. We'll go through this together."

Allison acknowledges Sandeson is trying to talk but can't because he's sobbing so hard.

"I think I'm going to pass out."

The officer tells him to sit up, acknowledging he's under a lot of stress.

"Tell me who was there besides you. Your next-door neighbour, was he there?" Sandeson doesn't answer the question, but his next-door neighbour will become a key player in his case.

"This is the moment of truth here, bud. I think it's time that you set the record straight here, right now."

When Sandeson says nothing, Allison presents him with still photos from his home-surveillance system, the one he'd suggested recorded over itself after twenty minutes. (Sandeson hadn't given them the password, but police had contacted the company that makes the system in China and found a back-door way to access it.)

"Do you recognize that as being from yours?"

Sandeson said that he did.

"And that's Taylor coming in, right?"

"Yes," he agreed.

Allison reminds Sandeson that the police are also talking to the other people seen on the video from his home DVR system. He notes the time stamp on the still images. It is 10:26 P.M. on August 15, 2015, when Taylor Samson walks into Sandeson's apartment carrying a big black duffle bag.

"I think you know exactly what happened to Taylor, right, Will? And I can tell by the way that you're acting right now that you feel horrible."

The crying starts again.

"When it was set up, was there intention to hurt him? To injure him? Were you told that they were gonna injure him?"

"No," is all Sandeson offers.

He puts his hand on Sandeson's shoulder again, telling him that he knows he's scared, but now is his chance.

"I want you to have your story of what happened inside that apartment out before somebody else gets it out and paints you with a brush that you're some evil genius."

Allison has been talking for nearly six hours.

"Whatever happened wasn't done very professionally, if you ask me. This looks like a bunch of amateurs." He notes there's blood on the table and chairs, the walls, and the money.

"Why don't you want to talk and tell me who else was there? Unless there was nobody else there." It's the first time he's mentioned the possibility Sandeson acted alone.

Sandeson rocks back and forth, his hands clasped between his legs now.

Allison explains that he can only give him so many opportunities to talk, and they're running out. He reaches for his stack of photos, flips to the images of Sandeson's phone, and begins reciting text messages Sandeson sent to Taylor Samson:

"I'm walking out now."

And later, "This isn't cool man. You said you'd be right back. Want that stuff."

"Do you know how bad this looks?" Allison demands, before returning to the texts.

"Yo man, Taylor's gone missing. Like he's being treated as a missing person by the police," Allison is reading a text someone else sent to Sandeson. "When's the last time you talked to him?" the person asks.

"Saw him Thursday to check out sample. Then nothing," Sandeson responds in the texts.

"Do you know how bad this looks?" Allison asks again. "Do you understand the predicament you're in, Will?

"Yes," Sandeson whispers, nodding with his head bowed.

"So why is it that you can't explain what happened? Why is it that you can't say who else was there? Why is it that you can't tell me where Taylor is? Who did he leave with, Will? Will, Will, who did he leave with?" Allison repeats it over and over like a mantra. It has no effect.

"Was it just gonna be a drug rip and then he got mad?" demands Allison.

Sandeson begins to get emotional again, and the officer pleads with him. "Stay with me...did he throw the first punch? He's a big man. Tell me about how it started."

Sandeson is now sobbing again.

"[Are] these guys going to harm somebody if you tell? Or are they really close to you, and you don't want to say?" Allison is throwing out every possible explanation.

Sandeson has now been under interrogation for seven hours.

"Let's get the people that fucked your life up. Who was it? Do you want to tell me what happened?"

"I want to say but I can't prove it."

"Don't worry about proving it," Allison says. "Who else was there? That's not for you to prove. That's for us to prove."

Sandeson cries harder.

"Okay, let's start with this—were they male?"

He nods.

"Okay, was one a Black male or a white male, or Hispanic?"

No response.

"Was there more than one male there? How about that?"

"Yes."

"Okay, so there's you, Taylor, and the two other males, so there's four people altogether?"

No response, but Allison forges on. He seems to be getting somewhere.

"Now, these other two males, are they friends of yours?"

Sandeson shakes his head no.

"Are they associated to you through drug transactions? How about let's start with one name? Just one name."

But the limited progress has come to a halt.

"Did you ever hear tell of the saying, 'hen's teeth. It's like pulling hen's teeth'? Very hard to get information," says Allison. "I'm trying to understand how this happened."

Then there's a knock on the door. Allison leaves and another officer enters. This is different. He's not patient, like Constable Allison, but firm, almost angry, from the outset. He's physically bigger, too, tall, with a commanding presence.

"Will, remember me—Detective Constable [Roger] Sayer? I spoke to you last night. Remember that?"

"Yup." (Sayer is a member of the Halifax Regional Police force. In Halifax, the RCMP and local police operate as an integrated unit.)

"I told you last night that I was one of the lead investigators on this file, and I've been here all day, all night, all week, okay? I've been watching you all day, and you've done nothing since I first saw you yesterday but lie. I told you that evidence would show that, and it has been doing it all day, and we haven't stopped collecting evidence. Do you understand that, Will?"

"Yes."

"Have not stopped," he continued. "And you sit in here and you keep going on and lying and lying and lying." He points to the growing pile of photos and documents on the floor and explains that, so far, the evidence disproves everything Sandeson has told police.

"Blood evidence. People come in and take twenty pounds of weed and $40,000 and they leave you what—a damage deposit? Not to mention the stack of twenties that's found in your bathroom underneath the garbage bag in your garbage can. Will, you need to start to get your head right, 'cause you think all this bullshit you're laying down—you think you're smarter than everybody that's working on this—you're making a very drastic mistake. Drastic."

Sandeson is quiet, listening intently.

"Jody believes in you. I tried to tell him 'cause I was in here last night and I saw what was what, but he believes that what you're trying to say is true. I don't."

It's clear Sayer is playing the "bad cop."

He picks up a photo. "There's blood on this table that somebody cleaned up and, like they always do because they all think they're smarter than they are, you wiped the top but don't think of the side. What's that going to be tested for?"

"DNA," Sandeson barely squeaks out.

"DNA," Sayer confirms.

"More blood," announces Sayer. "Blood on the chair. There's blood in your bathroom, on the floorboards, on the curtain. Your own words were that it happened in your kitchen area. How'd all that blood get in your bathroom?"

Sandeson keeps his gaze to the floor.

"Will, look at me. You're in here crying and going on, and you know what happened. There is nothing that I have seen in here today that suggests anybody showed up at that place. Nothing. That video runs for over an hour. No one comes, no one leaves. Then your system is turned off. If you think that people are that stupid, you're fooling yourself."

Sandeson is still silent.

"Listen, buddy, you don't have to be Columbo to figure out that between 11:33 and 1:00 A.M., when that system was turned off, is when he left—however he left."

Sayer tells Sandeson they've also seized his car. "How much of that do you think we need to find to get DNA," he asks, smacking a photograph of blood.

"Less than a drop," Sandeson replies meekly.

"Yup," Sayer responds. "And when we check your car, what if his DNA's in there? What's your story then? These mystery people made you drive him away?"

And then the interrogation takes another turn. "You're a liar—cold, calculating, and lying." He jabs at a photograph again, this one of Taylor Samson. "Where is this man?"

Sandeson sniffles and bows his head.

"Don't put your head down, man. Where is he?" He thrusts the photo of Samson under Sandeson's eyes. "What did you do to this man?"

He runs down the evidence police already have against him.

It's now almost 6:00 P.M.

"When you're in this room with people who are innocent, they kick and scream, bud."

Sandeson hangs his head.

"You crying and blowing in the Kleenex," he mocks, "like you're some kind of victim. You're a predator, bud."

Sayer's voice is aggressive, but slow and deliberate.

"I want to bring that man home to his family. Where is he?"

There is no crying now.

"You're done, bud. Done. There's no going past that, but you can do something right."

Sandeson still says nothing.

Another knock. Sayer gathers up the photos he's spread over the floor of the interrogation room. He places the one of Samson and his brother on the chair and sets it in front of Sandeson. "I'm going to leave and watch you push that away." He walks out.

Jody Allison is back in the room, playing "good cop." Sandeson is calm now. Allison wants to know more about the people who supposedly came into his apartment.

"Can you tell what time they showed up?"

Without hesitation, he responds, "Just after eleven."

Then he backtracks. "No, sorry, just after Taylor got there but they came through, they were in Dylan's room." Dylan Zinck-Selig was Sandeson's roommate, although he was rarely at the apartment, choosing instead to stay with his girlfriend.

"They were in Dylan's room?" Allison asks.

Sandeson explains that there's a window in Zinck-Selig's bedroom that can be used to access a roof where they used to keep a barbecue. Back with the good cop, Sandeson is telling his story, freely adding details. He says he knew the guys were in Dylan's room—that they were there as a "scare tactic"—to scare Samson out of dealing because he owed money.

"Okay, so these two guys that were in Dylan's room, so when you told me about—" Allison trails off.

"It's not the truth when I said they came through the front door," Sandeson finishes the statement. It won't be the last time he admits to lying.

"Okay, so tell me what happened when these two guys come out."

Sandeson stops now, bowing his head again.

"Was it the same as what you told me before?"

"Not exactly." He shakes his head. "I still retreated towards my room."

"And then what happened?"

"They were just talking to Taylor. Taylor didn't get up because they had a gun on him."

Then, he said, he shut off his surveillance system because these guys asked him to.

"So when they got you to do that, what happened next?"

A long silence ensues, and finally, "They put Taylor in the bag with the weed."

An outrageous twist.

"They put him in the bag with the weed?" Allison asks, incredulous.

Sandeson nods.

"Okay, what was going on with him when they put him in there? Like, was he dead or alive?"

Sandeson sinks his head into his hands again.

"'Cause a minute ago they were talking to him, right?"

"There was a gunshot. I didn't see what happened. Then there was a lot of blood. They put him in the bag and then went out."

"How do you know that they put him in the bag?"

"They left with the bag, and he wasn't there."

"How many gunshots did you hear?" Allison asks, pulling up a chair again.

"One."

"Now this bag, I remember you saying—"

Sandeson interrupts. "It was the biggest bag I've ever seen."

"Okay, so what kind of things are they saying to you when this is going on?"

"They weren't talking to me."

"No, but can you hear them? What are they saying to Taylor?"

"He was done."

"So they were saying to him, like you know, 'You're done,' and what was he saying back to them?"

"That he had money coming, like this was supposed to be a deal for both of us."

"What happened to the weed that was in that bag?"

"It stayed in the bag."

"And what did they do then?"

"They walked out the door."

"They went through the regular door, like down the stairs?"

He nods.

"Just pick one of them and describe him to me."

"Six-foot-ish, dressed all in black. They had like a Morphsuit face, like black Morphsuits."

"Morphsuits? I'm not sure what you mean by that."

Sandeson explains it's a spandex bodysuit that covers the whole body including the head, like members of the Blue Man Group wear.

"Did you see anything in their hands or on their hands?"

"They only had one gun between the two." (Sandeson had first told Allison there were three intruders.)

"Can you describe it to me, because I know you're familiar with guns?"

"It looked like mine except it was all black. The slide on mine's silver."

"So your gun is a Smith & Wesson gun. Are you familiar with the different types of guns?"

"Not at all. I went in and asked for a rookie gun, and that's what they gave me."

"Okay, describe the other person to me."

"He was bigger, like six-three or four."

"I know you didn't see the shot, but where was he hit?"

Sandeson reaches around and rubs the area around the back of his neck.

"And he was sitting in the chair when that happened?"

He nods.

"You're in your bedroom, you said. What did you do then?"

"I...I shouted out. Shouted to them."

"And what did they say?"

"Like, 'never mind, mind your own business. And you can clean up and you can keep that dirty money.'"

He said he started cleaning up.

"I mopped the blood with a Swiffer WetJet."

It must be enough. Allison leaves the room. When he comes back, he tells Sandeson he's arresting him for murder. After more than nine hours of interrogation, the young man pledging to save lives has been accused of taking a life.

CHAPTER 2

WHO WAS TAYLOR SAMSON?

My Plan

1. *1st $100,000+ investment by the time I am 25*
2. *I will give back everything I can to those who deserve it and more by the time I am 25*
3. *I will accumulate enough wealth early on so that I will never have to worry about money ever again.*
4. *I will Inovate [sic], develop and make the world a better place, as well as influence the lives of many before I die. (Hope to make it to 30. haha)*

The "Plan" was found scribbled on a piece of graph paper in Taylor Samson's bedroom after he disappeared. According to his friends, the note says a lot about who Samson really was: his entrepreneurial spirit, his desire to change the cycle of poverty within which he was raised, and his passion for helping others. The last line, no doubt meant as a joke by an invincible twenty-something, is now hauntingly heartbreaking. Samson wouldn't make it to thirty. He wouldn't make it to twenty-three.

Taylor Dean James Samson was born on March 2, 1993. The family was living in Tantallon, a Halifax suburb, at the time. It was a beautiful day, despite the season having not yet turned to spring; so nice his mother missed a barbecue when she had to go to the hospital. It was a fast labour—less than two hours before Taylor came into the world weighing seven pounds, fourteen and a half ounces, twenty-two inches long—his mother rattles off the statistics as though it was yesterday.

"Within six months, his doctor told me that he was going to be over six feet tall, the way he was growing," said his mother, Linda Boutilier, in an interview. And he was.

It was the middle of summer, 2017, and as we sat in Boutilier's kitchen drinking coffee, she told me she never thought she would have children. In fact, she didn't plan to have Taylor, but at thirty-two years old, she had been with his father, Dean Samson, for a couple of years and the news she was pregnant wasn't unwelcome.

Two years later she would go on to have another son, Connor, and the two boys could not have been more different.

Taylor never slept; he would be awake at 7:00 A.M. and not go to bed until 11:00 P.M., and he didn't sleep through the night until he was just over a year old. "He was too nosy," his mother laughed. Connor, on the other hand, slept like an angel and was always a quiet child.

Taylor, his mother said, was crawling at six months, walking by eight months, and running by ten months. "He was running all over the place; he was climbing chairs; he'd be up on the counter."

After being assessed as advanced for his age, Taylor began preschool early, at just three and a half years old, at the Peanut Butter Palace. He loved animals as much as he loved other children, but for some reason, he was always a protector. His mother recounted a story from those early preschool days when Taylor witnessed another boy push a little girl he believed to be his girlfriend.

"Taylor punched him in the nose and gave him a nosebleed," Boutilier said.

It could have been a sign of things to come. Taylor wanted to protect everyone in his life—his friends, his family, but most of all, his mother and his brother, who is autistic.

"As much as they argued, if anyone ever came near Connor that would be it—Taylor would be standing right there, protecting him," Boutilier explained. Life was not always easy for the family, and Taylor seemed to believe his hardship came with added responsibility.

Taylor's father, Dean Samson, "worked at everything," Dean said, until he suffered a stroke. He was a crew member at Dalhousie University's Rebecca Cohn Auditorium and at Halifax's Neptune Theatre, did stints as a photographer, and spent a few months as a reporter for a community newspaper. Later in life he did carpentry work. He started a degree in English at Saint Mary's University but never finished.

Taylor had just started school when his parents separated. He was five years old. When he was seven, Boutilier moved to Amherst with the boys—a community two hundred kilometres northwest of Halifax, near the New Brunswick border, population just under ten thousand.

Boutilier was trained as a certified nursing assistant (now known as a licensed practical nurse or LPN) and worked in geriatrics. She also has a diploma in business administration. For years she worked in a nursing home but said that got more difficult when she became a single mother because it was challenging to do shift work. On top of that, she had deteriorating discs in her back and there came a point when she could no longer handle the lifting required to do the job. While her children were growing up, she worked at Walmart and McDonald's, bringing in $24,000 a year, struggling to make ends meet.

It was a life she didn't want for her kids.

"When they were growing up, the first thing I always taught them: school is not done until you finish university or college. You're not done at grade 12. I put it in their heads for years because I didn't want them to end up struggling like I did," she said.

For all of the challenges, she takes comfort in knowing she raised her sons to be kind, loving young men who treated people well. She recalls a day when Taylor slipped a five-dollar bill to a panhandler as they walked by. When she gave him a questioning look, he said, "Mom, I know what it's like to be hungry."

She started to cry. "It was like I raised him right, you know?"

She said he didn't really know what it was like to be hungry.

"Sometimes there was whacks of groceries and other times I just couldn't afford to be out buying the steaks and expensive stuff, but you know, there was always something." And there was always something for everyone.

Described as a "community mom" by Taylor's friends, Boutilier's door was always open—literally never locked. Sometimes, as they got older, friends even slept there when Taylor wasn't home, and it wasn't unusual for him to come home ten minutes before supper with three other kids who hadn't yet eaten. "I had three pork chops, so I would have a piece of toast or a can of soup, while the rest of the kids all ate. I'd make goulash or something, just so they could all eat."

She doesn't think Taylor worried about money much as a child because he didn't understand it, but she does think he felt he had a responsibility to take care of her and his brother and recalls him telling her that he had to be the man of the house. He was twelve.

"I said, 'No you don't; you have to be a little boy and grow up.'"

It wasn't until he was around sixteen, she said, that he really started worrying.

His friend, Thomas McCrossin, who is also from Amherst, has the same recollection. McCrossin is the son of Elizabeth Smith-McCrossin, an independent member of the Nova Scotia legislature who represents the area in which Taylor Samson was raised, and Dr. Murray McCrossin, a family practitioner in the same community.

"I remember talking to him one night—we probably had drinks into us—and we were getting right passionate and talking about stuff, and he's like, 'Thomas, you have no idea what it's like to worry about whether or not you're gonna have heat or food.' That was what he was talking about back when he was fifteen or sixteen," said Thomas McCrossin.

Boutilier said she got behind in bills so that Taylor could play baseball.

"Amherst was everything about baseball," Boutilier said. So, when Taylor was in grade 1, his mother signed him up. He loved it.

Ryan Wilson met Taylor around that time. The two played on the all-star team together and became fast friends. "He brought me out of my shell. He introduced me to so many people," said Wilson. "He helped me be a better friend and showed me how easy it was to be a friend to someone else as well."

Wilson, who attended the trial with Boutilier and Connor, said he can't remember a weekend from the time they were thirteen until they were seventeen years old when one of them wasn't at the other's house.

"I was actually the first one out of all the guys to meet Dean. Nobody knew who Dean was. [Taylor] never spoke about him. I just didn't ask," he said. But then one day, when they were around fifteen or sixteen years old, Taylor called him up and asked if he wanted to meet his dad, so they hitchhiked to Cole Harbour, a Halifax suburb best known as the home of NHL superstar Sidney Crosby.

Taylor's mother didn't know about any of it at the time. "I found out a lot of things years later," she chuckled, but in a way that makes it obvious she doesn't really think it's funny.

During the last Christmas they had together, Taylor was home from university, and they sat and watched *Big Bang Theory* all day while a storm raged outside. "We just chatted and talked and talked and talked about everything," Boutilier recalled.

Then he asked her, "Mom, you remember that time when I went to Ryan's?" She hardly did. "Well, we kind of didn't," he said, and then explained that he and his friend had hitchhiked to his father's and camped out in his yard.

Boutilier insisted they could have made arrangements and driven him there, but Taylor said, "I wanted to go down and smoke a joint with my dad." She asked him why; his response was painful for her to repeat. "He said, 'I wanted to make him proud of me,'" she sobbed. "That's what he said."

Taylor's father said he doesn't recall the incident at all and said he didn't smoke with Taylor until he became an adult.

Boutilier believes her son started smoking weed when he was around seventeen years old, after being diagnosed with an auto-immune liver disease and realizing he couldn't drink.

McCrossin, who also met Taylor through baseball but didn't become a close friend until university, admits he bought weed from Taylor; he said pretty much everyone did.

His mother maintains Taylor didn't start selling until the summer before he moved to Halifax to go to university. He had been working at Walmart and asked her if he could take the summer off. She told him that he could but warned she would not have extra money to fuel his fun. He agreed.

"Then he started to have a bit of money, and then you'd see a couple of people come in I didn't hardly know, so I figured he was selling a few grams." She confronted him, and he confirmed it was true, but only small amounts.

She didn't know he continued selling in Halifax and didn't find out about it until his second year of school when he got sick and she ended up going to the city to spend a few days with him. Again, she noticed people she didn't know coming and going. She still believed he was only selling small amounts, and while she doesn't smoke herself, she said many of her friends do.

"I grew up with most of my friends smoking, so to me it's not a big deal anyways. Most of them own their own businesses."

Still, she asked him to stop and even got into arguments with him about it. It was his education she was worried about; she told him, "You're going to get kicked out of university and everything you worked for is just going to be gone."

But it always came back to the money. Taylor couldn't make ends meet with just his student loan. "I actually got behind in my own rent to help him out because he was behind. That's when he started to sell drugs, because I couldn't afford it, he couldn't afford it," she paused. "Then it got easier."

And when it got easier, Taylor could help his mom. When his brother, Connor, started his first job working at the lobster plant at Westmorland Fisheries in Cap-Pelé, New Brunswick, he needed steel-toed boots.

"We had the money for part of the boots. I was short like eighty bucks, and he had to start right away." Taylor sent them $100 to get the boots. But, she said, when Taylor's student loan didn't come through on time, she sent him money, and so they helped each other whenever they could.

Despite his illegal recreational activity, or perhaps because of it, Taylor seemed to be thriving at university. He did well in class, had a girlfriend, and joined a fraternity.

While he wasn't a great student in high school, he loved physics and believed he could use it to change the world. He talked about getting his PhD, finding a cure for autoimmune disease, and solving the equation that would facilitate teleportation.

At six-foot-five, Taylor was "tall, dark, and handsome" with a head of thick brown hair and a megawatt smile. His good looks seemed to work for him. His friends say he had no problem attracting many girlfriends over the years.

At the time of his disappearance, he had been dating Mackenzie Ruthven for six months, and his mother thought she was the one. Ruthven, a petite young woman with brown hair that hangs down past her waist, is from Harrow, a small community in southern Ontario on the shores of Lake Erie. She met Taylor when she moved into his old apartment in Halifax in the summer or early fall of 2014. They started dating in January 2015. Boutilier was excited because, while her son had dated several women, he had never brought one home to meet her. He brought Mackenzie home for his mother's birthday—bouquet of flowers in hand—and again for Mother's Day.

The first time she met Samson's mother, Ruthven explained that she was working toward a bachelor of science and had plans to go to medical school. "And I'm going, 'Oh my God, I'm gonna have a doctor in the family!' and Taylor's sitting there, 'Mom, you're embarrassing me,' and she's just laughing," said Boutilier, thinking back.

Ruthven said Samson was a great partner who was inspirational, brilliant, and irreplaceable.

"He was a lot more outgoing than I was," she said in her first-ever interview in fall 2023. "I don't want to use the word innocent, but like, I was an innocent kid. My idea of a fun Friday night was going to the library," she laughed.

In fact, when Taylor first asked her to go out one Friday night, she told him she was studying. He showed up at the library with coffee, and said, "I'm going to study, too, then."

She said he was thoughtful and cared deeply about people.

"He would go out of his way to do anything for those he cared about and was consistent and present and just ridiculous sometimes!" she said, adding that when they'd only been dating four months, he bought her a hedgehog because he knew she wanted a pet and couldn't have a dog or cat.

"Who does that?" she asked, laughing.

One day—during the particularly rough winter of 2014—after she texted him that she didn't want to go to work because she didn't want to shovel the driveway, he showed up with two other guys she'd never met and the three of them cleared the way. She said he would have done the same for his friends if they'd asked him to shovel snow for a girl he didn't know.

As so many others close to Taylor noted, she saw that he wanted to help people. She said he spent hours at his desk developing his tutoring business—Hfx Tutoring—doing recordings, trying to ensure the best quality, and figuring out how to get the most information into them. The videos are still on YouTube. His mother listens to them to help her fall asleep.

"He cared so much about it," Ruthven said, saying he thought it was a service he could have benefitted from in his early years at Dal; he wouldn't even charge for the service if someone was unable to pay. She said he did want to make money, but he also wanted things to be accessible.

She said he turned into "the biggest cheese ball" around kids and would let them put stickers on him and put hair extensions in as he went around the house wearing big, red, heart-shaped sunglasses.

"He would have been a really great dad," she said, wistfully.

"I really, really, really liked her," said Boutilier.

Taylor had joined the Sigma Chi fraternity in his second year of university. The Gamma Rho Chapter in Halifax was Sigma Chi's ninety-fourth installment and Canada's third. The fraternity's alumni include Brad Pitt, David Letterman, Tom Selleck, and the late Jack Layton, leader of Canada's New Democratic Party.

The organization's website says its purpose is to cultivate, maintain, and accomplish the ideals of friendship, justice, and learning. Samson had just moved into the chapter frat house on South Street in Halifax, a two-storey home with beige siding proudly displaying the frat's name and emblem on a bright blue sign.

Linda Boutilier wasn't so sure about the fraternity. She didn't understand it, believing her son was nothing like the "nerdy" people she believed to be among the group. "His honest words were, 'Mom, you don't realize how intelligent they are. I can learn so much from them,'" Boutilier said.

It was through the fraternity that Taylor would meet another close friend, Kaitlynne Lowe, who was a member of Alpha Gamma Delta, a sorority focused on scholarship, sisterhood, and philanthropy.

Lowe, who later became the president of the Dalhousie Association of Graduate Students, met Taylor during her second year at Dal at a party in January 2014. "He and I ended up talking the entire night and we just hung out," she said. "I had never felt so connected with a person so wholly. We jumped every conversation, everything from people that we commonly knew, what we liked to do and where we liked to go, to what we thought about life. It was a really impactful night."

She insists their relationship was always platonic. In fact, they were both dating other people. Still, just a couple of days after they met, she ended up celebrating her birthday with him.

"He didn't accept that my plan for my birthday was literally to work all day and then write an essay, so he had me over and we ordered Thai food and then we just hung out and watched Netflix." She was up until 3:00 A.M. and had a class at 8:00 A.M.

Five days after Samson disappeared and two days after William Sandeson was arrested, the Sigma Chi international fraternity issued a statement on its website:

Our collective hearts and prayers are with Samson's chapter brothers and the family and friends who survive him. We also send our sincere appreciation to the Halifax Regional Police for their tireless and expedient work in helping to bring clarity to an otherwise senseless tragedy. Our priority is to assist, in whatever capacity we can, in the long healing process which will now take place for those who will struggle with the reality of this tragedy. In the meantime, we ask for privacy and patience in the days and weeks ahead.

But the frat brothers have been largely absent ever since. They did not testify at the trial, nor did they attend. One of Taylor's frat brothers, who did not respond to a request to be interviewed for this book, posted a link to a news article during the first trial showing a picture of Sandeson. "Rot, you son of a bitch," he wrote.

Lowe said Taylor loved being a member of the frat and really believed in the organization.

"He loved bringing people together. He never wanted anyone to feel excluded. He literally went the extra mile to make sure people were trying to get along and having a good time. It was the perfect environment for him because he was such a leader organically like that."

His friends also say he was a natural entrepreneur who was constantly searching for legitimate ways to make money—not just by selling drugs.

In addition to his YouTube tutoring business, he joined Vemma, a multi-level marketing business that sold dietary supplements, started a smoothie business, and had just started to think about getting into real estate.

Lowe said it stemmed from his desire to make a better life.

"He wasn't satisfied with what he was seeing and what he had in life. Or it didn't match up with what he wanted, or [what] he felt like people around him deserved. I think that's really the most important part, is that he felt others deserved more," said Lowe.

Virtually everyone in Taylor's life knew he was selling drugs. They all say he talked about getting out of it.

"Oh my God, there's so many times we talked about that," said Thomas McCrossin. "I did his taxes every year, and every year I'd say, 'Taylor, we're saying zero here. Obviously, this isn't going to go on for the rest of your life.'" Taylor would always agree, yet he continued dealing.

His friends and family all agree he had no idea what he was getting into the night he died. On Saturday, August 15, when he left his South Street apartment and walked around the corner to 1210 Henry Street, he told Ruthven he was just going a couple of houses down and would be right back. The South End neighbourhood is heavily populated with students—home not only to Dalhousie, but two other universities: Saint Mary's University and the University of King's College.

Taylor left his keys, his wallet, and his medication on the living-room table and took only his cellphone and a black bag with him. Ruthven believed the bag contained a fair amount of marijuana—roughly four pounds.

Meanwhile, Taylor's brother, Connor, was already out at a bar with friends in Amherst, a somewhat unusual activity for the shy, withdrawn brother. Just before 10:30, their mother got a strange feeling—mother's intuition, perhaps.

"Something in my gut told me I better call Connor. Don't ask me why I never thought of Taylor," she said during our interview. "I figured Taylor was fine; it was Connor, because Connor never normally went out, and I thought, 'He's out with friends, they're drinking, they're going to a bar, something's wrong.'"

When Connor didn't answer several calls, his mother sent a Facebook message. It was 10:27 P.M., one minute after Taylor walked into Sandeson's apartment. "Answer the fucking phone," was all it took, before Connor called her back to let her know he was fine. Linda Boutilier was right to be worried, but she was worried about the wrong son.

When Taylor didn't return, his girlfriend and his friends waited at his apartment a while and then proceeded downtown. Ruthven began calling and texting around 12:30 A.M., but the phone just rang and rang before eventually going to voice mail. She called again around 2:45 A.M. This time the phone went straight to voice mail, leading her to believe it was either off or the battery had died.

The next day, Taylor, who had played baseball even with a broken hand, didn't show up for a game. That's when his friend, Shayn Power, decided the matter was serious enough to pay Taylor's father a visit. Karen Burke, who was Taylor's stepmother at the time, recalls that moment in August 2015 when Power showed up and gave them the news. "He came in the door and he looked like something's up and he goes, 'Taylor's missing,'" she said in an interview in the Halifax apartment in which she and Taylor's father lived in the summer of 2017.

Power did not provide the details of what Taylor had been doing the night before. Burke worried he had become ill after drinking alcohol, due to his liver condition, and decided to call around to see if he was at any of the area hospitals. He wasn't. Still, Burke thought he might be unconscious, so she called back again asking if there was anyone at the hospitals whose identity was unknown. That wasn't the case either.

"No, there's something really serious here, Karen," said Taylor's friend, trying to express the gravity of the situation. He suggested she should call the police.

"So I called the police," she said.

Officers first asked her if Taylor had suicidal tendencies. When she explained that he did not, they wanted to know if he had any medical conditions. She told them about the liver condition. "That's how it all started," she recalled. Her next move was to inform Taylor's mother. Burke said she tried to call, but there was no answer. It was now early evening on Sunday, and Taylor's mother and brother were at the grocery store near their home in Amherst. Taylor was supposed to be coming home for a visit that day, but they weren't sure what time.

Boutilier later recalled being at the store and thinking, "I wonder if Taylor's in town yet. He's got to be in town by now." She messaged him and didn't get an answer. "So I called him and it went right to voice mail," she said. She thought that must mean he was still driving and was unable to answer his phone.

A few minutes later, at 6:01 P.M., Connor got a Facebook message from his father:

connor, taylor has been missing since last night, we don't know where he is, not in the E.R. or jail...we want your mom to know. love you xoxo

There was no response before another message came in:

tell your mom to call us ASAP.

When there was no response again, the message got more frantic:

IF YOU HAVE A PHONE SEND ME THE #

That's when Connor finally saw the messages.

"I was kind of panicked, just like 'Mom, Mom, Mom!'" he explained, two years later.

"What?" his mother responded.

"Taylor's gone missing," he continued.

"What do you mean, 'Taylor's gone missing'?" his mother questioned, trying to comprehend what her younger son was telling her.

He showed her the message from his father. "She gave like that blank stare," said Connor.

"My whole body just went into a tremble," said Boutilier. "I've never experienced anything like it before in my life."

By this time, they weren't that far from home, but they ran the rest of the way and called Taylor's father and stepmother to find out what they knew. Then they packed up and drove to Halifax to meet up with Taylor's friends.

Taylor's friends clearly recall the moment they learned Taylor was missing—what they were doing and what they did next.

Kaitlynne Lowe was in Vancouver for a conference when she got a text from a friend on Sunday morning.

"Something's going on," it said. "Don't worry yet, gonna let you know when I know more."

Her friend called her a couple of hours later.

"I was standing near Stanley Park in Vancouver, and he was telling me essentially not to freak out, that something bad had happened. I had thought that, like, my cat had got out or something and that's what he was telling me, and then he's just like, 'It's Taylor.'"

"Where is he? Who was he meeting? What happened?" Lowe shot back, but there was no answer.

"I don't really know too much about Taylor's dealing. I saw some of it, and I knew about it, but it was never anything that he went into specifically. But what I knew and what I trusted was that they would all know; anyone that was involved with Taylor would know. I didn't expect it to be that much of a secret."

She tried desperately to get an earlier flight home but couldn't as she was already scheduled to leave the next morning.

By then, word of Taylor's disappearance was rapidly spreading on social media. That's where Ryan Wilson got the news.

"When I first heard about it, I was like, 'Why is this such a big deal? Why is this all over Facebook? He's been gone for not even a day.'"

Wilson said he saw no reason to be worried. He recalled other occasions when he and Taylor had been out having a good time and had not come home, and he believed Taylor would not get himself into a situation that would have repercussions. It wasn't until he found out where Taylor was going that night that he knew the situation was serious.

Thomas McCrossin got text messages directly from Boutilier and Connor but, thinking they were just messaging him some tax questions as he was also their accountant, he didn't look at the messages until Sunday evening. At that point, mother and son were already in Halifax, searching for Taylor. "We went banging on doors and I'm looking around, seeing if I can see Taylor's shoes," said Boutilier. They did that until one o'clock in the morning. She even unknowingly knocked on William Sandeson's door, but she recalls there were no lights on.

It wasn't until the next morning that Taylor's friends told his mother what he was up to that Saturday night. Thomas McCrossin said he was walking up to Taylor's apartment when Linda Boutilier came running down the street screaming his name and crying, "He's fucking dead!"

He was confused. "What? What's going on?"

"He had four pounds on him, and they didn't tell me until now. They killed him," she told McCrossin.

Taylor's other friends, who had tried to protect him—at first believing the drugs would get him in trouble—had genuinely believed Taylor had been trying to sell just four pounds of marijuana the night he disappeared.

McCrossin, who had no knowledge of Taylor's Saturday night plans, responded, "We're going to the fucking police station right now."

Sergeant Tanya Chambers-Spriggs later testified at the trial that Boutilier was at the front door of police headquarters with a friend of her son's on the morning of Monday, August 17, 2015, and was quite upset.

"There was nothing that initially stood out about his missing person report," she said in court. "When Ms. Boutilier came in, she was quite distraught."

Chambers-Spriggs said that's when Boutilier disclosed that her son had an autoimmune liver disease and could die within three to five days of not having his medication. She also disclosed that

Taylor's friends had told her that he may have had four pounds of marijuana on him. That information kicked the case up to the Major Crime Unit.

Boutilier said one of the officers told her, "I've been on the force for over thirty years; I'm telling you nobody dies over marijuana."

She responded, "And I'm telling you, something happened to Taylor."

The next day, officers told Boutilier she was right.

Boutilier was outside Taylor's apartment smoking a cigarette as Connor and McCrossin returned home from picking up a friend at the train station and two police officers came walking up the driveway. Boutilier said she knew something was wrong, so she sent the boys inside.

"He said, 'Come on, let's go talk,'" she said, as she started to cry. "I knew."

"Let's go get a coffee," the officer said, but Boutilier refused.

"Where is he?" she demanded.

"We don't know," said the officer.

Boutilier repeated evenly, "Where is Taylor?"

"We don't know," the officer said again, and as he walked toward her, he spoke the words that would change her world forever. "Linda, with the evidence we have collected, we think Taylor may have met with foul play."

Boutilier took off running, with the police following close behind—down the street, through the alleyway, toward the Asian grocery store, and up to the bright yellow apartments above it, where William Sandeson lived. "Don't ask me why," she said. "I went up the steps, trying to grab the door at Will's place, trying to get in."

She knew the police had already been there, but thought they were just looking for fingerprints to show that Taylor had been in that apartment.

Next came the terrible task of informing her son and Taylor's friends that their worst fears had been realized. After the officers had calmed her down, they all walked back to Taylor's apartment.

"Linda just sort of barged [in]," recalled McCrossin. "'I need you, you, you, you.'" Boutilier pointed at Taylor's closest friends. "'Everyone else, go!'"

Then she pulled McCrossin up the stairs inside Taylor's apartment. "I need you to sit by Connor right now," she told him. "They're charging somebody with first-degree murder."

Two officers had followed Boutilier inside, and the scene that was about to unfold would be dramatic.

"When Thomas held my hand and said it was going to be okay, it was that feeling that no, it's not," said Connor, describing the moment before police told the small group they were charging someone with first-degree murder in the death of his brother. Connor said he was in shock at first and then he "freaked bad."

"I'm sitting there, and Connor's just hyperventilating," said McCrossin. "I'm just sitting there, like, what the hell do I do? I'm like, 'I love you buddy' and he's like, 'Fuck off! It doesn't matter.'"

By then Boutilier had gone outside to speak further with the officers.

"I heard Connor in there just bawling and screaming," she said. "They had him, one on each side of him, trying to bring him down the steps. He could barely walk."

They took Connor to the hospital emergency department where doctors tried to explain how his autism would affect the feelings he was experiencing and gave him some medication to help him relax. Connor immediately believed his brother was dead, but his mother did not.

"I didn't feel it," she said, two years later, "I still don't." For Boutilier, it was just the beginning of a never-ending search for her son's body, without which she could not, would not, obtain the closure she needed.

CHAPTER 3
WHO IS WILLIAM SANDESON?

William Sandeson was born on September 27, 1992, the first child of Laurie and Michael Sandeson. They would go on to have three more sons and raise them on a small farm, where Michael also grew up, in Lower Truro, about one hundred kilometres northeast of Nova Scotia's capital.

They have mostly cattle on the farm, although the family also sells hay. They have approximately 150 acres in one lot, plus 60 to 70 acres of grassland in various spots, with the back half, or woodlot, mostly owned by William's paternal grandmother. The Sandesons bought the farm from Michael's parents.

By all accounts, William Sandeson and his brothers had a typical happy childhood, with dedicated middle-class parents who took them on family trips to Florida and the Dominican Republic. Sandeson also had the opportunity to visit Italy and Greece on a school trip, and he travelled around Europe while visiting a friend in Ireland.

Besides operating the farm at home, their father had a part-time job driving a truck, delivering bags of feed. Their mother had worked as a civil servant in the provincial department of agriculture for twenty-seven years in 2015. She was the coordinator of a 4-H program as well as the department's innovation coordinator.

Eugene Tan, who would become William's defence lawyer, was also his volleyball coach, through which he became a Sandeson family friend.

"Honestly, I don't think you could find a nicer family," Tan said during an interview in his office at Walker Dunlop, one of Halifax's oldest law firms, following Sandeson's first trial. "They're incredibly devoted to their kids."

Tan said all four Sandeson boys were very active, and their parents always attended their events. William, the eldest son, with dirty-blond hair, blue eyes, a closely trimmed beard, and a lean build, was boyishly good-looking, the epitome of clean-cut.

Tan first met him in 2009 or 2010 at a time when coaching volleyball was a significant hobby of his. Sandeson was attending high school at the Cobequid Educational Centre in Truro, but Tan's Halifax team was attracting players from outside the city and Sandeson was good enough to be one of them. Tan said that, despite not being overly tall at five-foot-ten, Sandeson was incredibly athletic and a tenacious player.

"He never gives up on anything; he just never ever stops moving," Tan said. "In any sport, you'll see plays where people will kind of give up, and most of the time, rightfully. You know, they'll see that this ball is just completely unplayable, they're not going to get it. He's the guy who's gonna jump over the first row of chairs through the stands to try and play that ball. That's the kind of player he was."

That said, Tan admitted he didn't know Sandeson overly well, having only coached him for about a year, but got to know him better when Sandeson moved to Halifax to attend Dalhousie University in 2010. Tan was then the assistant coach for the Dalhousie men's volleyball team. Sandeson tried out for that team but didn't make it. Instead, he was hired as the team statistician, a role he held for four and a half years.

Tan got to know the family better while coaching Sandeson's younger brother, Adam, on the Canada Games Team in 2013. At that level, he was doing three-hour sessions four to five times a week and said he saw Mike and Laurie Sandeson at least two or three times a week. He said the parents' devotion to their four boys cannot be overstated.

"They've all done well in school, they're incredibly kind, incredibly generous people," he said.

According to their parents, Sandeson was very close to his brothers: Adam, who was twenty when his oldest brother was arrested; Matthew, sixteen; and David, fourteen. David was once asked to write about his hero for a school project and chose to write about William. His brothers looked up to him—and why wouldn't they?

In a 2023 letter to the court in support of her son, Laurie Sandeson wrote that William has always been a "curious individual with a thirst for knowledge." His father similarly wrote that it was apparent early on in his son's life he was very inquisitive, thoughtful and determined. "He asked lots of questions about the world around him, had a keen interest in science, and was a problem-solver from an early age," Michael Sandeson wrote.

Cellphone reports I obtained following Sandeson's first trial show text exchanges between him and his parents that reflect a loving upbringing.

"We plan to watch Dal Tigers play MUN tomorrow evening," his mom texted one day after Sandeson had moved away to university. "Do you want us to bring anything along?"

"Hamburger soup is great thanks," Sandeson responded.

The report is riddled with typical messages a mother might send a son.

"Dr. Johnston's office is desperately trying to get you back in to fit your retainer. Please call their office and set up a time!"

"You forgot to take your pie," and "You left some of your clothes hanging on the drying rack."

"Just found the bunny, thank you and happy Easter!" Sandeson texted his mom in April 2015.

"Are you home safe and sound?" she asked in June 2015.

"Home safe!" Sandeson replied.

"Thanks I can go to sleep now. Hope you have a good sleep. Love mom."

A record of messages with his father also illustrates a typical father-son relationship.

"Heading to Cavendish in the early morning tomorrow. Stopping in to grab tent and sleeping bags on the way," Sandeson texted his dad.

"Tent and BBQ in wheelbarrow in basement. Probably won't be home when you get here," his dad responded.

"Coming to Hfx to fix Adam's door. Anything you want? Have truck," his dad asked another day.

Sandeson was everything any parent would be proud of. He did the International Baccalaureate program in high school—considered an advanced international education that seeks to develop "inquiring, knowledgeable, confident, and caring young people." He received the Lieutenant Governor's Education Medal, awarded to grade 11 students based on academic performance and qualities of leadership and service.

He volunteered as a swim coach with the Special Olympics, and at Ronald McDonald House, a charity that helps families with sick children.

He was also a palliative care assistant with the Victorian Order of Nurses as well as an assistant at the Camp Hill Veterans Memorial health-care facility.

In a statement to police, one of his teammates said he was "spoiled rotten"; that he was never "around drugs." Justin Blades, who would eventually play an important role in the case, also described Sandeson as "soft," saying he "couldn't fucking beat his way out of a paper bag." Blades said Sandeson did have an angry side while he was drinking—a side of him he believed came from the fact he was "suppressed at home growing up." He didn't offer any explanation as to exactly what that meant.

By 2015, Will Sandeson had completed his undergrad, a bachelor of science with first-class honours in kinesiology, and was about to start medical school. His mother said it was his intention to become a physician in a rural location where attracting doctors is a challenge.

It seemed that everything Sandeson was doing was geared toward his interest in medicine, specifically sports medicine. While doing his undergrad at Dal, he went to Ghana on a medical brigade mission to help treat people in a small village. In his letter to the court, Sandeson's father said the experience in Ghana left his son with an even greater passion for a career in health care. His mother wrote that it was in Ghana that William learned first-hand the difference he could make with simple interventions such as water purification, better nutrition, and good sanitation practices.

After failing to get into Dal's med school on his first attempt in 2013, he attended Saba University School of Medicine, a school located on the island of Saba, a special municipality of the Netherlands in the Caribbean. That's where he got his passion permanently tattooed on his body—a caduceus: the widely recognized medical symbol of two snakes wrapped around a staff.

It is not uncommon for Canadian students to attend medical schools in the Caribbean after being rejected at Canadian schools. It's also not uncommon for some to transfer back to a school like Dal.

Founded in 1818, Dalhousie is proud of its internationally recognized medical school, which it claims has the most up-to-date curriculum in Canada. Its website says that, while most doctors in Canada's Maritime provinces were educated at Dal, its graduates can also be found caring for people throughout the country and around the world.

After only five months on the Caribbean island, Sandeson returned to Halifax, where he completed a one-year certificate in disability management before being accepted to Dal's medical school. And while he didn't make the varsity volleyball team, he did make the track team, and would go on to run track for the Dalhousie Tigers right up until he was arrested.

Running track was a sport Sandeson shared with his girlfriend, Sonja Gashus, whom he had begun dating in January 2015. A commerce major from Dartmouth, NS, her specialty was sprinting.

Sandeson also began working as a personal trainer at Dal between December 2013 and September 2014, which is how he met Tanya Bilsbury. "I remember him as laughing and charming; we had fun," said Bilsbury, who was also a student at Dal and moved on to work for the federal government. "I really had fun in my personal training sessions with him."

In an interview, Bilsbury said Sandeson told her he was working twelve-hour shifts in an effort to pay off debt he had racked up going to school in the Caribbean. She said he was also paranoid she wasn't going to pay for her personal training sessions, which she thought was strange because she knew the payments went to Dal, not to him.

Sandeson quit his job as a personal trainer in September 2014 and began working for the Regional Residential Services Society, a non-profit organization that runs group homes and small option homes for adults with disabilities. He worked with three residents to help with medication, food, and personal care, and to help them move around the house and run errands.

At the same time, Sandeson also worked as a patient attendant in the emergency and trauma centre at the QEII Health Sciences Centre in Halifax—valuable experience while working toward the goal of becoming a physician.

Tanya Bilsbury ran into him at the Dalplex, Dal's athletic facility, in the summer of 2015, and he told her he had finally been accepted to Dal's medical school.

"I was so happy for him," she said. "I remember him running—he was so fast, he was like a streak—and I was watching him, thinking, wow he's really got everything he could want."

As the Sandeson case progressed toward a trial that would captivate the city of Halifax and much of the province of Nova Scotia, people wondered how a killer could have been accepted to medical school. Others expressed outrage when reporters associated him with the school.

"As a Dal med-school graduate, I find it offensive that William Sandeson is called a Dal medical student," one person wrote to me via social media. "He was accepted but never attended and was therefore NOT a medical student."

"Referencing Sandeson as an 'Aspiring Doctor' is an outrage to the medical profession," another man tweeted at me. "You grab a headline with a label that insults anyone who had put in the time and effort to earn the degree."

The fact remains, William Sandeson was a Dal medical student and was most certainly an aspiring doctor.

But eight days before his white-coat ceremony was to take place, Sandeson set in motion the series of events that would ensure he would never become a doctor.

For Sandeson, August 15, 2015, started out as a day like any other. He woke up with his girlfriend, who had spent the night; he went to work, and she went to the market before heading to Rainbow Haven Beach outside Dartmouth, where she spent the day with a friend. They both returned to Sandeson's apartment around 5:00 P.M. and watched an episode of *Scandal,* an American political thriller series, on Netflix, before heading to the Stubborn Goat, a downtown Halifax restaurant.

While they were eating dinner, Sandeson told Gashus he was going to have some people over that night and that she shouldn't be there. She made plans to visit her friend, who lived a few houses away from Sandeson's apartment, and they watched a movie, *The Fault in Our Stars*. She had to work early the next morning at Starbucks, so when the movie was over, she texted Sandeson that she wanted to come home. He responded, "Okay, won't be too much longer," until he eventually told her to come home between midnight and 12:30.

Gashus told police that when she arrived back at the apartment, it reeked of bleach, and Sandeson told her he had poured it all over the floor to clean up. "And he said that the guys that were there, one guy just snapped and just, like, attacked the other guy and he bled everywhere," Gashus recounted. She said she asked Sandeson if the guy was okay, and he said, "Well, he, like, stumbled out." She told police she thought it was sketchy, but she had to work early so she went to bed. She said Sandeson was pretty shaken up. "When we were in bed, like, I laid on his chest, and his was like, sweaty, and his heart was pounding."

The next morning, the couple woke up early and Sandeson drove Gashus to work around 5:45, picking up her co-worker along the way.

At 12:30 P.M., Sandeson went to work at the group home.

"When he came in, he told us that he had gone out with his girl-friend for food the night before," testified his co-worker Frances Myketyn-Driscoll. "And he was coughing a bit and he said he had been cleaning and might be coughing more through the day 'cause he inhaled some bleach fumes," she said, describing his demeanour as regular.

Myketyn-Driscoll said she and Sandeson took all three of the residents out to do errands at Walmart and Superstore, and he drove the van, interacting with the residents as he typically would. Later, as Sandeson and a co-worker were doing laundry for the residents, it was discovered he was also doing some of his own, but that was not entirely out of the ordinary.

Meanwhile, Gashus saw posts on Facebook that Taylor Samson was missing, so she shared that with Sandeson. "And I was like, 'This isn't the guy that got beat up, is it?'" she later told police. "And he was like, 'Thank God, no.'"

Gashus arrived back at Sandeson's place around 10:30 Sunday evening and waited a short time for him to get home from work. The conversation that night wasn't great, as Gashus, who had been angry at Sandeson for a couple of days was still pissed off, although she was also worried about him. She said he was on his phone a lot, and she told him, "You're just off." That night when they went to bed, Gashus asked Sandeson, "Do you know what happened to that guy?" and he said, "No, just cut off all ties to everybody." He thought she would be happy because she knew he was a drug dealer—in fact, Sandeson had done multiple deals in her presence, and she had repeatedly asked him to stop—and he had told her this was the end; he was getting rid of all of his product.

The next day, Monday, August 17, Frances Myketyn-Driscoll was back at work at the group home when two police officers showed up at the door. (Taylor Samson's phone would never be found, but police obtained the last number contacted by his phone from the telecommunications provider. They traced the number to the group home in Lower Sackville.) Myketyn-Driscoll and a co-worker answered questions for roughly two hours and showed one officer the staff computer, from which officers believed the message to Taylor Samson had been sent. When the officers left, a worker named Felicia Butler texted Will Sandeson and another colleague who was on shift at the time the message went out, asking if they knew Taylor Samson. It was 12:41 in the morning on August 18.

"Will this is Felicia. Do you know Taylor Samson? The cops just showed up saying the last known message to him was from here and now he is a missing person. They are going to contact you."

"Ok, thanks!" Sandeson responded, just before 8:00 A.M.

"No worries! Just thought I'd give you a heads up."

"Appreciated! I tried to get a hold of him when he wasn't answering anyone," Sandeson replied.

"Oh okay," answered his co-worker.

The following day, Sandeson's co-workers informed their supervisor about what had occurred. The supervisor, in turn, called the lead investigator at the time and informed her that the connection to Taylor Samson was Will Sandeson. The supervisor also called Sandeson and left him a voice mail to let him know the investigator was looking to speak with him. He texted her back around 10:15 Tuesday morning to let her know he had received the message.

The case was now connected to Sandeson, even if it wasn't exactly clear how.

CHAPTER 4
A VOLUNTARY WITNESS

Around 11:30 A.M. on August 18, RCMP sergeant Charla Keddy was asked to try to get in touch with William Sandeson. At the time, she was told police had determined the last number to contact Taylor Samson had somehow been related to Sandeson, and they wanted Keddy and her colleague to speak with him about when he last saw or contacted Samson.

Keddy called the number she was provided and left a voice mail; she also sent a text message, and Sandeson called her back shortly after, willingly agreeing to meet with her within twenty to thirty minutes. He arrived at Halifax Regional Police (HRP) headquarters, as promised, just before 1:00 P.M.

Keddy had been a police officer for just over fifteen years, starting out as a general-duty RCMP officer in Barrington, Nova Scotia, before transferring to the Organized Crime Branch in 2007. In 2014, she was named Officer of the Year by Atlantic Women in Law Enforcement. In 2015, when she was tasked with interviewing William Sandeson, she was the sergeant in charge of one of three homicide teams in the HRP/RCMP integrated homicide unit.

Sandeson was neither a suspect nor under any kind of suspicion during that first interview. Keddy noted he was polite and co-operative. It seemed he believed he was in control of the situation. Sandeson, however, had made a critical mistake during that interview—which would become apparent later when Keddy showed the video of the interview to the jury.

Keddy's interview with Sandeson takes place in a bright, open room with a couch and an armchair; the door is unlocked. Sandeson is wearing a T-shirt and shorts, sneakers, and a backward baseball cap.

Unbeknownst to both parties, it's only hours before the real interrogation will begin following Sandeson's arrest.

Keddy asks Sandeson to tell her a bit about how he knows Samson and the last time he saw him.

"Last time I saw him was this Thursday past," Sandeson begins, already lying.

"Okay."

"I didn't even know his last name until I saw him on the news, but I just think I met him three weeks ago—"

"Uh-huh."

"—through someone selling cannabis."

"Okay. All right."

"I wanted to see what he had."

Sandeson tells the officer that he and Samson talked back and forth a little since they had met through a mutual friend. When he saw him on Thursday, he was checking out a sample. Two other guys were with Samson, and a girl Sandeson thought was Samson's girlfriend. He tells Keddy he hasn't seen him since.

"And then he didn't respond to a text on Saturday night. I texted him Saturday night. I texted him again Sunday."

"So let's rewind for a bit. We're going to go back to the beginning. You said you first met him three weeks ago, approximately?"

"Uh-huh."

"Okay. So who introduced you to him?"

"I don't know his last name."

"That's all right."

"His first name's Jeff. I know where he lives."

He tells her Jeff is a Dal student who introduced him to Samson so Sandeson could buy some marijuana from him. (Police were ultimately unable to confirm whether Jefferson Guest was in fact the one who introduced Samson and Sandeson. Guest did not respond to a request to participate in this book.)

Sandeson tells Keddy that, after first meeting at Jeff's house, he and Samson exchanged sporadic texts for a couple of weeks before meeting again that Thursday night at an apartment on Robie Street at Samson's suggestion.

"He couldn't get in, and then we went to another apartment off Henry Street, close to my place—where all the police are right now." (Samson was in the process of moving out of an apartment on Robie Street and into the frat house off Henry Street, on South Street. His girlfriend says he probably didn't have his key to the old place because she had taken his keys and car to run some errands.)

Keddy tells Sandeson he can scroll through his phone to find the exact address of that Robie Street apartment if he can't remember it.

"As, as soon as he went missing—I had a texting app and I deleted the texting app," Sandeson stammers.

"Okay. And why did you delete it?"

"I got nervous about selling marijuana."

Keddy wants to know who was at the second apartment when they went inside.

He tells her there were several people, but he didn't know any of them.

"All right. And so what happened when you were in the apartment?"

"He went upstairs to the right and came down with a duffle bag and just opened it up and basically showed what he had."

"Okay. And how much marijuana do you think was in the duffle bag that he showed you?"

"There were two big—what's it called—vacuum-sealed bags. Probably was two pounds at one point but it looked like they'd been dug into a bit."

Sandeson says he didn't take any that night because the quality wasn't very good.

"I mean, the introduction was to meet someone with something really nice, and that wasn't, so I just didn't take anything," he says.

He says Samson was disappointed that he didn't want the weed and was going to look for something better.

"I worked Friday, Saturday, Sunday, yesterday, out in Sackville. I don't think I heard from him Friday. I didn't hear anything, and then Saturday he was anxious to meet me, but I was at work pretty much all day."

"Uh-huh."

"And then after work, I went out for dinner with my girlfriend and—"

"Where did you go to dinner at?"

"The Stubborn Goat."

Sandeson tells the officer he had some drinks at the restaurant and then went home and had a few more. His girlfriend went to a friend's apartment across the street to watch a movie and he went to hang out with his neighbour.

It's here that Sandeson begins to veer even further from the truth. He tells her Samson had been texting, wanting to show him the new weed that he got, and he had said he would take a look, but because he was drinking and his phone was on silent, their communication was bad.

He starts to ramble.

"I think I missed a call from him and then I called him back and he said he had to run somewhere for a while and then would be back. So I think we decided—we had a time set. At some point there was a time, and then that time passed. I texted him wondering where he was, no answer, and then I texted him the next morning too, wondering, and then a friend, Jeff, told me that he was missing."

Keddy asks him to go back over his Saturday a little more. He says he left the Stubborn Goat around nine.

"So during this whole time, is Taylor still messaging you or are you messaging back and forth while you're having supper?"

He says he didn't have his phone out.

"I did today at lunch, and I got grilled for it," he laughs. "No, I don't think I even got a message waiting because I said I couldn't meet until a lot later that night."

He was supposed to meet Samson around 10:00 or 10:30, after his girlfriend, Sonja, left, he says. When she did leave, he continued drinking by himself, watching Netflix, and cleaning, and then when Samson said he'd be a while longer, Sandeson went to see if his neighbour, Pookiel McCabe, had anything to smoke. McCabe didn't have any drugs, so Sandeson had another beer and went back to his apartment.

"I think I saw a missed call from him, so I called him back again. He said, 'Oh, you missed your window' or whatever. 'Now if you want any, I have to go get more.'"

"Uh-huh."

"And I went, 'Okay, yeah, like I'll wait. Go get more.' And then I waited around. He didn't come, still didn't come. Then my girlfriend came back and then, well, 'You can't—you can't come now.'"

He says he texted Samson that if he could get some the next day, he would still take it.

"At around what time?"

"I think it was like 1:30. I was awake still."

"Okay."

"And then the next day I messaged wondering if he could bring it and then no response and then we found out he's missing."

Keddy wants to know what Sandeson knew about Samson.

"So little. I know that Jeff was good friends. He'd been dealing with him for a long time. He was into network marketing, is what I understood, because he said Jeff is starting a T-shirt company. So I thought he'd be a good friend to have, because my roommate, Pookiel, is starting a T-shirt company." (Pookiel McCabe, who also went by Pookie, actually lived across the hall from Sandeson in another apartment.)

"Yeah. And what kind of quantity were you looking at buying from him?"

"I just wanted a few grams for myself." (This statement would eventually lead to Sandeson's undoing.)

"Uh-huh."

"But I know people who are looking for pounds, so I was curious if he had a good price on something then I could just put people in contact with each other."

"Did you ever share his information—his phone number or any-thing—with anyone?" It's a question that indicates police do not yet suspect Sandeson of anything other than buying and selling marijuana, to which he freely admitted.

"No, no, I didn't share it."

Sandeson explains that he has a talk-and-text application called Nextplus on his phone that only works with wi-fi and uses a num-ber with an out-of-province area code. This is when he tells Keddy he's a student at Dal.

"Okay. So what are you taking at Dal?" she asks.

"Medicine. Starting on Sunday."

He willingly tells her he's from Lower Truro, just outside Truro, and that he's been in Halifax on and off for five years. "I did my bachelor's in three years at Dal and then finished up. Worked a weird summer between Sackville–Truro, not Halifax. 2013 summer I lived—you probably don't need this much detail."

"No, that's okay."

"Anyway, sorry. I worked at GoodLife. I got hired at Truro GoodLife. I got trained in Sackville GoodLife."

"Uh-huh."

He explains that he had to quit that job as soon as he finished training because he got accepted into medical school at Saba. "It's a very, very small island," he says.

"Where is it near? Is it near St. Kitts and all that?"

"Yeah. St. Maarten—I fly into St. Maarten, and from there, either—it's the smallest commercial airway in the world—so you either take a twenty-person plane over or an hour-and-a-half ferry."

"Yeah, okay."

"And did a semester there. Hated it on the island." He explains that he returned to Halifax around Christmas 2013 and took a job at the Dalplex, which he held until that summer, when he got the job at the group home.

"And this will be your first year of medical school here—"

"At Dal."

"Did your stuff in the Caribbean count towards credits?"

"No. Kind of soars my debt." Another point that will come back to haunt him.

"So you have your motorbike. Do you have any other vehicles?"

Sandeson tells Keddy he had two other vehicles—a truck for the farm that stayed in Truro, and a Mazda Protegé, for which he had an appointment to get the brakes fixed that afternoon.

"Okay. And how long have you been kind of in the marijuana scene for, do you figure?"

"I knew people before I left for the Caribbean, but I hadn't, like, made any money off of it."

"Yeah, okay."

"And I hadn't smoked anything until January, last year, [which] was the first time I tried it."

"Uh-huh."

"And then from January, I just met a few people because I was always interested in trying new things."

The officer tells Sandeson she is going to take a break and he can just think while she's gone, but he continues talking.

"I don't know if Jeff's been in, but Jeff was asking me about seeing Taylor, and I was like, 'Well, where do you think he was trying to get weed from that night?' and he said he's never known who Taylor got weed from. Protecting his profit; wouldn't tell anyone, but he said he seemed to think it was Sackville, and all he said was that the guys were in deep, or 'pretty serious.'"

"And when do you first find out about Taylor missing?"

"Saturday."

Samson wasn't missing on Saturday.

"Saturday?" the officer questions.

"Or the—the day after," he stammers. "I had three un-responded-to texts the next, that day when I was at work. So Sunday." (These are the texts he sent as part of his cover-up.)

"And who told you that he was missing?"

"Someone else who sells."

"Okay. And who was that?"

"His name's Jordan. I don't know his last name, but I also know where he lives. He said that he was missing, or do you know where Taylor is? And I said, 'No, why? And Taylor who?'"

(The young man would later be revealed to be Jordan MacEwan, and he would tell the court a dramatic story of his own about dealing drugs and being robbed and beaten in his own apartment.)

Sandeson tells Keddy that MacEwan told him Samson was supposed to drop off some money the night before—$900—but he didn't show up.

"And I said, 'Well, I was supposed to see him, too, and he didn't come around.' But that was it and I didn't know if they knew each other until that day."

Keddy leaves the room and comes back ten minutes later. By now, Sandeson has been in the interview room for nearly forty minutes. He seems to believe he has totally outsmarted the police.

"I just have a couple other questions for you, Will, and then we'll finish up."

Keddy wants to know more about Sandeson's texting app.

"So when did you just delete the app?"

"Yesterday."

"Okay. And how come you deleted it yesterday and not earlier?"

"Because [Jordan] told me, he said, 'The police have his phone. I'm worried. Do you think we'll get in trouble?'"

"Okay. And meaning 'will we get in trouble' over what?"

"For weed. Selling it."

"Okay."

"I'm like, 'Well, I haven't even thought of that. I don't think. I think they're just trying to find him.' And he said, 'Well, I'm probably going to ditch my phone,' and 'okay, well I think I'll delete the app then.'"

"And after you delete that app, you can't recover it and get all your contacts?"

"I'm not sure. I haven't tried." (Perhaps he should have tried, because it was the recovery of that app that would allow police to begin to unravel his web of lies—an unusual mistake for someone of his apparent intelligence and of a generation typically very tech savvy.)

Keddy continues questioning Sandeson about who was aware of his drug involvement.

"And you said you have a girlfriend, right?"

"Uh-huh."

"Is she aware of your weed involvement?"

"Yes. She knows that if I ever needed any I had no problem finding it."

"And did she ever put you in touch with people, or—"

"No, actually she's completely dead set against it, hates to hear about it, so that's why I was waiting for her to be gone." (But his girlfriend would later testify that she had seen him sell weed many times.)

"Is [Taylor] into any other drugs besides marijuana that you know about?"

"I know he bought mushrooms from Jordan."

"Okay. And have you ever had any other involvement with any other type of drug except for marijuana?"

"Last summer, a year ago, I had a couple of grams of MDMA that I bought personally."

"I just want to make sure that you're being completely honest about the marijuana part, because that's not what we're investigating."

"Yeah."

"So if you were to sit here and tell me that you were buying pounds at a time and you were selling pounds at a time, you're not going to get in trouble for that."

"I never did through Taylor. I have, but I'd never done it through Taylor."

He explains that he had another person that he usually purchased from but had been shopping around for a new supplier.

"Would you ever pick it up and deliver it to each person?"

"I have."

He says he's never had more than a pound, but people have asked him for more, up to ten pounds, so then he would connect them with his dealer directly.

"So when he brings down his stuff to show you on Thursday when you're at his apartment, he's showing you because he knows that you're dealing potentially in pounds of marijuana."

"He knows, yeah."

"Okay. So initially when you were looking to meet up with him Saturday night, how much were you supposed to pick up from him?"

"I just wanted something for myself that night."

"Okay."

"Because I'd been drinking."

"Oh, okay. But you had been in touch with him earlier during the day right, while you were at work, when you weren't drinking, and you were supposed to meet him later that night."

"Yeah."

"So what was that for?"

"That was a sample on a large amount again that he wanted to show me."

"All right. So how much of a large amount?"

"Twenty pounds."

"Okay, so he wanted to sell you twenty pounds?"

Sandeson nods. "And I couldn't take it. I didn't have anyone interested in it."

"Yeah, but he still wanted to meet you to give you a sample, right?"

"He still wanted to give me a sample, and then as I started drinking, 'Well, sure, I'll take a sample.'"

"Okay. And then when you wrote back and you said, 'I can't meet you now because my girlfriend is back' or whatever, 'But I'll meet you to get it tomorrow from you.' So how much were you supposed to get from him the next day?"

"The sample."

"Just the sample?"

"I hadn't seen it yet so I couldn't verify that I could—I wasn't going to get it and hold onto it, and basically it was supposed to be, like, the end because I started school on Sunday."

"You were going to stop this."

"Not doing it anymore, and when I was drunk that night, I texted my girlfriend, 'Good news, I'm all done.'"

Keddy asks Sandeson to tell her the story backwards. He does this with ease. She then steps out and asks him to try to recover the texting app he deleted.

"If I just hop on any wi-fi—" he starts.

"Yeah, so maybe you might have to do it like when you're home or whatever to see if you can bring it back up," Keddy interjects.

"Or if there's wireless here, I could do it right now," Sandeson offers helpfully, seemingly unaware the app would restore all of his text history. Keddy eventually brings in someone to help Sandeson establish a personal hotspot. While they wait, she continues questioning.

"How much was Taylor looking for, pricewise, for what he had that you saw Thursday night?"

"Two thousand dollars each."

Sandeson tells Keddy that when he met Samson on Thursday night, he had only two pounds on him, and he was asking different prices for each because they were two different types.

"Do you know what he was calling them? You know how some people call them grapefruit or kush or—?"

"I don't know what the expensive one was because it was already outside my price range, and the other one was one of the gun ones, like AK-74 or M19 or something like that."

"So what do you think happened to Taylor? Have you heard anything?"

"I don't really know. I haven't heard from him, so I assume he's hiding, but I don't really know."

There's a knock at the door. It's the tech officers asking questions about Sandeson's efforts to connect to the internet. They're trying to figure out a way to access the texting app he keeps referring to but says he's deleted.

They leave the room together, hoping the connection is better. Six minutes later, they return, with Keddy explaining on the recording that they were able to recover the Nextplus texting app and the tech guys are going to take some screenshots of his messages from that night.

Sandeson helpfully searches his phone for the numbers of the contacts he and the officer had been discussing previously, and she asks to look at his conversations with Samson. He hands over the phone, pointing out that the app shows the times on the side of the conversation.

"He says at 10:24 P.M., 'I'm out back of the building now. Is that your bike parked by the door?' and you said, 'I'm walking out now.' So, what happened then?" asks Keddy.

"I went out and there was no one there." (Not true.)

"That's when I went over to Pookie's, and I guess he's not coming."

"Okay. And then you said, 'This isn't cool, man. You said you'd be right back.' So what happened in between the time you walked out and the time you sent the message, 'This isn't cool, man. You said you'd be right back.'?"

"I think I talked to him on the phone. There should be a phone—"

"Is that incoming at 10:24? Yeah, incoming. So he called you at 10:24?"

"Right."

"So at 10:24 he says, 'I'm out back of the building now. Is that your bike parked by the door?' You say, 'I'm walking out now' at 10:25. But he must have called you because there's an incoming call at 10:24."

"Yeah."

"What was that call about?"

"I think that was him saying, 'Too late.'"

"Even though you messaged back like one minute—"

"Yeah, one minute," Sandeson interrupts. "If you just scroll down to get more of the conversation. He was in, like, a weird hurry."

Keddy is holding strong, questioning all the odd things that don't add up in Sandeson's story. (What she doesn't know yet is that Sandeson's own video camera shows him leaving his apartment and coming back with Taylor Samson at 10:26.)

There's another knock on the door and an officer enters the room to photograph the phone. (Police had asked Sandeson if they could have his phone for a few days so they could make a digital copy of it. He declined but agreed to let them take the photos.)

Keddy tells Sandeson to call her if he hears anything else about Taylor Samson.

"I have asked quite a few people to look around, so if I do, yeah, absolutely, if I hear anything."

They begin to leave together, with Keddy planning to follow him to his car appointment, when Sandeson backtracks into the room, glancing at the cameras and smiling, before telling Keddy he plans to go camping with his girlfriend at Kejimkujik National Park the next day. "But this Saturday I have to be back in Halifax. There's registration at the Med campus at noon on Saturday." (William Sandeson would never make it to med-school registration. He would be behind bars before the end of that very night.)

That Tuesday afternoon, just before 3:00 P.M., after he dropped off his car to get the brakes fixed, Sergeant Charla Keddy and another officer drove Sandeson in an unmarked vehicle to his apartment on Henry Street before returning to headquarters, where investigators were now poring over the text messages they had photographed on Sandeson's phone—and discovering they didn't quite match his story. The texts made it clear Sandeson was *not* expecting Samson to show up with a sample to smoke that Saturday night; he *was* expecting him to show up with twenty pounds of marijuana. The fact that he'd lied about it made him a suspect.

Several hours later, while he was at his girlfriend's grandmother's house in Dartmouth, William Sandeson was arrested. Sonja Gashus testified that as they were walking out the door after dinner, police officers who had been hovering around the driveway handcuffed them both. "I was confused, and I asked questions about what was going on," she later told the jury. "They said that he was arrested for abduction, I think, and that I had to come with them."

Gashus was questioned but never charged. Sandeson was initially arrested for kidnapping, trafficking, and misleading police.

The next day, as evidence began to emerge, William Sandeson was charged with first-degree murder.

CHAPTER 5
PREPARING FOR TRIAL

Two days after William Sandeson was charged with murder, Eugene Tan was driving back to his office in downtown Halifax after an appearance in family court, when he heard the news on the radio.

"I heard it, and my first reaction was—no, it must be same name, someone else," he said during an interview. He called a friend who confirmed it was the same Will, but Tan still couldn't be convinced. "I said, 'That can't be right. Something's gone wrong here.'"

Tan, who said he was never on track to become a lawyer, was called to the bar in 1996. In high school, he was scientifically and musically minded. After deciding his dream of becoming a musician wasn't practical, he attended the University of Western Ontario, where he completed a degree in neuroscience.

Although he was not on track to become a lawyer, it seems it was always meant to be. "I guess when they say the apple doesn't fall very far from the tree, it doesn't."

His father was a Chinese man living in Singapore at a time when civil rights were in the forefront; he was part of a movement that was trying to establish greater civil rights and defend the existing Chinese culture in Singapore when it was being increasingly repressed. After seeing friends and family thrown in jail, Tan's father decided he couldn't stay any longer.

"He was quite an activist, through all his days," said Tan.

Together with his mother, Tan's father began roaming the globe before settling in Guelph, Ontario, where Tan was raised. He said his father, a professor, was always community minded. That fact would inspire Tan to apply for law school at a time when he was trying to determine his path in life. "I always had this sense of justice which, over time, I realized was a little bit different than all my friends," he says.

He and his wife, who is also a lawyer, have called Halifax home since 1996. He spent his first ten years practising civil litigation, personal injury, and corporate law, but he was always fascinated by criminal law and aspired to argue exactly the kind of case William Sandeson presented.

But that day in August 2015 when he heard Sandeson had been arrested, he called Sandeson's father, only as a family friend. Michael Sandeson also didn't seem to know much about what was happening, but called Tan back not long after and told him his son wanted to see him. Tan went to the Halifax provincial courthouse on Spring Garden Road.

"[Will] was really bewildered at that point, had no idea what was going on," said Tan.

Tan told him he didn't know anything about what had happened but could try to find out. He said there was no discussion about what had happened during that first meeting, and he didn't ask.

"I think he just wanted to know that there would be somebody with some knowledge who he knew who could potentially be out there, and who might also be able to answer some questions in the long run for his parents," he said.

A couple of days later, Tan got a call asking if he would take on the case. He handled the matter on his own for the bail hearing and the lengthy preliminary inquiry, at which point Brad Sarson, a managing lawyer for Nova Scotia Legal Aid, offered to be his second chair.

"Eugene really did not look physically well," Sarson said, referencing the intense workload associated with the case.

Tan jumped at the chance to work with Sarson. "Brad is among the best lawyers I know," said Tan. "He'll never tell you that, but he is truly among the best criminal lawyers I know."

Sarson, who was born and raised in Bedford, a suburb of Halifax, wanted to be a criminal lawyer from about the age of nine. He considered becoming a cop, a teacher, and a doctor, but eventually, after about a year and a half of practising family law, he would indeed become a criminal lawyer.

Despite eighteen years in criminal law under his belt, William Sandeson's case was the first murder he took to trial, which he attributes to the fact Legal Aid used to have a policy that allowed people charged with murder to choose their own counsel. That policy changed in 2014.

Sarson could not have picked a more high-profile, labour-intensive case in Nova Scotia—a case which would eventually involve surprise witnesses, calls for a mistrial, and a private investigator who would end up working against the team that had hired him. It was a trial that involved some unlikely players—people who were young, attractive, and from all appearances, headed for success.

Susan MacKay was first assigned the case for the Crown. MacKay, a veteran prosecutor who had been practising for twenty-three years at the time, was born in Cape Breton and had arrived in Halifax around the same time as Eugene Tan. As the lead Crown attorney on the case, she brought on Kim McOnie as second chair. McOnie, a Halifax native, had eighteen years under her belt, and was in her tenth year with the Crown office after working with Legal Aid in both Nova Scotia and Calgary.

As the evidence was trickling in, both legal teams set about preparing the case.

The first major proceeding was the bail hearing, which took place in the fall of 2015, when Sandeson had been incarcerated for just over two months at the Central Nova Scotia Correctional Facility, a provincial jail in Dartmouth, and Nova Scotia's largest. It houses provincially sentenced offenders, those on remand—incarcerated for things like parole suspensions and immigration violations—and newly sentenced federal offenders who are awaiting transfer to a federal penitentiary. Commonly known as the Burnside jail, it has been plagued by violence, with both guards and inmates being attacked.

And so it was that Will Sandeson wanted out. On October 21, the parties gathered in Nova Scotia Supreme Court on Halifax's Lower Water Street, with Justice Jamie Campbell presiding. At the time, everything discussed and all evidence presented were subject to a publication ban. As is typically the case, it was lifted once the trial jury was sequestered.

In most circumstances, the onus is on the Crown to show why a person should be detained pending trial, but the Criminal Code recognizes that an allegation of murder is different. Because Sandeson was charged with murder, he had to show cause as to why he should be released.

Detective Constable James Wasson, the lead Ident officer in the case, and Detective Constable Kim Robinson, the lead investigator at the time, both provided a sample of the evidence—which was already extensive—police had collected so far. They admitted they still hadn't found the body, and that DNA evidence was still being analyzed.

The defence also had two witnesses: their client's parents, Michael and Laurie Sandeson.

It was late afternoon on October 22 when Michael Sandeson took the stand in what was obviously an emotional time for all of the Sandesons, including William, who cried while his parents testified.

"Mr. Sandeson, you're familiar with what brings your son before the court, are you?" Eugene Tan began his questioning.

Michael Sandeson said that he was.

"And you've got some knowledge about the allegations against your son?"

"Yes," he replied, before testifying that despite that knowledge, he was putting himself forward to be a surety for his son, pledging to guarantee he would not leave the country, would report to court on time, and would be watched always.

It quickly became clear that this was a man who had no prior experience with the criminal justice system. Michael and Laurie Sandeson appeared to be a typical middle-aged couple—she, with short blond hair passed on to her boys; he, with dark hair and a moustache. They appeared in court together, well dressed, supporting their son in any way they could.

Michael Sandeson explained to the court that he drives a delivery truck three to four days a week and spends the rest of his time looking after the livestock, fixing machinery at home, doing household chores, and taking care of his other sons who still live at home.

Tan asked him to describe his relationship with William.

"I guess, in a nutshell, we love each other," he said.

He told the court he would talk to his son once or twice a week since he went away to university in Halifax.

"Mr. Sandeson, you understand that the charges of which he stands accused are extremely serious?"

"Yes."

"Okay, and you also understand that, in addition to these charges, there are allegations that he's been involved in some other wrongdoing, including the drug trade. Are you familiar with that?"

"Yes."

"Now what, if anything, is your knowledge of his involvement in this kind of behaviour?"

"I had no knowledge until I got a phone call after he got arrested." (He also hadn't had any cause for suspicion.)

"Mr. Sandeson, I wonder if you could tell the court a little bit about the authority you have over your son. How would you describe that?"

"He was always very obedient. I was able to discuss stuff with him and he could see some logic in anything that I wanted to discuss with him as long as I had a logical argument."

Michael Sandeson told the court if his son was released, he would put William to work on the farm and they would work side by side so he could watch him at all times. He had also made arrangements with his part-time employer.

"If need be, he can come with me on my delivery days," said Michael Sandeson. "The other option would be that I would quit the job and stay home to make sure he's watched."

"When you say that you would quit your job, are you able to financially do that?" asked Tan.

"It would be stressful, but that would mean I could get more work done at home," Sandeson replied.

"And you said it's a possibility. How willing are you to do that, sir?"

"Well, I'll have to do it if that's what pleases the court."

Eugene Tan also presented the court with the Sandesons' property assessment, continuing a series of personal, probing questions, all with the intention of helping their son. Sandeson's father explained that their property was assessed at $264,000 for the house, $115,900 for the barn and $15,200 for the pastureland. He testified he also had a number of other small parcels of land, valued at $100,000, and that the family had a small mortgage with the Farm Loan Board, but they owed less than $1,000 against it.

He had grown up on the property and purchased it from his parents in 1994. It had been previously owned by his grandfather, so Michael Sandeson was a third-generation owner. He had built his family's home in the corner of the property, but the old original farmhouse he had grown up in was still there.

"It's home. It's the only home I've ever known," he said.

After doing the math that the Sandesons owned roughly $440,000 worth of property, Eugene Tan asked the question that would illustrate just how far they were willing to go in support of their eldest son.

"Mr. Sandeson, if I were to ask you how much you would be prepared to risk, how much essentially you'd be prepared to bet on your son, is there a figure that you'd be prepared to offer?"

"I guess I'd have to say we're all in," he said, as though there were no other possible answer.

"And you understand what that might mean, sir?"

"If he messes up, we're out of a home."

He said his son had expressed a desire to live on the farm again someday.

"He really loved the old farmhouse; he said, 'Someday I'd like that as my house when Grammy goes.'"

Tan switched gears, asking Michael Sandeson whether he was aware of his son's financial resources. His father explained that when Will was accepted into medical school, his son got a line of credit at the bank and that it was currently higher than his parents had anticipated. But the elder Sandeson said his son told him he had spent some of the money on med-school application fees, which he hadn't realized were so expensive, and that he'd invested in stocks at CIBC.

He continued that his wife was the co-signer on the line of credit, but they agreed it needed to be closed. He also told the court his son's passport was in the basement of his home and he was prepared to deliver it to the court to ensure his son could not leave the country should he be released from jail.

"Mr. Sandeson, have you ever known your son to have been in trouble, in legal trouble, in the past?"

"No. Other than parking tickets."

"Thank you, Mr. Sandeson. Those are my questions."

Then it was Susan MacKay's turn to cross-examine Michael Sandeson.

"Are you aware that your son is alleged to have had arranged a drug deal for twenty pounds of marijuana with a street value of about $90,000?"

"I didn't know the street value. I was made aware that there was a drug deal," Sandeson replied.

"That's all you were made aware of? You didn't know how much?" MacKay challenged.

"No," came the reply.

"And are you aware the allegation is that your son shot the victim at, basically, within his own apartment in Halifax?" The cross-examination was blunt.

"I've been made aware of that, yes."

He agreed with the Crown that he had three other sons who were financially dependent on him and his wife, and that, while his wife also worked outside the home, they also relied on his income to support their family. He further agreed that the traditional family farm could not entirely support the family.

"Not at the lifestyle that we want to live," Sandeson told the court.

"Sure. So basically you're saying that you would be prepared to put your whole livelihood on the line for him, because if he was to get out and you were ordered to take him with you—you'd quit your job if you had to—but if something happened you'd be left with nothing, in fact. No farm, and if you quit your job, you'd have no job."

"Mm-hmm," was all that Michael Sandeson could mutter.

MacKay pointed out that Sandeson now had less contact with his son than when he was living at home, that his son was a smart young man, and at this point did what he wanted to do when he wanted to do it, giving his father no ability to exercise control over him.

"He's an adult," Sandeson agreed.

Susan MacKay then questioned Michael Sandeson about his son's line of credit, which would become all-important evidence as the case progressed.

"Sir, are you aware of how much is on the line of credit at present?" she asked.

"Approximately $78,000."

"Okay. And, even though medical school fees are expensive, I take it they're nowhere close to $78,000 to apply, correct?"

Sandeson said his son also used part of that money, roughly $30,000, to pay for the semester he did at Saba University. According to the school's website, tuition for the first semester of med school is $16,000 plus other student fees, travel, and accommodation. In 2015, first-year medical school at Dal cost $19,440, including tuition for two semesters and other student fees.

"So you agree with me, sir, that your son was acting on his own in deciding that he was going to, as he told you, invest money from that line of credit? He wasn't doing that in consultation with you or your wife, to your knowledge, correct?" MacKay continued with the line of questioning, seemingly intended to illustrate Michael Sandeson would not be able to control his son's every move as he was suggesting.

"He asked me what I thought about borrowing money to invest to make more. And I said it's a little risky, but if the interest rates are low and you can put it some place pretty secure, then there's a benefit to it in the longer run."

The cross-examination concluded with Sandeson telling the court his wife's salary was $80,000, with him earning an additional $30,000 from his part-time job.

Then it was his wife's turn.

"Okay, Ms. Sandeson, I'll get right to the point," Eugene Tan began. "You're familiar with why your son is currently in custody?"

"Yes, I am," she responded.

"I wonder if you might be able to describe for me your understanding, generally, of the allegations against your son?"

"First-degree murder charge, that's what I understand."

"So, what does that mean to you?"

"It's about the worst charge anybody could have, from what I understand."

Tan also wanted her to describe her relationship with her son.

"I've been very proud of William for the accomplishments that he's made in his relatively short life. Love my son, just as I love all my other boys."

"In terms of parental authority, or really any authority, how would you describe your ability to control his behaviour or hold him accountable for his behaviour?"

"Well, certainly when he lived under our roof, we held him accountable, and he lived by our rules. When he went off to university, we gave him advice on how to cope away from home. And I mean he was certainly back and forth—it wasn't that far away from Truro. And then when he became an adult and went off to the Caribbean for instance, that was a pretty big leap for a young man to do, and we got a sense he was doing okay." (Sandeson's parents obviously had no idea he wasn't doing okay—not okay at all.)

As he did with her husband, Tan asked Laurie Sandeson about the property on which she lives with her family.

"Is there an emotional connection at all?" he questioned.

"Oh, I grew up on a farm in PEI, and I was happy to marry a farmer and live in Truro—and happy to be on the farm again."

Then back to the money: "What knowledge have you got about that line of credit?"

"Receive a monthly statement because I'm a guarantor on that line of credit, so I see the monthly statements."

Mrs. Sandeson said her son would have qualified for the line of credit without her if he had needed a line of credit in Canada, but because he was leaving the country, the bank needed somebody in Canada to be the guarantor. She said she had begun to worry about the line of credit back in the spring.

"I noticed that the line of credit had jumped from about $25,000 to about forty-some-thousand, so I was concerned."

"Okay. So, did you act on that concern?"

"Yes. I confronted William right away, and I was concerned. I said, 'I don't understand why this jumped that high,' and he explained to me the reasons why it had gone up."

"So what were his reasons, ma'am?"

"Just that...because the line of credit interest rate was so low, he thought if he borrowed on that to make investments, that would work, would make more money.... And he was talking to somebody at CIBC about what smart investments looked like at that point in time."

"Ms. Sandeson, do you know what it means to be a surety?"

"Caretaker? Kind of supervisor?"

"Do you understand what your role is to be or [what] your obligations are?"

"Yes. You have to ensure the terms of the bail are met."

"Ms. Sandeson, you're working, so you're not able to be home during the day. Your husband is able to be home. If your husband were to leave his job, his part-time job as a driver, how would you feel about that?"

"We'd be okay. We might have to let some things go in terms of lifestyle habits, but we'd be okay."

"Let's talk about the land and the farm and whatnot—the financial value of all that. How much are you willing to bet on your son?"

"All of it," Laurie Sandeson replied, echoing her husband's earlier testimony.

Eugene Tan argued Sandeson should be released into the custody of his parents on a bond of $100,000, but reiterated the parents would be willing to pledge in excess of $400,000 if the court wished.

"That would likely be the largest bond that certainly I've come across in similar circumstances," said Tan, pointing out Dennis Oland, who was charged with the second-degree murder of his father, Richard Oland, in New Brunswick, was released on bail with a $50,000 bond. (Oland was eventually acquitted after a retrial in 2019.)

Sandeson was, in fact, so desperate to get out of jail that his lawyer argued he wasn't even asking for the three to four hours a week of personal time that people seeking bail often request. Tan argued the file was going to go on for a matter of years and would not be proceeding to trial anytime soon, noting disclosure had just been received and contained several thousand pages, that a preliminary inquiry alone would take weeks, and that dates had not even been set, let alone for a trial, which hadn't even yet been thought about.

"Mr. Sandeson has a Charter right, a basic entitlement to be granted reasonable bail unless there is just cause to do otherwise," Tan argued.

The Crown, in turn, pointed to the significant amount of evidence the police had already amassed in the two months since Taylor Samson had disappeared, including the accused's own numerous self-contradictory statements to the police.

There are three grounds under which lawyers can argue to keep people who have been charged with an offence in jail. In this case, the Crown argued it could meet all three. Susan MacKay told the court the Crown was worried Sandeson was a flight risk, that detaining him was necessary to ensure both the protection of the public and public confidence in the administration of justice.

But in the end, the decision was Justice Jamie Campbell's.

The judge began by acknowledging the accused was about to enter Dalhousie Medical School at the time of the alleged crime.

It's reasonable to infer that he is of above-average intelligence and perhaps that he's not afraid of hard work, he said.

But Campbell noted that just because Sandeson had no criminal record, that didn't necessarily mean he had never been involved in a crime—just that he had never been caught. He said:

The evidence is substantial that he was a drug dealer who had, to this point, evaded detection. There's an old saying that there is no honour among thieves. There's none among drug dealers either. Dangerous people are part of that life, and nice guys don't succeed.

Will Sandeson was not, it is evident, the kind of person whom his parents believed him to be. He was involved in a drug business where, if he had been caught, he would have found himself spending some years in jail rather than going to med school. He is a high risk–taker.

There's some evidence as well to suggest that he is impetuous. His response to his girlfriend's cheating on him was to threaten to kill her and dispose of her body. Smart people don't usually say those kind of things to others unless they're very much caught up in a moment.

Campbell was referencing unsettling evidence presented in the bail hearing by then-lead investigator Detective Constable Kim Robinson. Robinson had told the court that five or six weeks prior to the murder of Taylor Samson, Sandeson had become upset because he thought his girlfriend had cheated on him. In a text to another friend, he said that he would kill her and discard her body at the back of his parents' property so the coyotes could get it. He also mentioned he would cut off her head and her hands and put them in a bucket of lye.

Lye is a metal hydroxide most commonly used to cure many types of food and make soap. It can also be used to digest tissues of animal carcasses by placing the body in a sealed chamber, adding a mixture of lye and water, and applying heat to accelerate the process. After several hours, the substance will take on a coffee-like appearance, with the only solids remaining very fragile bone hulls which can be mechanically crushed to a fine powder with very little force.

"Rather than realizing that something very bad was going down and telling the police what happened, he tried to fix it," said Justice Jamie Campbell. "Either he was trying to hide evidence of his own crime or was trying to hide evidence of someone else's crime."

Campbell said the Crown's case was a strong one, but he also acknowledged that so was the release plan Sandeson's defence team and parents were proposing. "Their confidence in him is as it should be," he said. "Parental love is not supposed to be rational, but entirely unconditional."

But the complete devotion of William Sandeson's parents would not be enough. Campbell said he was concerned Sandeson could be motivated to tamper with evidence or even intimidate witnesses, given that Taylor Samson's body still hadn't been found. Campbell said:

> No one knows what cash he might have or what contacts he might have...He knows he's facing a strong case and a potential twenty-five–year jail term. He would be eligible for parole sometime in his late forties. He is a person who is prepared to take high-level risks. He lived a risky lifestyle. He's prepared to act without giving matters much thought. He would be highly motivated to make an attempt to escape, intellectually capable of devising a plan to flee without a passport, and impetuous enough to potentially try it.

Campbell denied Sandeson's application for bail.

No sooner had the judge left the courtroom than Taylor Samson's mother called out, "Maybe you'll do one decent thing for your fucking family and give my son back to me!"

There was no response.

William Sandeson would remain behind bars until the start of his trial a year and seven months later. The lawyers were likely not aware at the time, but the case would become the lengthiest matter they had ever handled.

CHAPTER 6
THE CROWN'S CASE: FAMILY FIRST

On April 20, 2017, Crown Attorney Susan MacKay stood in courtroom 301 in Nova Scotia Supreme Court for the start of the first-degree murder trial of William Sandeson. She introduced herself and her co-counsel, Kim McOnie, and wasted no time in addressing the jury directly.

"No doubt you've all seen TV shows like *Matlock, Law & Order—LA Law,* maybe, if you're as old as I am," she joked. "Or maybe even *Perry Mason*. Well, those shows can offer good entertainment, but what happens in courtrooms like this one is not quite as smooth as what you see on TV or Netflix."

She was certainly correct; the trial that was about to ensue would be anything but smooth. Riddled with delays and interruptions, it would stretch on for two months, making it one of the longest trials in the province's history.

Blair Rhodes, a veteran Nova Scotia reporter, had been covering the courts off and on for thirty-seven years and had been dedicated almost exclusively to court coverage for CBC News for six years. He'd seen his share of high-profile murder trials. He says this one spiralled out of control—so much so that the judge appeared to be exasperated as he tried to protect the jury.

"It's the worst trial I've seen in that respect—the number of interruptions. It was like they were getting hammered from all sides," Rhodes told me.

MacKay explained to the jury that the Crown had the burden of presenting the evidence necessary to find Sandeson guilty and that he did not have to prove his innocence. "He is presumed innocent unless, and until, you decide otherwise," she told the eight men and eight women gathered before her. (Two of them were alternates and would be dismissed before the first witness was called. Two more would leave before the jury began deliberating. Only twelve could decide the case as per the Criminal Code.)

The monumental task before them had to be settling in. They would either put a killer behind bars and give a young man's family justice, or they would leave that family searching for answers and set a young doctor free—potentially to save hundreds of lives.

"While this task may be a bit nerve-racking, all that's required [are] your eyes, your ears, and your good common sense," said MacKay.

Then, so there could be no question, she read them the charge: "William Michael Sandeson stands charged that he, on or about August 15, 2015, at or near Halifax in the county of Halifax in the province of Nova Scotia, did unlawfully cause the death of Taylor Samson and did thereby commit first-degree murder."

She explained that there are central elements that the Crown must prove—that the murder took place within the province of Nova Scotia, the date on which it occurred, that William Sandeson was responsible, and that the first-degree murder of Taylor Samson actually took place. MacKay also explained that in order to be first-degree—as opposed to second-degree or manslaughter—the killing must be planned and deliberate.

"Each piece will come together from all the evidence presented in the Crown's case, which we submit will form the clear picture of William Sandeson's guilt beyond a reasonable doubt," she said.

Samson's mother sat with some of his friends on one side of the courtroom's public gallery. Samson's stepmother and stepsister were also present. Sandeson's family was not present. (They later said they did not attend because they believed they were not allowed as they may have been called to testify. The Crown later said that was not the case.) Members of the media sat together, filling several rows of seating, on the other side of the courtroom.

The trial attracted a large media presence—more than other Halifax murder trials had—with most outlets providing coverage every day.

The Crown's first witness was Taylor Samson's mother, Linda Boutilier. Boutilier told the jury she had last heard from her son on Thursday, August 13; that he had texted to say he would be home to Amherst for a visit the following Sunday, but he didn't arrive.

She testified she was very close with her son and saw him on a regular basis. She said sometimes he would go home once a week, but sometimes she wouldn't see him for a month. Even then, they would talk on the phone or text.

"I'd call him and say, 'Whatcha been up to?' Sometimes he would just message me and say, 'I love you, Mom.'"

"And were you aware of whether Taylor had any future plans?" MacKay asked.

"He planned on getting his doctorate in physics," Boutilier replied before being cut off by Eugene Tan.

"I'm going to object, My Lord," he said, getting to his feet.

The judge asked the jury to leave. (It would be the first of many objections that saw the jury entering and exiting the courtroom.)

"Not sure that that question is probative in any way. It's not relevant and it seems designed to elicit some form of emotional response," Tan continued.

"M'Lord, the defence has indicated in the past that they don't concede that Taylor Samson is dead," argued MacKay. "We are attempting to elicit evidence that might show that if he had been alive, he would be in touch with his mother."

"They haven't objected to any of the information regarding communications," said Justice Arnold.

"We'll withdraw the question," MacKay conceded after conferring with McOnie. "When did you first become aware that Taylor Samson, your son, was missing?" continued MacKay when the jury was once again seated before them.

"The following Sunday, August 16, around five o'clock. Connor, my younger son, and I were up getting groceries and we were walking home, and Connor got a message through Messenger on Facebook from his father saying, 'Just wanted to let you know, Taylor's been missing since last night.'"

"So what did you do when you heard about this?" MacKay asked.

"I went right home. I called a few friends to find out if they'd seen him because I knew that Taylor was coming up on Sunday to pick up a friend of his that had been out West. He was going to bring him down to Halifax and it was going to be after a ball game."

Boutilier testified she got on the phone and started messaging people on Facebook before going to Halifax that night. She arrived around 11:30.

"I called the police officer that was handling the missing person case, and honestly, I don't remember the whole conversation 'cause it was a long time ago and I was still in a panic," she testified. "Then I started searching."

Together with one of Samson's friends, she walked the streets, up and down sidewalks, looking under bushes and in dumpsters. The next morning, she went to the police station and gave a statement.

"I wanted to tell the police that I knew it was more than just a missing person, that something had happened to my son. I felt something had happened to my son because he had no contact with anybody within twenty-four hours."

"And did you consider that, yourself, to be unusual for your son?"

"Very unusual."

"At any point in time, were you contacted by the police in regard to providing a sample for DNA analysis?"

Boutilier confirmed that she was.

"I was out searching for Taylor that day; I'm not sure which day it was. I got a call from [an officer who] asked me to come back to Taylor's apartment, where we were staying, with his brother; they wanted to get a blood sample from both of us."

Susan MacKay produced two photos and asked Linda Boutilier if she recognized the person.

"That's Taylor, my son."

"Do you know who that is?" MacKay asked, pointing to the next photo.

"Taylor, my son," Boutilier responded, but her voice broke, and she started to cry.

"Thank you, Ms. Boutilier. Those are my questions for you."

Now it was Brad Sarson's turn, and he wasted no time.

"One thing Ms. MacKay did not touch upon was Taylor's involvement in selling drugs, and my understanding is that you were aware that, at the very least, when Taylor moved to Halifax, when he started university, he began selling marijuana?"

"I was aware; I didn't like it, but I was aware, yeah."

"Right. And he was supporting himself somewhat through student loans?"

"Through student loans and other things that he was doing, yes."

"Did you know who Taylor's supplier was?"

"No."

"Did you know who Taylor was selling to?

"A few, yes."

"A few, as in you knew their names or you knew them personally?"

"I knew their names and a few I knew personally."

"You also were under the impression that Taylor was only selling small quantities of marijuana, correct?"

"Yes."

She said when she initially learned that he might have had four pounds of marijuana on him the night of August 15, she was shocked. It was far beyond any quantity of drug she thought he might have.

"I'm guessing that you later learned that the quantity of marijuana that he had with him that night was not four pounds, but was twenty pounds, correct?"

"Yes, in court I did, yes."

In a series of questions, Sarson asked Boutilier whether it would be news to her that her son was involved in either the sale or possession of mushrooms, cocaine, MDMA or ecstasy, or prescription drugs, indicating police had information he was. In all cases, she responded that it would indeed be news to her.

"Another thing that didn't come up when Ms. MacKay was asking you some questions was with respect to Taylor's medical condition. My understanding was that around the age of fifteen it was discovered that he had an autoimmune disease of some sort that affected his liver."

"Autoimmune liver disease, yes," she responded, explaining that he was taking daily medication.

"You also shared with the police the fact that not having his medication for a couple of days wouldn't present any serious difficulties for him, correct?" Sarson was setting the scene to argue that police had no urgent need to burst into Sandeson's apartment without a warrant.

"I said to two different officers two different things really."

"Okay. Do you remember what you told the officers?"

"The first one I told, I remember saying that if he had no alcohol into him that he could go three or four [days], sometimes a week. I think the other officer I told him three or four days before it actually started affecting his liver if he didn't take his medication."

"And is that the extent of what you remember telling the police?"

"To my knowledge, yes, because it was like seven or eight o'clock that night when I started giving the second statement and I had been without sleep for over thirty-six hours. I was more worried about finding Taylor than anything else. I don't recall exactly what I said in those statements."

Sarson then quoted Boutilier's statement to police, asking her if she recalled saying, "'After probably five or six days, his liver, the enzymes will start going up and his liver will start getting enlarged.'"

Boutilier said she did.

Sarson went on, still quoting the transcript of Boutilier's statement to police.

"'If he's out, like, a week or so, he'll probably start having a little bit of jaundice or whatever, and I'd say within two weeks, then he could be starting [to vomit] up brown bile.' Do you remember saying that?"

"Yes."

In the transcript, the officer said, "But, we're talking forty-eight hours right now, so he should be okay medically wise?" and Boutilier replied, "No, he's fine."

"Yes, I did say that," she agreed in court.

"Finally, Ms. Boutilier, do you recall talking to the police about Taylor having a temper?"

His mother said she did.

Sarson read from Boutilier's statement: "'Taylor can fight. I'll tell you, and everybody will tell you, Taylor can fight. Taylor, if someone is picking on one of his friends or downtown at a bar,

Taylor can take on three people and put them down flat. And I'm talking like thirty-year-old guys when he was sixteen years old.'"

His mother also agreed she had said that, and then it was over.

Linda Boutilier took her seat in the public gallery, but not before the defence tried to have her removed from the courtroom for the duration of the trial, arguing she had been disruptive and "making comments" during the bail hearing and the preliminary inquiry, and suggesting that the consequences of that kind of behaviour were far greater now that the case was in front of a jury. Justice Arnold ruled the victim's mother should be treated like any other witness and permitted to sit in the public gallery after she had testified. "I don't know what happened in those other courts, but...I can assure you that, during this trial, there won't be anything like that tolerated at all," Arnold said.

Boutilier would, in fact, be present during every day of the trial, even when the jury wasn't, and the lawyers were making legal arguments. She was Taylor Samson's most visible advocate, and she developed online followers who felt her anguish as a mother. Some of them reached out to her directly, and a few showed up at court at various points throughout the trial. There were no other outbursts—at least not inside the courtroom.

Taylor Samson's girlfriend, Mackenzie Ruthven, took the stand. She was twenty-one at the time and told the jury she had just graduated from Dalhousie University with a bachelor's degree in physics with a minor in math. She started to cry as soon as she was asked where she studied.

"I'm sorry, I just need a minute," she said. It was a reminder that this trial was presenting a lineup of smart kids who had bright futures ahead of them before they got tangled up in this mess— some through no fault of their own.

Ruthven had been dating Samson for six months when he was killed.

"How often would you see him?" asked Susan MacKay, still handling questioning for the Crown.

Ruthven testified she would stay at his place most nights throughout the week, but she was working full-time at the Health and Safety Office at Dal and going to school, so she didn't see him throughout the day.

"So, when is the last time that you recall seeing Taylor Samson?" MacKay asked.

"Saturday, August 15, 2015, at 10:30 P.M."

But she testified it was two nights earlier that the suspicious circumstances had really begun. She said a group of people were sitting around the common room at Samson's apartment on Thursday evening when a person who went by "Devon" showed up with a black bag. Ruthven testified she had never seen the guy before, that Samson immediately took him upstairs to his bedroom, and when they came back down, they did not have the black bag. Ruthven told the jury the man stayed only a short time and Samson made an awkward introduction.

"Devon reached across the table to introduce himself, and paused with, 'My name is—' and Samson filled in with 'Devon,'" she explained. She described him as tall and socially awkward with short brown hair and a dark face that looked rough, with unkempt eyebrows. "He was just really awkward," she continued. (Later, in our interview in 2023, she said she had never learned who Devon was, or whether that was his real name.)

She didn't see Samson much throughout the day on August 15 because he had baseball and went to the gym. She had woken up early and gone back to her own apartment because an exchange student she was hosting from Italy wanted to ride the Harbour Hopper—an amphibious vehicle that takes people on tours around Halifax—and go to Peggys Cove. They were planning to go out together with friends that night. Samson wanted to give the exchange student a taste of downtown Halifax, and Samson was rounding up a group of friends to go to Pacifico, a local nightclub. But Ruthven said Samson seemed antsy and disengaged and was on his phone a lot.

"I don't know how to label it," she told the jury. "He didn't seem particularly focused on going out. He seemed a little bit distracted."

Samson was in the process of moving into a new apartment in the back of his frat house, and that's where he was with his girl-friend that night, before leaving just before 10:30 P.M.

"He said he was just going a couple houses down and would be right back," Ruthven testified, telling the jury he left his keys, his wallet, and his medication on the living-room table and took only his cellphone and a black bag with him. She believed it was the same black bag "Devon" had arrived with two nights earlier but couldn't be sure. She believed the bag contained a fair amount of marijuana; roughly four pounds.

She knew Samson was involved in the drug trade and had seen him use drugs but didn't really know much about his dealing. "He tried very hard to hide it from me," she testified.

"And how long were you expecting Taylor to be gone when he left?" MacKay asked.

"He said he was just going a couple houses down and would be right back."

"And have you had any contact from him since?"

"No."

There was the ever-present issue that Samson's body had not been found, and the Crown did not want to leave any possibility for the defence to argue he wasn't dead.

"Did you try to contact him?" MacKay went on.

"Multiple times," said Ruthven.

"When did you do that?"

"That evening and multiple times after that. I tried calling him twice that evening and I tried texting him probably about seven times."

"Did you get any response from him?" the Crown asked, her voice softening.

"No."

"Those are my questions for you. The defence may have some questions for you, Ms. Ruthven."

Brad Sarson began by asking Ruthven about the three statements she had given to police, two on August 17 and one on August 18. She admitted she had been less than forthcoming with police the first time but said she gave them as much information as she could after that.

Sarson asked Ruthven if she had any direct knowledge about how much money Samson made through the drug trade.

"I know that he had a list that he kept about like, if people didn't pay him right away, but that was about it. He would never tell me how much."

Sarson then quoted Ruthven's statement to the police in which she had been asked if Samson made a lot of money selling drugs and she had responded, "More or less, yeah."

"What was the basis for your answer?" Sarson probed.

"That he was, from my understanding, trying to pay his way through university," Ruthven responded, agreeing with the defence that she was aware her boyfriend had a safe in the apartment and that he kept his money in it.

She said she had no knowledge of Samson selling drugs other than marijuana but that he did act as a go-between for MDMA and 'shrooms. She wasn't sure whether he got paid for that.

"And although he used marijuana with the people he was selling to, he also would use cocaine on occasion, correct?"

"If we were going out or something like that, yes."

Ruthven also told Brad Sarson she was aware of Samson's auto-immune disease and that he was supposed to take his medication once a day. She told Sarson about a time he hadn't taken his meds for a couple of days and he'd started getting heartburn, so she went to get his prescription filled for him. Sarson asked her if Samson could go months without the treatment, but the Crown objected, saying the question wasn't relevant and was also based on hearsay.

By this time, Ruthven was getting emotional again, so the judge suggested she leave the courtroom to compose herself while the objection was discussed. She leapt at the chance and ran out of the courtroom crying.

It was decided that the defence could proceed with the questioning about Samson's medication but only in the context of what Ruthven had told police. Ruthven returned to the stand and Sarson began quoting her earlier statement: "'The way that he's explained it to me, because I've gotten very mad at him for not taking medication before, is that it would have to be a long period of time—so a couple of months to a year—in order for there to be any real discrepancy in like, his health.'"

Ruthven pointed out she'd gotten this information through an argument with Samson in which he'd been trying to calm her down, to defuse the situation. She seemed to be implying it may have been exaggerated.

Ruthven's testimony ended and she returned to the gallery.

CHAPTER 7

THE CROWN'S CASE: POLICE WORK

The quality of the police work would be questioned repeatedly throughout William Sandeson's first-degree murder trial, but the Crown presented a lineup of officers who defended the investigation.

Sergeant Tanya Chambers-Spriggs, a shift supervisor for the Halifax Regional Police at the time of Taylor Samson's disappearance, testified she was one of the officers who had met with Linda Boutilier when she'd shown up at headquarters very upset.

"There was nothing initially, I guess, that stood out about his missing person report," Chambers-Spriggs testified. "The young man hadn't been seen for about a day and a half at that period of time."

But that was when Boutilier disclosed to police that her son's friends had told her he may have had marijuana with him—a significant amount. As a result, Chambers-Spriggs had Samson's phone pinged to determine its location.

It didn't work.

"We had information come back shortly after that—that the phone was either out of range or off," the officer testified.

Police were concerned about Samson's health due to his auto-immune disease, and the urgency of the situation was increasing so they asked for the last number contacted by Samson's phone. Chambers-Spriggs testified she got the number, but it was a 705 number (an area code from northeastern Ontario), not the 902 area code from Nova Scotia police had been anticipating. Around the same time, police received some data from the CPIC (Canadian Police Information Centre) operator indicating the phone was being operated with some sort of internet-based telephone service. This was not within Chambers-Spriggs's area of expertise, so she forwarded the information to Detective Constable Todd Blake.

Blake testified the cellphone number was used through a carrier called Iristel, a voice-to-internet service provider based in Ontario. Blake explained to the jury that the company has a group of phone numbers that they provide to resellers to use for different mobile applications. The 705 number that had been contacting Taylor Samson had been resold to an app called Nextplus, a free web-based phone provider. Blake explained that if you have a phone or a tablet that is not set up on a cellphone contract, you can use a wi-fi-capable device and get a free phone number.

"You can put any name you want; you can put any date of birth you want; you can put whatever you want on there because it's not verified because it is a free application," he testified.

William Sandeson sat paying close attention and taking notes, wearing the Dal track suit he would often wear. His legal team told reporters covering the trial that he was very involved in his own defence, having read every scrap of paperwork related to the case.

Blake told the jury he wrote a production order, which he served on the internet provider, Eastlink, to get access to the IP (Internet Protocol) address which would provide the location from which the internet was being accessed. That led him to Regional Residential Services, based on Cavalier Drive in Lower Sackville, where Sandeson worked.

Eugene Tan rose to cross-examine Blake, but his questions were not about any of the information elicited by the Crown. Tan wanted to know about a search warrant Blake had executed on Taylor Samson's apartment in the back of the frat house on South Street. Tan produced the evidence-processing sheet completed during the search.

Blake confirmed the list, explaining that he and another officer seized 185.5 grams of marijuana, four cellphones, a digital scale, Samson's passport, a tin case containing $1,680 in Canadian currency, and a safe containing several more envelopes of money totalling $6,350 Canadian and $20 American.

"They were all very neat; it was a very tidy set, and each of these envelopes had the writings, which I have marked on there, 'Blue Dream,' 'Diesel,' 'WR,' 'OG,'" testified Blake. (Blake didn't testify as to the meaning of the labels, but an internet search indicates they refer to particular strains of marijuana. "WR" stands for "White Rhino," "OG," or "OG Kush," as it is more commonly known, stands for either "Ocean Grown" or "Original Gangster." The purpose of the testimony seemed to be to further establish that Taylor Samson used and sold drugs.)

Tan moved on.

"It doesn't appear in the exhibit log, and I don't believe it's in your notes, but did you at any time come across a prescription bottle for Taylor Samson?"

"No, I don't recall a prescription, no."

Tan was again setting himself up to argue that Taylor Samson didn't need his meds as urgently as had been suggested, and therefore police had no right to burst into his client's apartment searching for Samson.

❖

As the trial continued, the lawyers whipped through testimony from various police officers fairly quickly. Detective Constable Randy Wood testified he was with HRP's general investigation section at the time and was one of the officers who attended Sandeson's workplace after police connected the address to Taylor Samson through phone records.

Sergeant Bobby Clyke testified he was brought onto the case on August 17.

"First, I reached out to some confidential informants to see if we could ascertain any information on missing person Taylor Samson," he told the jury. He said when that didn't turn up anything, he accompanied Detective Constable Wood to Lower Sackville.

Sergeant Charla Keddy testified she was the one who took Sandeson's first statement, when he was still considered a witness, not a suspect.

But it was Sergeant Sandra Johnston who would give the jury the first glimpse into just how much evidence police had compiled against Sandeson.

Johnston told the court she had been a police officer for twenty-five years. In August 2015, she was in the forensic identification section with Halifax Regional Police. She was called to William Sandeson's apartment on Henry Street on August 17 to photograph a bag that had been located outside the building that contained four unopened one-litre bottles of formamide. Formamide is an industrial chemical, a clear liquid with an ammonia-like odour, used in the manufacturing of pharmaceuticals, herbicides, pesticides, and other chemical substances.

Johnston seized the items and took them back to police headquarters. Two days later, she went back and forth to the Henry Street apartment three times, staying for most of the day. "I arrived at 5:26 A.M. until 12:07, then I returned at 3:06 P.M. I left at 6:30 P.M. I returned at 8:20 P.M. and I left at 9:10 P.M.," Johnston testified with precision.

It was still dark when she arrived at that early hour and there were officers stationed outside in an unmarked police car. "You go up two flights of stairs and down a hallway. The scene was a two-bedroom apartment," Johnston told the jury.

Two officers who had been guarding the apartment overnight left as Johnston entered the apartment alone.

"I put booties on, which are the large slippers, Tyvek booties, that go up to your knees," Johnston continued.

"What did you notice when you went in there?" questioned MacKay.

"The apartment was neat."

Johnston testified she then began photographing and video-taping the scene with the assistance of Detective Constable Rob Furlong.

"We examined the scene looking for anything that would be related to evidence as to what happened to Mr. Samson," Johnston said.

The Crown provided a book of Johnston's photographs to the jury and the officer began detailing what she had captured in each one. Johnston described exterior shots of the apartment building on Henry Street, the grocery bag from Pete's Fine Foods containing the formamide, and the stairs leading to the apartment.

"Do you see, in the top corner, a round black circle? Do you know what that is?" MacKay interjected.

"Yes, that's a security camera," answered Johnston, before moving on to the next photo. That camera, and the video it was recording, would become critical evidence.

Johnston said when she looked in the open doorway of apartment 2, she was looking directly into the kitchen and dining-room area and could see a table and two chairs and a black silhouette that Johnston said was a shooting target on the door.

There were photos of the hallway going to the bathroom, the toilet, the tub, garbage can, closets, the kitchen, and each of the bedrooms.

"I found blood spatter in the bathroom," Johnston continued.

But Eugene Tan was on his feet. "Sorry, M'Lord," he interjected.

"What appeared to be blood spatter," Sergeant Johnston corrected herself, before Tan could go on to make the point that when Johnston was at the scene in those very early days the substance had not yet been tested.

Johnston continued that she believed there was blood on the window curtain in the bathroom, on the bathroom floor, the wall, and the vanity. When she lifted the garbage bag out of the can in the bathroom, she found a bundle of money beneath it.

There was also a skateboard, a bat, and an axe in the apartment.

MacKay turned her attention to a photograph of a chair at the kitchen table.

"If you come in the front door, this chair would be immediately to your left," Johnston testified, explaining it also appeared to have bloodstains.

She also found a black backpack with a Canadian flag on it in Sandeson's bedroom, containing a black garbage bag in which she found money, mostly twenty-dollar bills, totalling $2,270.

"They appeared to be wet and stained red," she told the jury.

"Okay, did you notice anything else about that bag of money?"

"There was a strong smell coming from the bag."

"What smell?"

"I could best associate it to decomposition."

Johnston then described photos that show her hand holding a Hemastix, a test strip that can be used as a presumptive test for blood. She used it on the liquid found in the bag and explained that it did test positive for blood, but that the test strips can also test positive for other substances.

"What are you wearing on your hand?" MacKay asked.

"A glove; a nitrile glove," she said, explaining the synthetic gloves police use for handling evidence.

MacKay was trying to pre-empt what she knew was coming in the cross-examination by the defence.

"And why do you wear gloves and booties?" she asked.

"Gloves so that my hand doesn't come in contact with the exhibits and booties so my feet or the bottom of my boots don't come in contact with the staining on the floor."

Police also found an empty Smith & Wesson box in Sandeson's room, as well as two laptops and a sword. In the centre of the bedroom, she said, there was a chair with a pair of khaki pants on top of a pile that had small stains on the front.

The next photos Johnston showed the jury were of a roll of duct tape, two new hammers with plastic bags still over the ends, a knife inside a sheath, and vinyl exam gloves.

And if there was any doubt about in whose bedroom all of these things were found, Sergeant Sandra Johnston further dispelled it when she found a photo ID on the dresser from Capital Health, the former name for Nova Scotia Health.

"Okay, and do you recall whose name it was in?"

"Yes, William Sandeson," the officer replied.

She found certificates with his name on them, and a wallet, also containing ID.

It seemed every inch of the apartment had been photographed. Johnston was now on photo #109, an image of the kitchen table showing what she described as "white marks" or "wiping patterns" on the top. She said the same marks were visible on the front right table leg, and there was what appeared to be bloodstaining on the table, the chair, and the front door.

Meanwhile, Detective Constable Furlong (who by the time of the trial had retired) was searching the dining-room area.

"He located what appeared to be a bullet hole in the window frame," Johnston testified.

That was at 10:45 A.M. on August 19.

Johnston said she and her partner contacted Sergeant André Habib, who was in charge of the force's forensic identification section, and had him attend with a trajectory kit to map the bullet's path.

Habib was the next officer to testify. He used photographs from the scene to explain to the jury how he placed a rod in the hole determined to be the bullet's entry point in the window frame. At the end of the rod, he placed a laser.

"Having the laser kit on the end of that trajectory rod allows you to project a spot into space to kind of give you an idea of where that projectile may have come from," he explained, elaborating that the projectile he referenced would be a bullet.

He said police also placed a fluorescent string along the line projected by the laser to help people visualize the bullet's path.

But the officers didn't just find the hole; when Furlong removed the window casing around the hole, he found the bullet itself in the frame.

Johnston testified she was the one to seize it.

When they returned to the apartment just after 3:00 P.M., Detective Constable Furlong sprayed the area with a protein-staining reagent called Amido Black. It stains the proteins in blood but it's also not a perfect test.

"It's not a presumptive test for blood like the Hemastix was, so it would stain any proteins that are in the blood or other bodily substances," explained Johnston. "You spray it on and then you let it sit for a little bit and then you wash it off with distilled water and the staining remains."

The jury looked at photos of the kitchen after it had been sprayed.

"And what, if anything, did that process indicate to you?" MacKay asked.

"There's a possibility it could be bloodstaining in that area," Johnston testified.

With the inside of the apartment examined, the officers headed outside. Johnston took photos of the vacant business to the left, a former laundromat and video store.

The scene, where Sandeson lived, was very close to the campus on which he was about to start medical school. The university's

Schulich School of Law and Rebecca Cohn Auditorium were one block north of his apartment, a Dalhousie residence one block to the west, and the Dalplex fitness centre was just beyond that.

There were also photographs showing the exits and entrances to the apartment. Those would turn out to be critical later in the trial, especially the photo of the exterior of the window in Sandeson's roommate's bedroom.

"How did you get to that spot?" Susan MacKay asked. That "spot" was a ledge or roof outside the window.

"I crawled through the window," said Johnston.

The officers left the Henry Street apartment again but returned one more time later that evening at 8:20 P.M., when they gained access to the code for the safe in Sandeson's bedroom. Inside, they discovered a 9 mm handgun with a trigger lock and a box of American Eagle 9 mm rounds.

She said she and her partner opened the box of ammunition and there were two rounds missing. Johnston also took photos of two jugs of bleach when she went back that evening because she had been told they could be of interest.

Detective Constable Furlong brought a reciprocal saw, which he used to remove several portions of the flooring in the kitchen that evening to see if there was any pooling of blood underneath. Johnston said the protein staining had reacted to an area about two millimetres down in the wood.

Then it was time for show and tell.

Sergeant Sandra Johnston began producing items, one after another, she and her partner had seized from Sandeson's apartment, and one after another they were entered as exhibits in his murder trial.

First, the gun.

There seemed to be a collective gasp in the courtroom as those seated in the gallery realized this was the murder weapon—the smoking gun, so to speak—that had been used to kill Taylor Samson.

"Did it have any bullets in it?" MacKay asked.

"It did. It had one live round," Johnston testified, explaining she was wearing gloves to handle the gun because it had what appeared to be blood on the slide, and had also been treated with cyanoacrylate.

"It's basically superglue, and you heat it up and the vapours adhere to fingerprints on non-porous surfaces," she said.

Officers found some fingerprints and some small, red staining along the gun's slide near the muzzle and at the tip of the muzzle.

Johnston also produced the trigger lock (the device that locks over the trigger making it impossible to fire the gun), the gun box, the box of bullets, the bullet found inside the gun, the bullet found in the window casing, a piece of the window casing itself, a piece of stained seat-cover cut from a chair at the kitchen table, three pieces of stained flooring, the $5,000 found beneath the garbage bag in the bathroom's garbage can, and the stained bathroom window curtain.

Johnston testified she and her partner double-checked each other's work and did a walk-through of the scene with the forensic investigator and the lead investigator before securing the scene.

Then it was Brad Sarson's turn to cross-examine her.

"I'm a little bit curious," Sarson said. "As I understand it, you can not only wear booties made of Tyvek but there are also entire suits made of Tyvek, is that right?"

"Yes," Johnston agreed.

"And as I understand it, it's kind of like a snowsuit?"

"Yes."

"It includes a hood?"

"Yes."

"All right. What determines whether it's appropriate simply to wear Tyvek booties as you did in this case, or whether it's appropriate to wear an entire suit made of Tyvek?"

"It depends on the scene. If you're in a vehicle, it's a smaller area, you're more likely to come in contact with other surfaces. So

I'd be more likely to wear a full suit when I'm in a car. If it was a large bloodletting scene, I would wear the suit."

"Why do you say that for a large bloodletting scene you would wear the suit?"

"When I say 'large' I mean large splashes on the wall or pooling or any potential where I'd have to be in contact with the stains."

The defence would go on to ask nearly every officer about the protective clothing they were wearing, often suggesting it wasn't enough. They also asked nearly every officer about the notes they took throughout the investigation.

"As a police officer—as a beginning police officer—I assume that you are taught the importance of taking notes?" Sarson asked Johnston.

"Yes."

"That information, which has to be relayed at a much later date, should be recorded very soon after the fact that it's learned so that, when you're in court many, many months later, you have something to assist you in refreshing your memory with respect to events of that time period, correct?"

"Yes."

"Okay. In spite of the fact that I would anticipate that that would be sort of one of the first things you'd be taught as an officer, in this case, my understanding is that you did not have any notes. Is that correct?"

"I don't have any notes with me, that's correct."

"Okay. Do you have any handwritten notes at all?"

"I do have handwritten notes."

Sarson asked for a moment in the absence of the jury before stating neither he nor Eugene Tan were aware that Sergeant Johnston had handwritten notes. The Crown has a general duty to disclose all material it proposes to use at trial.

Justice Arnold asked the Crown to step in.

"Perhaps we can ask Sergeant Johnston about the notes?" asked MacKay. And the trial entered a voir dire. (A voir dire takes place in open court but in the absence of the jury, so what takes place is protected under a publication ban until the jury is sequestered. Unlike in the United States, Canadian juries are rarely sequestered until they begin deliberating the verdict.)

"I've misplaced that notebook," said Johnston.

"After this file happened, I was finishing off my time in Ident and I had just been promoted, and I packed up my desk of ten years and I don't know where the notebook is."

"Okay. And have you made any computer [notes]?"

Johnston said that when she returned to the police station just after noon on August 19, 2015, she wrote notes in Versadex, an internal database used by police. The Versadex file had already been disclosed to the Crown and to the defence.

Johnston said her Versadex notes are usually much more detailed than her handwritten notes, and noted Furlong had been with her all day so the timeline would match the notes in his notebook, which she now had.

It wasn't enough for Brad Sarson.

"Had you ever disclosed to the Crown that you couldn't find your notebook?" he asked, still in the absence of the jury. Johnston testified she had told the Crown the previous week, as she had continued searching up until that time.

"And what efforts have you made to try and locate that notebook since that time?"

"I went through my entire locker. I went through—I have a drawer in the office, went through that. And I have gone through my house. I've gone through pockets, I've looked extensively."

Sergeant Johnston was asked to step out of the courtroom.

"M'Lord, defence obviously caught by surprise by Sergeant Johnston's testimony with respect to a lost notebook," Brad Sarson began, still in the absence of the jury.

"Let me stop you there," Justice Joshua Arnold cut in. "Had you received any of her handwritten notes by way of disclosure at any time?"

Sarson and Tan agreed they had never received any handwritten notes from Johnston, but Arnold challenged them, pointing out that if they had never had any notes and they still didn't have any notes, they shouldn't be surprised. (He was tough on both the defence and the Crown throughout the trial.) But Sarson didn't back down. He argued the issue was that the notes had been lost and that the Crown was aware and did not disclose the matter.

Susan MacKay said she had only known for a week and, with a lot of things going on in relation to trial prep, she had simply forgotten to tell the defence. The defence was eventually satisfied and agreed to proceed after further investigation into Halifax Police's electronic note-taking process and how it corresponded to the handwritten notes.

At this point, the judge pointed out that, six days into the trial, not a lot had been accomplished.

"The ongoing issue that we've had so far is that we have a jury of fourteen people who are involved in this case and are not really being able to participate yet at this stage," Justice Arnold told the lawyers, asking if they were confident they would be able to complete the trial in the thirty-two court days that had been set aside. The trial didn't sit on Fridays. The lawyers agreed they were on track. The jury returned and the trial continued.

Constable Alicia Joseph told the court she went to Sandeson's apartment shortly after 6 P.M. on August 18. She said she was told she was entering the apartment under exigent circumstances under the preservation of life. (The Criminal Code of Canada authorizes warrantless searches when necessary to prevent imminent bodily harm or death or the imminent destruction of evidence.) Joseph testified she went into the bathroom, looked around, and looked behind the door. She was looking for Taylor Samson.

"I remember noting that the bathroom was kind of grimy, not well kept, but I remember thinking, the bathtub's spotless and there's no shower curtain. I thought that was kind of odd."

On cross-examination she testified she didn't notice any signs of foul play in the apartment.

Detective Constable Jason Shannon testified he was on his way to Truro on the evening of August 18. He had been asked to go there to look for a vehicle, but he didn't get far. He got a call from the lead investigator informing him William Sandeson had been located at an address on Leaman Drive in Dartmouth. He went there instead, to assist other officers in making the arrest. It was around 8:00 P.M.

"As I was pulling up there, Mr. Sandeson was exiting the residence there, and by the time I got turned around he was already under arrest."

As Sandeson was taken away, he left behind a backpack, which Shannon seized. It was a black Dal Track and Field bag. Shannon produced the contents for the jury. Inside a Winners bag there was a bath mat and a shower curtain, along with a receipt dated August 18. One by one, the items were marked as evidence for the jury to consider later, when they began deliberating the verdict: a protein shaker, protein, an iPhone charger, black gloves, a wallet, a Dodge Ram decal, Axe body spray, a Visa card in the name of Sonja Gashus, and sixty-six dollars in Canadian currency. Finally, Shannon handed over the empty backpack to also be entered into evidence.

On cross-examination, the defence began by asking Shannon if he knew the importance of taking notes, whether he did take notes, and what he was wearing. Shannon did not take notes because he was just assisting and also didn't realize the case would "balloon." He testified he was not wearing gloves or a so-called "bunny suit" typically worn by forensics officers. He was not asked why and did not offer an explanation.

He also testified he did not see any signs of foul play.

Next up was Detective Constable Roger Sayer, who was now the lead investigator in the Samson homicide. He began by telling the court he had been a police officer for fifteen years, including seven years on general patrol before becoming a detective in the criminal investigation division. He worked in the drug unit for a brief time before transferring to the general investigation section, handling break and enters, robberies, and arson. Following that, he worked in the sexual assault unit for four months before he was transferred to homicide, where he had been for four and a half years. Sayer had pretty much done it all.

He told the jury he was called on August 17, 2015, to assist with a missing persons file. It was deemed to be of concern because of a pre-existing medical condition and because police had information a large drug transaction was occurring at the time of the disappearance. He was asked to be a part of what police call the investigative triangle. His first role was as the file coordinator, the officer charged with preparing and issuing tasks to other investigators as well as preparing documents that would be put into the file. The other members of the triangle were Detective Constable Kim Robinson, who was then the lead investigator, and Sergeant Derrick Boyd, team leader. As he sat directly addressing the jury, Sayer explained that Boyd's role as team leader was to obtain resources. Robinson, he said, was responsible for the flow and direction of the case. Robinson was promoted to sergeant two months later, at which time Sayer took over as lead investigator.

Sayer said he was the first to interview William Sandeson following his arrest on August 18, 2015, and into the early morning hours of August 19. This interview took place before then Constable Jody Allison arrived and the two started their good cop/bad cop charade, and before Sandeson started talking about Morphsuited intruders bursting into his apartment to kill Taylor Samson. Sayer told the court Sandeson was polite, very quiet, calm, and appeared to be paying attention.

The Crown then began playing for the jury the video of Sandeson being interviewed.

❖

The video begins at 9:41 P.M. on August 18. Sandeson is in the interrogation room alone. There are two chairs in the room, but they are both empty. He's lying on the floor on his stomach, face down. Within a couple of minutes, Constable Jason Shannon enters the room, takes Sandeson's particulars, and tells him he's under arrest for kidnapping, trafficking, and misleading the police. (He was never actually charged with those offences.)

Sandeson remains calm as Constable Shannon reads him his rights and asks if he wishes to call a lawyer. He says yes. The two leave together at 9:47 P.M. and come back at 10:20 P.M.

In the video, Sandeson is again alone, his head in his hands.

Detective Constable Sayer enters the room at 10:27 P.M. (Only short snippets of the conversation were played for the jury, the remainder having been deemed inadmissible. The judge told the jury they should not guess or speculate about what had been removed or why. The publication ban on that material has now been lifted.)

The interview shows Sandeson in that same empty interrogation room.

"I want you to know, William, I've been part of this investigation from the beginning. I'm one of the officers that's taking the lead in this investigation," Sayer begins. "I had an opportunity to see almost everything that was done in relation to this investigation, and I've been doing this stuff for a long time, William."

Sandeson sits, nodding as Sayer explains that many officers are working on the case, putting together the pieces of the puzzle.

"I'm a firm believer, William, that people make choices in their life, and when they do, sometimes they're good choices and sometimes they're bad. Does that mean that good people can make bad choices? Yeah, it can."

Sandeson remains silent.

"After putting all these pieces of the puzzle together, there's no doubt in my mind that you were involved in what happened to Taylor. There's no doubt."

Sayer explains that he doesn't think Sandeson is evil, unlike many of the people he sees in this room. Using a sports analogy, he references the Toronto Blue Jays's improbable winning streak in 2015, explaining no one player can do it all, but rather they each have a role on the team.

"You have a role in this file," he tells Sandeson. "What I don't know is how deep your role is."

As it would again and again in this case, the conversation returns to William Sandeson's chosen profession. "If you want to be a doctor, there's some part of you that wants to do some good in this world."

Sayer has printouts of Sandeson's texts with Samson in his hand.

"I know what was on your phone," he tells Sandeson. "And you know I know. So I need to know where he is." Sayer pauses. "You know where he is, Will." (Police had seized his phone and obtained a warrant to search it for other evidence, but he had refused to give them the password. So for six to eight hours a crime analyst watched the video of Sandeson typing in his password during his interview with Charla Keddy, playing it over and over until he figured it out.)

Sandeson shakes his head. "I don't know," he barely whispers.

"Or you know what happened," Sayer continues.

"I don't know," Sandeson mumbles, his hands clasped together at his mouth.

"I understand that you're scared. I get that. People do things for certain reasons, and fear is one of them, but you have to understand that there's a man's life at stake."

He tells Sandeson he's a young man and there's still time for him to move forward from this, but he has to start doing the right thing. "This is the biggest day of your life moving forward and you need to make a choice of what you're going to do."

Sayer is all but pleading for answers, speaking in a gentle, coaxing manner. "What are you going to do, Will? Are you going to let that family suffer? Are you going to let that mom grow old with a broken heart? Never knowing what happened to her son, over some weed? Is that who you're going to be? Are you a monster?"

But it is of no use. Sandeson continues to exercise his right to silence.

"How does a guy go from being a student athlete, going to university, wanting to be a doctor, to not giving a shit about leading a man possibly to his death? How does that happen?" (This is the stuff the judge did not want the jury to hear.) "You haven't even been willing to tell me if I'm being a fool in thinking I could still help this man."

Eventually, at 2:07 A.M., Sandeson is taken to police cells, where he is provided a bed and food.

This is also when police try a technique called a cell shot—embedding an undercover officer in cells with a suspect to see if they can strike up a conversation and get them talking. It doesn't work. Sandeson says nothing of value.

Back in the courtroom, Sayer explained that Sandeson was very upset the next morning at 9:50 A.M. when the RCMP's then Constable Jody Allison took over the questioning.

Sayer said that during that interview, Sandeson was crying, sobbing, and at times finding it difficult to breathe. That stopped later that evening when Sayer returned to question Sandeson once again.

Sayer said he used two different approaches when interviewing Sandeson on August 18 and 19. On August 18, he used an emotional approach, mentioning family and appealing to Sandeson's desire to help people. "It's a calmer approach," said Sayer.

"The second night when you see me go in, I take a firmer, direct approach, and I'm factual and I'm talking about evidence." This is when he played the role of bad cop.

Sayer explained that, while police did get a search warrant to enter Sandeson's apartment, they didn't wait for it to be produced, citing exigent circumstances as other officers had. Sayer explained that to have the warrant written, produced, and executed took nearly ten hours, and at the time police believed they might still be able to save Taylor Samson's life. Police didn't actually seize items until they received the warrant around 5:30 A.M. on August 19.

One of the items seized was a DVR, or digital video recorder. With Sayer on the stand, the court played video for the jury showing the hallway outside Sandeson's apartment between 10:19 and 10:41 on the evening of Saturday, August 15. Sayer walked the jury through what they were seeing as Sandeson came and went. This is the video Sandeson told police had recorded over itself every twenty minutes.

Sayer told the jury the first thing they should notice was Sandeson going downstairs to the entrance of the apartment building around 10:20. He comes back with two other young men, whom he escorts to his friend Pookiel McCabe's apartment across the hall from his own. The two individuals are only there for two or three minutes before they leave the same way they arrived.

Sayer told the jury this was important because the time frame corresponded with a text message on Sandeson's phone when he told Samson, "Actually hold dude bunch of traffic."

At 10:26, the video shows Sandeson going downstairs again. This time he comes back up with Taylor Samson. Samson is carrying a large black duffle bag. The two enter Sandeson's apartment. Sayer pointed out that the time stamp corresponded with text messages between the two: "I'm out back" and "I'm on my way down."

Next, Sayer told the jury to notice Sandeson's apartment door opening. The video shows a shoulder in the jacket Sandeson was seen wearing a few minutes prior. The door is only open for a couple of seconds and then it closes.

At 10:30, the door opens again. Sandeson goes across the hall. The two people in that apartment enter the hallway looking inside Sandeson's residence. They would become the trial's star witnesses.

At 10:40 Sandeson steps out, not wearing a shirt now, and places something in a shoe rack that can be seen in the hallway. He goes back inside. Later, another man arrives at the apartment and picks up the item. It is not clear in the video, but later testimony indicated that the item was marijuana, which means Sandeson effectively did a drug deal in the midst of the murder, or at least the cleanup.

The Crown skipped the video ahead to the next morning—5:52 A.M. on Sunday, August 16, 2015. Sandeson is seen leaving his apartment with his girlfriend, Sonja Gashus. He's wearing a sweater and a bright orange toque. At 6:05 A.M. Sandeson returns to his apartment. The jury later heard he drove his girlfriend and her co-worker to work at a Starbucks in downtown Halifax.

Sandeson leaves again three minutes later. At 9:38 A.M., he returns, now wearing a white tank top, having shed the toque and sweater. A minute later, he leaves again, carrying a green compost bin and a spray can. He takes the materials back inside four minutes later, along with a large black bag.

The video switches to a different camera. This one shows the exterior of the building. At 9:41, Sandeson gets out of his car—a black Mazda Protegé—and heads for the trunk, taking some items out, and placing others inside.

In court, the Crown zoomed ahead to Monday, August 17, at 7:52 A.M. Sandeson is leaving his residence wearing a black Dalhousie University backpack and carrying a large KitchenAid box with a grocery bag on top.

Sayer explained that the items shown were important because they were seized when police executed a warrant at an address on Chestnut Street four days later. Inside, officers found the twenty pounds of marijuana believed to have fuelled this crime.

It was found at the apartment where William Sandeson's younger brother, Adam, lived with his roommates.

There was one more video.

On Tuesday, August 18, at 8:09 A.M. Sandeson puts some items in the trunk of his car, leaves with the trunk still open, and comes back again two minutes later to put more items in the trunk. They include black garbage bags and a blue Adidas bag. He's wearing bright reddish-orange gloves.

The video presentation complete, Susan MacKay had one more question for Sayer.

"Is this or is this not still an active investigation today?"

"It is," Sayer replied.

"Why?"

"The remains of Mr. Samson have never been located."

"Thank you. Those are my questions for you."

Brad Sarson handled the cross-examination of Detective Constable Sayer for the defence. He began by pointing out that Samson had been reported missing nearly twenty-four hours prior to Sayer's involvement, so information was already coming in.

Sayer agreed. "In a missing persons file what happens, and did happen in this matter, is that family and friends are quite concerned about why their loved one is gone missing, so there is a heavy flow of information coming in of friends, contacts, anywhere they could be. So when you first begin your investigation it's like a large net you throw out because, when you have a missing person, time is of the essence. So if you want a positive result you have to have it quickly."

"You've made reference to that, or said that a couple of times," said Sarson, "that in a missing person file that time is of the essence. Isn't it fair to say that time is of the essence only if foul play is involved?"

"No, not always," Sayer disagreed, saying sometimes people go missing and are injured accidentally or attempt to take their own lives.

Sarson also asked Sayer about how Sandeson went from a "person of interest" to a suspect and how and why police began surveillance on him. Sayer testified it was Sergeant Derrick Boyd who, while keeping an eye on Sandeson's first interview, noticed that something wasn't right. As police began obtaining Sandeson's text messages, Boyd picked up on the fact Sandeson hadn't mentioned Samson messaging, "I'm out back of the building now. Is that your bike parked by the door?" Instead, he'd told police Samson didn't show up.

Sarson asked when police felt they had reasonable and probable grounds to arrest Sandeson. Sayer explained that during Sandeson's interview with Jody Allison, Sandeson had said Samson was shot in the back of the head. At that time, evidence against Sandeson was already stacking up, and police had found no evidence anyone else had entered the apartment.

"Myself and Sergeant Boyd were watching the video and we looked at each other and we were like, 'His jeopardy's changed.' And we determined it was time to arrest him for murder."

"Even though the information he provided was that someone else had shot Mr. Samson, you and Sergeant Boyd agreed that, at that point in time, Mr. Sandeson was arrestable for the murder of Mr. Samson?" asked Sarson.

"We did."

Sarson also asked Sayer about what he knew about Samson's liver disease, asking him to recount the information provided to police by a pharmacist, Samson's mother, and his girlfriend in that regard. There had been conflicting information provided about the medical condition at various times. His mother first said he would be okay without his medication for three or four days. She later told police he would be okay for five or six days. Samson's girlfriend, on the other hand, thought he would have to be without his meds for a year in order for it to have a serious impact. Sayer said he placed more weight on Linda Boutilier's testimony because he believed she would be more familiar with his health than a girl he had dated for only a few months.

Sarson pointed out that Samson had been away at university in Halifax for four years and his mother lived in Amherst.

"I would agree with that, sir," Sayer said to Sarson, "but where his mom resided and how many years he had in university would not change his health condition."

"Except you're not a doctor, correct?" Sarson countered.

"No, but I don't think living in Halifax or Amherst, if you have an autoimmune disorder, is going to change that. That's my opinion."

Sarson continued, asking Sayer about names provided by Samson's mother and stepmother regarding possible people Samson was supposed to meet with the night he went missing.

"The evidence led us in a certain direction," Sayer testified. "You put your resources into that direction, and you come back if that proves to be not the right direction to go in."

Sarson also asked about attempts to identify the socially awkward man named "Devon" who Samson's girlfriend told police had arrived with a black duffle bag matching the one Samson was last seen carrying. Police spoke with two individuals named Devon, but they could not be linked to the person Mackenzie Ruthven described. Sayer said police did not make further attempts to identify the Devon she referenced.

"We already knew that Mr. Samson was at Mr. Sandeson's residence and that's the last place we could put him. And the evidence that police gathered continued to come in after that in that same direction."

Sarson reiterated that Sandeson was charged with murder around 6:45 p.m on August 19.

"I'm going to suggest to you, Detective Constable, that from that point forward all of the police efforts were dedicated to locating and obtaining evidence in an effort to prove that charge against Mr. Sandeson. Would you agree or disagree?"

"I would disagree, sir. You go where the evidence goes. However, our first concern has always been trying to find Mr. Samson. And so even when Mr. Sandeson had been arrested for his murder and Mr. Samson's remains had not been found, our first priority in the evidence that we were gathering was trying to locate him."

Sarson asked Sayer about reported sightings of Samson.

"There were tips coming in from the time that the media release was made of Mr. Samson being missing and they have continued today," Sayer said on the stand. It was May 8, 2017, nearly two years after Samson had disappeared, and his body still hadn't been found. "Also, since then we've received reports on body location, even psychic reports," Sayer said.

One of those letters was admitted as an exhibit in the case.

Saturday, August 22, 2015

To whomever it may concern,

I am writing to you regarding the case of Taylor Samson. I did not know him personally nor was I aware of who he was until he was reported missing.

Two or three days after his disappearance I was on my way to the supermarket and came across a notice on a telephone poll [sic] advertising his disappearance. I seldom look at ads stapled about the city. However, I happened to look in the direction of this one and it instantly grabbed my attention. I starred [sic] at his picture and read the information on the paper. After having looked at it for only a few seconds I knew he was dead.

Later, either before or after the case had been changed to a homicide investigation (I cannot remember exactly), I had a vision of the Northwest Arm from the perspective of someone standing on the shore of the peninsula. The vision was focussed on a spot in the middle between the Armdale shore and the peninsula. This spot was darker than the rest of the water, implying that this is where his body was. I also had a vision of him lying on his chest, with his face turned to the left, and his left arm above his head with his palm face down.

I have a strong feeling that his body is there and also have felt that his spirit has been around me. He has been interfering with my ability to fall asleep and when I woke up today, I realized that he was urging me to write this to you. I don't know what you make of this kind of information; whether you value it or dismiss it. However, if all else fails, I highly recommend looking in the Northwest Arm.

Regardless, I wish you well in your investigation.

It was perhaps a sign of the public's intense interest in the case. Some members of the public who had no connection to those involved showed up in court to witness the drama first-hand. On more than one occasion there was a lineup outside the courtroom. One day a deputy sheriff asked for volunteers to leave because the courtroom was full and immediate family members of Taylor Samson didn't have a place to sit. Still others followed along as reporters covering the case live-tweeted the testimony, many so intrigued they admitted to ignoring work and other responsibilities; journalists picked up hundreds, in some cases thousands, of followers as the case progressed. A Facebook group emerged called "Taylor Samson: Case Discussion—trial watch." Its members seemed to be obsessed with the case, following every word and sharing speculation.

Reporter Blair Rhodes says it was the mystery around what happened to Taylor Samson that not only maintained the interest but caused it to build throughout the trial. Where was his body? "How could [Sandeson], who appeared squeaky clean and beloved, turn out to be a stone-cold killer?" Rhodes asked.

CHAPTER 8
THE CROWN'S CASE: WITNESS TO MURDER

I n the summer of 2015, Justin Blades and Pookiel McCabe were enjoying life. McCabe, who also goes by Kahmall, had just graduated from Dalhousie University with a business management degree. He was bartending at the casino and running day camps at the Dartmouth Sportsplex. Blades had been pursuing an arts degree but had dropped out because he didn't have enough money to finish. Both were members of the Dal Track and Field team.

"Always track, every day," Blades would tell a jury nearly two years later.

According to the team's website, Blades was still the record holder in the 400 metres, having run 48.76 in 2012.

On August 15, the two teammates were anticipating a good night. Blades was at home waiting for McCabe to get ready. "He takes forever, so eventually I got fed up. I don't have a phone that texts, so I messaged him on wi-fi, through Facebook or whatever. I have no patience, so he didn't text me back quick enough, so I just took off down to the house."

Justin Blades was twenty-six years old at the time he testified in May 2017. Like many of the others whose lives had been turned upside down by the case, he was young and fit. With short brown hair and closely trimmed facial hair, he stood six-foot-one. He wore a dark grey Roots hoodie to court, where he testified he'd grown up in Yarmouth, in southwestern Nova Scotia. It was clear he hadn't had an easy life, his upbringing entirely different than the friend against whom he was testifying.

Pookiel McCabe was twenty-four at the time of the trial. McCabe is from Brampton, Ontario. He's six-foot-three with short black hair and neatly trimmed facial hair. He wore a collared shirt to court.

When Blades arrived at 1210 Henry Street, apartment 1, it was 9:55 P.M. McCabe and William Sandeson, his neighbour from across the hall, were already drinking, smoking weed, and playing video games. The music was a little loud, but not so loud they couldn't have a conversation over it. Sandeson had just arrived moments before Blades. Blades and McCabe were heading out to a track and field party.

"We asked if he wanted to come out," McCabe testified. "He didn't want to come out with us." Sandeson left fifteen minutes after Blades arrived.

Blades had had three-quarters of a bottle of red wine by the time he arrived. Pookiel McCabe was just getting started. "He usually is a late starter," Blades told the jury. "'Course, when I got there, I'm gonna rev him up to get in the zone, party."

Blades and McCabe continued alone for a while until Blades got a text from a friend named Adrian asking for some weed. He told him to come and get it. Adrian and his friend, not known to McCabe or Blades, arrived at McCabe's apartment at 10:21 P.M.

"He picked up a gram of weed, wasn't there long. He didn't pay for it, I just gave it to him whatever, it's only weed."

Surveillance video shows the boys leaving just three minutes after they arrive. Two minutes after that, unbeknownst to McCabe and Blades, Sandeson enters his apartment followed by Taylor Samson. Just three minutes later the evening starts spinning out of control.

"It wasn't long and then we heard a loud bang, real loud," said Blades.

"We didn't know what it was," said McCabe. "We just looked at each other, like, 'What was that?'"

"We were ready to jump out the window," said Blades.

Instead, the two froze for a moment, then jumped up, ran to the door, and locked it.

"Put my head against the door frame, not directly against the door, just to listen," said Blades.

"Didn't hear really anything, just like a little small scuffle, like a table or chair moved." The noise was very quick. We listened, it was quiet and then we heard his door open."

Then there was a knock on their door.

"He said, 'Hey, it's Will,'" Blades recalled. "We didn't open the door, we just waited a second, and he said, 'It's Will. It's okay, open the door.' So I unlocked the door and opened it."

"He seemed like a little shocked, I dunno," said McCabe.

"There he was, just standing there," said Blades. "Quick as I opened the door, he turned around and went back into his apartment. He didn't say anything to us."

He said Sandeson was at the door less than a minute after they heard the loud bang. When he left, they followed him across the hall.

"I went first and Kahmall was right behind me. As soon as you went through the door you could just see the scene."

But four days after their shocking experience, when police first questioned them, Justin Blades and Pookiel McCabe had told officers they saw nothing at all.

❖

Pookiel McCabe was questioned first, on August 19, 2015, at Halifax Police Headquarters, days after Taylor Samson vanished. It was just before 5:00 P.M.

A transcript of that interview shows Detective Constable Jonathan Jefferies explaining to McCabe that police are investigating the disappearance of Taylor Samson and have some questions for him. By now the police have secured McCabe's apartment and he can't get back in.

He tells police he has been living in apartment 1 alone for two years and that Will Sandeson and Dylan Zinck-Selig live together across the hall in apartment 2. They've only been there for a year.

"Do you know Taylor Samson?" Detective Constable Jefferies asks.

"No, I don't," says McCabe.

"Have you heard about his disappearance?"

"I've heard, I've seen like, on Facebook and stuff like that, yeah."

"All right. Have you heard anything about it through the grapevine or through friends, or have you talked about it with anybody or anything like that?"

"No."

McCabe insists repeatedly that he doesn't know Samson at all. About that much at least, he is telling the truth.

"I got off work at 5:30, took the bus home, went upstairs to my room," he continues when Officer Jefferies asks him about the previous evening, August 18.

"And then, like ten minutes after I got in the door, I hear, like, cruisers or whatever come up. So I looked out the window and there's like a bunch of cops down there. And I was like, 'Holy shit, what's going on?'"

He tells Jefferies he was kind of nervous.

"They just, like, ran up to the door, knocked on the door, said, 'Police, police.' So I was like, 'Shit.' Opened the door and I was like, 'What's going on?' And then they just, they didn't really tell me what was happening. They came into my house, asked me some questions, took my name and stuff like that, checked my apartment, said they were looking for a body and they didn't—like, I didn't understand that."

"Okay."

"But like, yeah, I let them walk around my house or whatever, and then like, my door was open still and they just kicked down the next door, like next-door neighbour's door."

McCabe says he asked the officers if he could close his door and they told him he could, but he decided he couldn't stay there.

"My heart's just jumping," he tells Jefferies. "Like, what's going on? And they don't want to answer anything."

He takes the officer through everything he had been doing for the past couple of days, just going to work and to the gym, his regular routine.

"So with regards to Will and Dylan, do you know of any criminal stuff that they're into?"

"Criminal? Like...maybe, like, sell a little weed."

"You know that they sell a little weed?"

"Not Dylan. Will, like, sold a little weed, but like, that's all."

"All right, so let's go back to the weekend when you're home. Anything out of the ordinary happen when you're home? Did you hear anything?"

This is where McCabe stops telling the truth.

"Like, um, no," he responds.

"No?" asks Jefferies.

McCabe shakes his head.

"So, when you were home did you stop over to the neighbour's—"

McCabe cuts him off.

"No, no. I didn't."

"...Will and Dylan's and say hi or anything like that?" Jefferies continues. He knows McCabe went across the hall because he's seen him on surveillance video, but McCabe sticks to his story.

"I didn't stop in, no. I don't think anybody was home."

Jefferies has to be disappointed. He has reason to believe McCabe might have witnessed something crucial.

"Okay, so you never heard anything out of the ordinary?"

"No."

"Never saw anything out of the ordinary?"

"No."

Jefferies tries one last time. "Anything else you can think of that might have popped in your head the last couple of days that you think I should know?"

"No, it was just that that lawyer called was kind of weird." Sandeson's lawyer had called Pookiel McCabe asking him to go into Sandeson's apartment, get all the cash he could find and bring it to the courthouse. "And ah, yeah, the cops being there," McCabe continues. "Nothing much else."

It was a week later when police interviewed Justin Blades, who had been with McCabe that night. He had gone home to Yarmouth with his girlfriend to visit family, so police travelled to Yarmouth to question Blades there. It was August 26. The RCMP's Jody Allison (he was still a constable at the time) conducted the interview with Detective Constable Scott MacLeod of Halifax Regional Police.

It starts out much the same way as the McCabe interview, with the officers explaining they're investigating the disappearance of Taylor Samson, asking Blades how he knows Sandeson, and what they were doing the previous Saturday night. He tells essentially the same story as his friend, only Blades admits he was talking to Sandeson at his apartment door.

Otherwise, Blades is no more forthcoming than McCabe.

"Do you remember anything out of the ordinary there that you saw?"

"No. Will kept his stuff, like his drug deal stuff, on the down low."

"Okay, did you see anybody in his apartment?"

"No one, not a person," Blades says, before trying to change the subject. "All the boys got together after all this and we talked because we're all fucked up from hearing, like..."

But Allison quickly returns to his line of questioning.

"Did you see anything on his table?"

"No, if he had product, like, he wouldn't leave it out."

"You're not going to be in trouble for that stuff, like if you saw something, or—"

"No, I will try to help you guys out," he says.

Allison reminds Blades he's already spoken to Sandeson and already watched the surveillance video. "I want you to think about it because it's very important that you tell us the truth."

"Well, the only thing I was sketched out about too is when Dylan came in and talked to us...he said he went home and showered and there was no fucking shower curtain."

"Yeah."

"That's just unsettling."

"I don't want you to think that, you know, you had any kind of knowledge about this. That's not what I'm saying. But if you saw something, if the door was open and you saw somebody in there or if you saw something on the table or something like that, then I mean, you know, you're not in trouble for seeing that kind of stuff."

"Yeah, like seeing drugs and stuff."

"Yeah," Allison agrees.

"Well, I honestly didn't see anything," says Blades, and the police have struck out once again.

The next morning, they try with McCabe again. Allison's handling this one too. This time, McCabe is warned he can be charged for misleading police, but it's no use.

"The door is wide open," Allison is taking McCabe through the sequence of events seen on the surveillance video. "So there's yourself and Justin standing there."

"Okay."

"Okay? So tell me what you saw."

"I didn't see anything." Again. For the next fourteen months Justin Blades and Pookiel McCabe will maintain their silence.

In October 2016, the two young men were approached by a private investigator working for William Sandeson's defence team. He wanted to know their stories and, for the first time, Blades and McCabe wanted to talk. They told the private investigator everything they knew, and he encouraged them to go to the police, even going so far as to help arrange an interview for Blades. (This was a move that later almost derailed the case—one that would cause a retrial and be debated for at least the next seven years. But all of that was still in the distant future.)

On October 20, 2016, the police paid Justin Blades another visit, drove him to police headquarters, and Jody Allison, who had now been promoted to corporal, found himself once again interviewing Blades about that still-mysterious summer night in the South End of Halifax. Both the officer and the witness knew this would be a very different interview.

"It is 12:46 in the afternoon," Allison begins. "And this video is in reference to an investigation by Halifax Regional Police into the homicide of Taylor Samson, okay?"

"Okay," agrees Blades. After more than a year of keeping this terrible secret, he's ready to tell the truth.

"I want you to understand that severe criminal sanctions exist for the making of a false statement," says Sergeant Derrick Boyd, the Commissioner of Oaths. "Do you understand that lying under oath constitutes perjury which may be punished by fourteen years' imprisonment?"

"I do. That's heavy."

Blades affirms the oath, signs the paperwork, and gets down to business with Allison, admitting he didn't tell him the complete truth the first time.

"Okay, and can you explain why you decided to provide police investigators with information regarding this information now?"

"Tired of being scared."

Blades's story starts out the same as the first time. He was at his friend Pookiel McCabe's getting ready for a track party.

"I show up at Kahmall's like I always do and, yeah, Will is in there and we're all playing video games. And I just remember Will saying he just came back from supper with Sonja and they said they loved each other for the first time. I remember that really stood out to me."

Blades says a friend texts him looking for some weed and two guys come by to get some. They leave at 10:24 P.M. Seconds later, Sandeson leaves too.

"Wasn't long man, like heard the gunshot go off," Blades told Allison. "I ran over and locked the door. I remember that and just being like, 'What are we going to do? What do we do? What do we do?' Pretty much, like, fuck, we're going to jump out the window. And I was putting all these scenarios in my head, like, 'Oh my God, are we next? Do they know we're over here?' And then we just stood there and stood there, like, tried to listen to see if we could hear anything."

At first he said they couldn't hear anything, then they heard the door open. "And then we were, like, 'Oh fuck!' and then Will knocked on the door."

Blades said he was already shocked.

"He opened the door, and then his door was open, and then as we went to the doorway, like, Will is panicky. He's panicky obviously, like he's going to be panicky, and he's like, running around his apartment with," he trails off. "I guess it was Taylor Samson. You couldn't see who he was because he was slumped over like"— Blades leans forward and bends over—"head down, suffering from a gunshot to the head, blood all over the floor, money all over the place, drugs all over the floor."

"Okay."

"Just like a scene out of a fucking movie, man."

"And when you saw it, you could still see, like, the blood pouring down?"

"Yeah, it was still coming out, but there was pints and pints of blood on the floor.

"And we just stood there in the doorway, being like, 'What the fuck?' At this point, like, everything's running through my head."

"Do you remember seeing a firearm? Because you heard the shot—"

"No. That's what freaked me out like…like, he wasn't the shooter."

"Okay, now as far as who else was there, anybody else around besides you and Pookiel?"

"No, just us three, I guess."

"There wasn't anybody, like you couldn't see anybody in the hallway, down the hallway or anything?"

"No, I only had the doorway image. And I just remember being like, don't even know what I said to him. I didn't even know if I said anything. Like, 'What the fuck happened?' pretty much and he just didn't say anything, just running around, like, 'I got to clean this up. I got to clean this up.' And we went back over to the apartment, and I was like, 'Kahmall, man, like, we got to call the police. What are we going to do?' And we were just like, 'We'll just go tell him he's got to figure this out. He's going to call the police. We need to get out of here.'"

The two young men glanced inside Sandeson's apartment again.

"And the second time though, like what really fucked me up, is like, when I knock on the door and be like, 'Will, we're leaving,' and like, you could veer [*sic*] in and he moved the body from the position and dragged it into the bathroom. You could see the streaks of blood."

"Did you go in very far?"

"No, I just stopped at the doorway, no fucking way, man. I wasn't passing there."

"Can you tell me what else you saw in the room at the time?"

"He was just picking up bloody money."

"Still doing the same thing."

"Yeah."

"I know this is tough, Justin. I just want to make sure we get everything covered off," Allison explains to an obviously emotional Blades. The officer asks him to go through everything again, but this time backwards, explaining that sometimes it helps people remember details they hadn't before, but Blades is struggling to keep it together.

"If I wouldn't have been so frigging impatient, I wouldn't even have been there. I would have been still at home, sitting there playing Xbox, waiting for Kahmall to hurry the fuck up. He's always like a girl and he just wants to get pretty."

"But the main thing to remember, though, is that you didn't do anything wrong. You didn't do anything wrong." The officer tries to console him.

"I did though; I should have at least, I know I feared for my own life, but like, fuck, man, that poor Taylor's mom didn't deserve to look at any of that."

"No," the officer agrees. "The thing is, though, you didn't do anything wrong. He did that; he did it, and he brought you into it."

At this point, the "remembering backwards" idea seems to work.

"Even the weirdest part is that he asked me to bring the car around," Blades recalls.

"What? When—when was that?" Allison asks.

"That was the first time he came and got us, and he was like, panicking, and he was just like, throwing shit out of his mouth."

"So did you bring the car around?"

"Fuck, no."

"So what did he mean by that?"

"I don't know."

(Only three minutes actually passed between the time Sandeson first knocked on McCabe's door and the time McCabe and Blades left the building.)

"I was in a panic," Blades tells the police this time. "Like, left everything going, video game is still going, it was just like, 'Will, man, we're leaving. You need to call the fucking police.'"

They headed to Blades's apartment just a short distance away.

"I was sick the whole way, like throwing up and shit, fucking power walking, like didn't know what to do, and then I went in the house and had a poop."

Blades and McCabe continued on to the track and field party as planned because they wanted to be around people. They hung out at the party for a while and then waited for their girlfriends, both bartenders at downtown Halifax nightclubs, to get off work.

"I couldn't wait for her to get off," Blades tells police. When she did, they went to her place for the night.

"I didn't sleep; she slept, and I just laid there, and then at like 10 A.M. in the morning, [she] wanted to go to the beach and, like, she knew I was upset, but I didn't tell her why."

He told his girlfriend he wanted to stop at Sandeson's on the way to the beach to get some weed, but it wasn't really about that. He needed to assess the situation, see if he could figure out what had happened and whether the police had been by yet.

"I went inside, knocked on the door, like—I had no idea what the fuck I was going to walk into again."

But to the untrained eye, the apartment was sparkling clean, as though the horrific murder scene had simply vanished.

"He was in his apartment and it just like, smelled like fucking chemicals, and they were so hard. So obviously when I walked in and realized he cleaned the place up, I was in shock again. I was like, this is not right; this isn't right."

His girlfriend was waiting in the car, so he didn't stay long.

"I remember just saying like, 'You're supposed to start med school.' I remember like, pep-talking him and being like, 'You're fucked.'"

Blades has been talking for a while now. Allison doesn't even have to ask questions.

"[Will] says, 'I got this, I'll figure it out. I'll take care of it.'" But to Justin Blades, it very much appeared that his friend, the aspiring doctor, had already taken care of it. What "it" was, he still didn't really know.

"I was scared to come in contact with him because I didn't know what the fuck was going on, so I messaged him on Facebook. I wanted to get him in a public place, where I knew I could talk to him without an environment like that, so I told him I wanted to go kick-boxing with him."

Sandeson said he couldn't go kick-boxing because he was at work.

"And I was like, what in the fuck is he doing at work?"

He told Blades he would get in touch the next day and maybe they could go kick-boxing then, but that was August 18, the day Sandeson was arrested.

"That's crazy; that's crazy, eh?" says Allison. It's the first time he's spoken in a while.

"Yeah, it's so fucked up, man."

"I mean for him to put you in that position is pretty selfish."

"Oh, if I was left in this room with Will right now, I'd rough him up for sure. I don't know how, like, any of the justice system works here, but I almost wanted to go into the jail, and be like, 'I'm tired man, what's going on? You need to come clean, like tell me if I'm being pursued.'"

"That was something you were thinking of doing, you mean?"

"Yeah, stuff like that played in my mind all the time."

But he figured any conversations in prison would be recorded, and since he hadn't told the police what he knew he might get in trouble.

"So Justin, back around that time, why didn't you tell us that then? What was going on?" asks Allison.

"There's hearsay through a lot of people. I knew Will was affiliated with, or whatever, was working for the Hells Angels," Blades says. He says he knew there was a large quantity of drugs involved, and thought it was more than Sandeson was capable of dealing with himself.

"You don't fuck with the Hells Angels," says Blades.

"Right. I mean, I can understand that, and I can empathize with your position there. This must have been weighing on you for a long time."

"Yeah, I'm so tired of putting a face on the whole time, man, like, fuck. I'm so hurt but I have to hide it."

"Yeah, it's tough and I'll tell you something—you gotta make sure you talk to some people about this when we're done, you know, you make an appointment and talk to the right people, okay? Because something like that, that sticks with a person forever."

"Yeah, I don't know what's going to make it better."

"Justin, by doing what you did right now, you have made some good steps."

"Yeah, poor mom, man, fuck, Taylor's mom, like, obviously I feel for people, I work helping save people's lives." At the time, Blades worked in the emergency department at a Halifax hospital. "I see a family come in to see their hurt loved ones, and I've been to so many funerals in my family."

"Yeah, so if you could do something to help his mother. It's obviously why I'm here."

"That's the reason you're in here," Allison repeats.

"As long as my name doesn't come up in all this shit," Blades says.

"I can tell you right now that if you're concerned about the Hells Angels that he has no connection to the Hells Angels."

"I want to believe you."

"I can tell you that whatever he was telling people, or whatever people believe, I can tell you that is not the case," Allison tells him. "There is no connection. If there was, they would have come after his family for the money and all that. They could have got him in jail if they wanted to."

"Yeah," is all Blades can offer.

"I'm not saying that some of the stuff that he didn't buy some-how made it to them, or some of the money didn't, but I can tell

THE HELLS ANGELS MYTH

Stephen Schneider has been researching organized crime in Canada since the late 1980s. He teaches in the criminology depart-ment at Saint Mary's University, and he's written three books on the subject, including *Iced: The Story of Organized Crime in Canada*.

Schneider disputes Sandeson's claim that he travelled to Montréal to deal with the gang. "If he was dealing with the Hells Angels, he wouldn't have gone necessarily to Montréal," he says in our interview. "He would have gone to Ontario, because Halifax and Nova Scotia were being controlled by the Gatekeepers [an affiliate club] out of London, Ontario." He points out that while the Angels are well represented in Quebec, they deal mostly in hash and cocaine there, not marijuana.

Schneider also says the Angels have distanced themselves from street-level trafficking because it simply isn't profitable. "They tend to be more just involved with financing of grow ops, things like that, and most of the marijuana trafficking that the Hells Angels do is exported to the United States. They don't do a lot of trafficking in Canada, because they get bigger money in the US—double what they would make here."

Schneider says the Angels have learned from the past and would now have three to four intermediaries between them and a street-level dealer. "They would be so far removed that generally speaking I can't see any full-patch member of the Hells Angels in Quebec or Ontario having a relationship with this guy."

Plus, he says, "the Hells Angels, when they do deal in pot, deal in tonnes, not pounds. If you had twenty pounds of heroin or fentanyl or cocaine, then, yeah, that's huge, but not marijuana."

you right now that the stuff he had you can get from people that have no affiliation to the Hells Angels right here in this city."

"I just heard because he was fucking, like, they needed someone smart like Will; it just made so much sense when you looked at it."

"They usually look for dummies," Allison says.

Many of the rumours that William Sandeson was involved with organized crime seemed to have been fuelled by Sandeson himself. Blades tells police Sandeson had told him a story about going to Montréal to do a deal with the Hells Angels.

"I can tell you that they wouldn't be dealing with him," Allison reaffirms. "I can guarantee they would not. A patched Hells Angel member's not going to deal in twenty pounds of weed, not even a hundred pounds of weed. If you're bringing in maybe fifty keys [kilograms] of coke, they wouldn't even touch it themselves."

"It's not worth it for them?" Blades asks the officer, seeking reassurance.

"It's not worth it for them," Allison confirms. "Plus, they don't want to go to jail."

"There is nothing that we have found in any part of this investigation that would lead us to think that there's anybody from the Hells Angels or any other criminal organization that's interested in him," Allison tells Blades.

"So stupid," Blades mutters. "I don't know why I deserve to even—"

Allison interrupts him. "You don't want to think like that at all. You didn't go and put yourself in this situation. This is the other guy. For whatever reason, who knows why he did it, he pulled you and your friend into it. He ruined—"

"Ruined Kahmall's life," Blades interjects. "Like, fuck, he's not the same, and he was my best friend, too. We just can't even look at each other the same."

"So, Pookiel, he saw everything that you pretty well saw, did he?"

"Yeah, he was with me there."

❖

Days later, Nova Scotia police travelled to Ontario and surprised Pookiel McCabe early one morning as he was getting ready for work. He agreed to go with them to a local detachment for the third time. Like his friend Justin Blades, this time, McCabe was also in a truth-telling mood. (The two would go on to testify at William Sandeson's trial in the spring of 2017.)

McCabe's story was not as detailed or dramatic as Blades's, but the facts were similar. "We just, like, walked across the hall and looked in his apartment and saw a man there sitting in a chair. He had blood on him. Me and Justin looked in there. We didn't look that long."

McCabe could not back up Blades's account of Sandeson running around in a panic, cleaning up bloody money.

"I wasn't focussed on him. I was just, like, in shock."

Like Blades, McCabe also cited fear as the reason he didn't tell the truth for more than a year. "I didn't know if he was affiliated with anybody, like if he was affiliated to any organized crime or something," he later told the jury.

As Blades had, Pookiel McCabe saw Sandeson after he witnessed the horrific scene in his apartment, but the circumstances were different. McCabe went home later that night. He admitted he was intoxicated.

"When I got there, I had received a text message from William. He just wanted to know if I was still up. I said yes and he came over and, like, we just played video games." Surveillance video shows Sandeson entering McCabe's apartment at four o'clock in the morning, and for an hour and a half the two played *Call of Duty* and listened to music.

"Did you talk about anything?" asked Crown Attorney Susan MacKay.

"We didn't," said McCabe in court.

"And how did that feel to you? That interaction with him at that time?"

"From what I can remember it was a weird feeling."

At 5:28 A.M., Sandeson went home, but it would not be the last interaction between him and McCabe. They continued corresponding as Sandeson awaited trial behind bars.

"He wrote letters to me," McCabe told the jury.

Sandeson's letters were not introduced as evidence, but McCabe's responses were.

"Ay, homie," he wrote in a typed letter in November 2015, three months after Sandeson was arrested for murder.

I would never chuck out your letter without reading it or replying. I just hope you're staying strong and safe, so I'm happy that I did get your letter, and that you've got some people you're cool with keeping you fed. Yes, and I've talked to Sonja, she says she speaks to you frequently now, that's awesome. She cares about you a lot man. But $20 for 7 minutes? They don't have any better phone plans than that?! No discounts?!? Ya leave it to Andrew to snag your liquor, using it to wine and dine Bianca, no doubt. We'll definitely get some shots of Glen Fiddich when all is said and done. You're right, fuzz and media had been annoying trying to talk to basically anyone you came into contact with. I wish you the best of luck in finding someone else to represent you, if that's still your goal.... The crew misses you and we'll always be here for you. Keep your head up, Guillermo.

He closed the letter with the Spanish form of "William."

"You have to understand that me and Will had known each other for five years," McCabe told the jury. "So we had grown really close, and our whole team, we had a group of friends, he was part of our group of friends so I just wanted to let him know that there was other people that missed him."

Just over a year later, in January 2016, McCabe responded to another letter from Sandeson. Again, it's not known what Sandeson wrote, but we can gauge some of the conversation by McCabe's response.

"Waddup cuz," he wrote, this time in a handwritten letter. He told Sandeson about his Christmas, some music he was interested in, and asked if he could send him some books.

re: Lawsuit at the end of this—Yah, that's fucked, they literally tested everything in that apartment, I was wondering what you would do about that, Dylan too. A lawsuit for the time and loss of your personal belongings sounds about right to me. Good to hear you're staying on top of it and thanks for explaining the legal procedure of the case. You & Eugene put in work."

He continued writing about some new card games he had learned before signing off. "Work on your handstand pushups, those are challenging. Until next time Amigo. Hang in there, the crew is waitin for ya."

McCabe testified he also got a phone call from Sandeson from the Burnside correctional facility after he had given his final statement to police, sometime near the beginning of 2017.

"First when he called me, he said, like, right off the bat, he said, 'I'm allowed to call you as long as we don't talk about the trial.'"

He said they mostly spoke about mutual friends.

"Did you want to speak with him?"

"It was really weird having him call. I didn't really know what I would say to him, you know what I mean?"

He said they spoke for about ten minutes.

In contrast, Justin Blades testified he had no contact with Sandeson after he was arrested. He told the jury he went off the map, moved to a new address, got rid of his phone, didn't really see anyone other than his girlfriend—not even his family—and tried to suppress his memories of what he witnessed the night of August 15, 2015.

"Still to this date, I still have a lot to explain to them. I've just been bitter. I don't trust anyone." And then he repeated, "I don't trust anyone."

Despite his best efforts, he testified, he still hears about Sandeson everywhere he goes. "I can't even go outside to Sobeys and not hear about it. I was there yesterday and heard about it. It's everywhere. It follows you like the plague, man."

On cross-examination, defence lawyer Eugene Tan tried to poke holes in Blades's story, but Blades held his own, at times sparring with the lawyer in front of the jury. Tan pointed Blades to a photo that showed some dark staining in the kitchen of Sandeson's apartment.

"Do you recall if there was a pool of blood near that location?"

"Huge pool of blood. Literally it covered pretty much the whole half kitchen."

"Okay, so where would the biggest concentration have been? Right about where that staining is?" asked Tan.

"I don't know what you mean—it's an abundance of blood all over the floor," said Blades, his frustration building.

"I guess what I'm asking you here is: is there like a fairly significant pool right here?"

"There's a significant pool on the whole floor!" Blades nearly shouted, exasperated. "Is there a point to this? You just want answers?"

The judge interjected. "Mr. Blades, Mr. Tan will ask questions, and if they're questions that are not appropriate the Crown will object or I will intercede. Otherwise, you're to answer the questions."

Blades obliged, but before long, he was again frustrated.

"You don't have to [create] smoke and mirrors, it's cool," he told Tan, and was again admonished by Justice Arnold. Eugene Tan was undeterred.

"Okay, so Mr. Sandeson's running around without any particular purpose or direction at this point, is that right?"

"Yes, sir."

"Okay, is he stepping in this?"

"Definitely. There's no way not to step in it. If you're inside the apartment, you're stepping in it."

"Is it possible through that time period, that either being forced to relive this or after hearing other people talk about it that your recollection may have changed over time?"

"Well, of course, like anything you play certain things in your head. I've researched like the human psyche and if you think about things a certain way, you change things in your head, but when you see a horrific scene like that, that is burned into your head."

It was a cross-examination that seemed to help the Crown's case more than William Sandeson's.

CHAPTER 9
APPLICATION FOR MISTRIAL

On the morning of May 9, 2017, Pookiel McCabe was about to resume his testimony from the day before about what he'd witnessed in William Sandeson's apartment on August 15, 2015. Everyone was expecting he would pick up where he had left off. Instead, defence lawyer Eugene Tan rose to address the judge with what would become the trial's most significant twist.

Tan explained that the defence had been informed the day before that an informer was inquiring about confidentiality. One of the officers working the case had advised the Crown someone was asserting that privilege. Informer privilege imposes a duty on the police, the Crown, and the courts not to release any information that risks revealing the identity of a police informer. However, Tan went on to say that it had been confirmed to his colleague, Brad Sarson, via text message the previous evening after 10:00 P.M., that the informer was now waiving any privilege claims. That's also when the defence learned the informer's name was Bruce Webb.

"Problem with that, My Lord, is Bruce Webb is an investigator who had been employed by the investigation firm retained by defence counsel."

Bruce Webb was a retired police officer who had served thirty-five years with the RCMP and was now working as a part-time private investigator for Martin & Associates Investigations, owned by Tom Martin, who was also a retired officer, having spent thirty years with Halifax Regional Police. He had been in business as a private investigator since 2011.

Lawyers often hire private investigators to take statements from witnesses so that the lawyers themselves don't end up as witnesses. For example, if a witness ends up on the stand saying something different than provided in the statement, the lawyer could also be called to testify, but that can't happen if the lawyer wasn't the one speaking with the witness in the first place.

So it was that in the early fall of 2016, while William Sandeson's defence team was frantically preparing for his trial, Tom Martin tasked Bruce Webb with tracking down key witnesses to find out what they might say under pressure.

"Shortly thereafter, and perhaps a little suspiciously, Mr. Blades and Mr. McCabe came forward and they provided statements to the police," Tan explained. In November, when Tan received copies of the new video statements in which Blades and McCabe now claimed to have witnessed the aftermath of murder, he confronted his private investigator.

"My instruction had been, 'When you interview them, make sure that you press them a little bit so that we have a sense of what they may say under pressure.' Basically [Webb] shrugged his shoulders and he said, 'I must have leaned a little too hard.'" Tan said he asked Tom Martin to investigate further and was given the same assurances. So it seemed it was an unfortunate coincidence for the defence that the witnesses had so drastically changed their stories and the defence would just have to live with it. Tan continued his work on the case.

But now, three weeks into the trial, it appeared that Sandeson's own investigator had turned against him and started working for the police.

On the morning of May 9, Eugene Tan told the judge that Webb had sat in on strategic defence meetings; that the defence now had no idea what information Webb had shared with witnesses and the police; and that he believed solicitor–client privilege had been breached. (Solicitor–client privilege is a right protected under the Canadian Charter of Rights and Freedoms that protects all communications between a professional legal adviser and his or her client from being disclosed without the permission of the client.) He also told the judge that Webb's employment had been terminated the night before and he was no longer taking calls from the defence.

"So in light of all that, My Lord, we would be seeking a motion for a mistrial."

Justice Joshua Arnold interjected immediately. "Aren't you ahead of yourself on this?"

"Well, I would suggest, My Lord, that the damage, frankly, has been done," replied Eugene Tan.

"I don't see how you're at a stage to request a mistrial when you don't know the facts yet either."

And so the court entered into another voir dire to determine who said what and who knew what when. It would be the seventh of eleven voir dires in the Sandeson trial.

Bruce Webb was subpoenaed to testify in the voir dire the next day. He told the court he had been tasked with interviewing Justin Blades and Pookiel McCabe as well as others, including Sonja Gashus, Sandeson's girlfriend at the time. He acknowledged he had signed confidentiality agreements with Martin & Associates and that any information he would obtain would be the property of that firm.

"You understand that you had been retained by the defence?" asked Eugene Tan.

"Yes," came the response.

In fact, it was Adam Sandeson, William Sandeson's brother, who put Webb in touch with Blades. Blades also testified in the voir dire that Webb told him he was trying to help Sandeson and his family. The two met on October 18, 2016.

"Do you recall how you introduced yourself?" Tan asked Webb on the stand.

"I introduced myself as a private investigator for Martin & Associates."

But what Tan really wanted to know was if Webb had encouraged Blades to go to the police.

"Mr. Blades, during the interview process and at the end, wanted to come clean. He had a real burden on his shoulders," replied Webb. "He was really, really messed up. He said, 'I'm sorry that I didn't tell the police everything at the time.'"

"All right. My question was, Mr. Webb, whether you encouraged Mr. Blades to go forward and speak to the police?"

"I said, 'Would you like to speak to the police?' and he said, 'Yes.'"

"And that's all you said? You asked him?"

"I said, 'I know a fella, and I can put you in contact.'"

"So you facilitated a meeting with the police. Is that correct?"

"Yes, I did. I felt really bad for him because he was in such a messed-up situation."

Blades corroborated that story when it was his turn on the stand.

"He wasn't just like, 'You need to go do this, but it's in your best interest.' And I think he's right," he testified.

Later the same day, Webb was driving down the road in his own neighbourhood when he saw his neighbour, a police officer, out walking with a new puppy. Webb waved him over.

Staff Sergeant Richard Lane was in his twenty-eighth year as a police officer in Nova Scotia and was a watch commander for Halifax Regional Police at the time. He testified he wouldn't consider Webb a friend but that he would wave or say hello if he saw him in the neighbourhood. He knew that Webb worked for Tom Martin.

"How did you broach the subject with Staff Sergeant Lane? What'd you say?" Eugene Tan asked Webb in court.

"I told him that I had interviewed Justin Blades and he wanted to come forward 'cause he has more information on what occurred."

"Okay, is that all you said?"

"And I said that when he looked in the room he saw Taylor Samson's body slumped over in a chair." (Blades had actually said he saw a man slumped over in a chair—a man he couldn't identify. He had never met Taylor Samson.)

"Okay, did you express to Staff Sergeant Lane that in your opinion the police weren't doing enough to further their own investigation?"

"I don't believe I did."

But Staff Sergeant Lane's testimony was contradictory.

"He knew what position I held at the time, and he wanted to express a concern, I guess, that he was afraid we weren't doing enough to the investigation."

"During that conversation, did he relay to you any other information such as contact information for Mr. Blades or what Mr. Blades might have to say to you?" asked Tan.

"He did at that time tell me that Mr. Blades had seen the victim dead at the table. In the same conversation, he didn't want to be involved, basically remain anonymous, so I didn't want to talk to him too much about it."

Eugene Tan wanted to know what motivated a man working for the defence to effectively switch sides.

"I was motivated by helping this young guy get his life back on track 'cause he was harbouring what he saw that night for over a year."

"Okay, so you're motivated by your desire to help Mr. Blades?"

"Yes."

"Is it also fair to say that you're motivated in part because you had come to the conclusion yourself that Mr. Sandeson was guilty?"

Long pause. "A strong likelihood yes, based on what Mr. Blades told me."

Sandeson's girlfriend, Sonja Gashus, testified that she had also met with Bruce Webb and that he had encouraged her to remove herself from the situation as much as possible, supporting her decision to decrease her communication with Sandeson. "He said that it didn't look good for Will," Gashus told the court.

Webb admitted he "might" have been breaking confidentiality rules, that he was really torn over what to do with the information he had received, and that he wished he had talked about it with his boss.

Martin testified he had been retained by Walker Dunlop, Tan's law firm, to do a case review and locate and interview people in relation to the Sandeson file, beginning in the fall of 2015. He testified Bruce Webb had been one of his senior investigators for nearly four years and would have signed a confidentiality agreement drawn up by his firm's lawyers, an agreement he believed Webb had breached in a serious manner.

Martin also testified he was aware Blades and McCabe had gone to the police shortly after Webb interviewed them.

"It caused me to have a conversation with Mr. Webb in which I asked him, did he in any way, shape, or form, suggest or direct Mr. Blades to contact the police?"

"And his response was?"

"Absolutely not."

Martin said he believed Webb and it was because of that belief, he said, that he didn't share this information with defence counsel. He did speak with Webb about the matter again, but not until two nights before this testimony.

"I told him that I wasn't happy learning that he was a confidential source for the police."

He testified that Webb told him he was not.

"He explained to me that he had interviewed Mr. Blades. Mr. Blades was the only individual discussed. He had interviewed Mr. Blades and Mr. Blades had said he'd wanted to contact the police and he wanted Mr. Webb to make that happen for him. I asked Mr. Webb, 'Why didn't you tell me about this?' And he said he made a mistake."

Webb admitted that throughout the course of the investigation he would have been privy to strategic meetings and information that would have been considered to be privileged.

Lane said Webb told him he had interviewed Blades—he didn't say in what capacity, but Lane assumed it was as a private investigator working for Sandeson.

"Okay, did that raise any concerns with you, the fact that somebody retained by the accused was offering information to the police?" Tan asked.

"I got the feeling he knew the accused was guilty and didn't want him to get away with it. That's the perception I got from him."

"The fact that this information came about as a result of his retainer by the accused, did that weigh on your mind at all?"

"I'm more of an as-long-as-the-truth-gets-out kinda guy so that's basically why I said, 'I'll get somebody to get in touch with ya.'"

Lane spoke with Corporal Allison and another officer working the case. Allison, who admitted police otherwise had no plans to speak with Blades again, called Bruce Webb the following day.

"He didn't give me many details, just that Justin had disclosed to him something that was very troubling to him," Allison told the court. "He said Justin was messed up from what he witnessed. He also said that Justin witnessed something that happened in the apartment."

They all agreed to meet at Blades's house. Webb made the introduction and then Blades left with Allison to go give his statement.

The same day, Webb would track down another witness, Pookiel McCabe, who had since moved to Ontario. Three days later, the two would speak over the phone.

Webb told McCabe he had been talking with Blades and relayed some of the information Blades had given him. He said he did not tell McCabe that Blades was going to be in touch with police. Again, Webb encouraged the witness to go to the police, but this time, received no commitment. The investigator passed on contact particulars to Corporal Allison.

"What motivated you to do it on that occasion?" Tan asked while Webb was on the stand.

"I wanted to do the right thing."

"You wanted to do the right thing. And by doing the right thing you had concluded that Mr. Sandeson was guilty?"

"A strong possibility."

"A strong possibility. Right, so that was your conclusion."

"There were two witnesses," Webb offered.

"Right, but my question being that you had reached your conclusion, is that correct?"

After a long pause, Webb quietly responded, "Yes."

Detective Constable Roger Sayer, Sergeant Derrick Boyd, and Corporal Jody Allison all testified that they travelled to Toronto to interview Pookiel McCabe and showed up at his home unannounced with the assistance of some Ontario officers.

In court, Tan asked McCabe if he believed he had any choice but to go with police to provide another statement when they showed up at his door. He said that he believed he did.

"Why did you choose to participate?"

"Because it was the right thing to do."

But in his testimony, Webb admitted that on some level he knew going to the police with what he had learned wasn't the right thing for him to do.

"And that's borne out in the fact that you were asking for confidentiality from the police," Tan suggested.

"Yes," Webb replied.

Corporal Allison had previously told the court that Webb had been requesting confidentiality from the beginning and that he had asked that his name not be used in any fashion. Detective Constable Sayer had also said he was aware Webb had requested anonymity. "If somebody makes that request, I will honour it," he had said.

Somehow, something still got confused.

"You asked for privilege, which you've since waived," Tan continued probing Webb on the stand.

There was no response.

"Since that time, you have elected not to pursue that?" Tan pressed.

Again, there was no response. Tan waited.

"I don't recall that," Webb said finally, and everyone in the courtroom knew there was another problem.

"Sorry, My Lord, I was advised that it was no longer being asserted," Tan offered the judge.

"We're going to stand down now. Mr. Webb, you'll remain under oath, and I'm just going to have you wait outside the courtroom while I chat with the lawyers."

"Well, My Lord," Tan began.

The judge interrupted, firmly.

"We're going to take a break right now, Mr. Tan, and you and the Crown are going to have a chat and you're going to sort this out, you're going to find out where this information came from and where the assertion that confidentiality and privilege was waived [came from], because clearly Mr. Webb is indicating that it was not. And then we're going to resume and you're going to explain to me what's going on here."

Susan MacKay jumped in. "I can do that without a break, My Lord, right now."

"Okay, Ms. MacKay."

"My Lord, I spoke with Corporal Allison, I think it's two nights ago now, around suppertime. He indicated to me on the phone that Mr. Webb had agreed to waive privilege, the claim of privilege, confidentiality. That's what I was told."

"This is not a knee-jerk-reaction situation. We have somebody on the stand who has just said under oath that they were not waiving their confidentiality, their privilege," said the judge.

He took a break and ultimately decided to enter into a voir dire within a voir dire—essentially a trial within a trial within a trial—to determine whether Bruce Webb could claim informer privilege.

"It's a sensitive issue and, although it may be trying to put the cat back into the bag, that is not possible," said Justice Arnold. Although Webb's name had already been published, Arnold held the voir dire in camera, excluding the press and all members of the public from the courtroom. (At this point all live reporting had ceased, and social media was rife with rumours as to what was taking place. Many thought Sandeson must be changing his plea.)

Lawyers were directed not to discuss Arnold's decision, and it was not released publicly until August 25, 2017, well after the trial had concluded.

Justice Josh Arnold ruled Bruce Webb could have no expectation of privacy under the circumstances.

"While the identity of confidential informers must be closely guarded, if Webb ever was a source or confidential informant in these circumstances, once he met with the police and Blades together to introduce them and to assist in making Blades comfortable such that he would provide a statement to the police, he lost any possible status as a confidential informant," Arnold wrote.

"Webb was not merely a citizen who quietly provided the police with information about criminal activity with the expectation of confidentiality. Instead, he became an active participant in the criminal investigation and as such is not a source or a confidential informant."

Back in May 2017, with no explanation as to why or how, the original voir dire continued, and the public was welcomed back inside the courtroom.

Bruce Webb took the stand again, but this time he was not questioned by Eugene Tan. In yet another bizarre twist, the lead defence lawyer announced he would also become a witness, meaning he could not be present while Webb was being examined by his colleague, Brad Sarson. Sarson could also not be the one to question Tan, so yet another Halifax lawyer joined the growing chorus of lawyers who now had their hands in the Sandeson trial.

Sarson began by reminding Webb he had previously testified that he had stopped to speak with Staff Sergeant Richard Lane while he was out walking a puppy. He asked if he also had an earlier conversation with him at Lane's house. Webb agreed that he went to Lane's house to try to "get a feel" for the investigation and that he told him things didn't look good for Sandeson based on the facts he had.

All of this was happening without the presence of the jurors, who had been sent home.

Seated beside his legal team, Sandeson took notes.

"I also felt at that point that if I didn't come forward then I would be obstructing justice," Webb continued.

He agreed he'd sat in on several defence meetings about the case.

"It would have included discussion of defence strategy?" Sarson asked.

"I really wasn't sure what the defence strategy was," Webb replied.

When pressed he said he was party to discussions including legal arguments about the defence's plan to attack the search of Sandeson's apartment as well as the statements he gave to police.

Webb testified he was aware Justin Blades had previously told the police he hadn't seen anything on the night in question, but he didn't believe Blades had been truthful.

"And what did you base that on?"

"The look on their face when they looked in the apartment on the video."

Webb was referencing the surveillance video captured in the hallway outside Sandeson's apartment building in which Justin Blades can be seen looking inside the apartment in the minutes following the murder. He appears to be shocked.

Following Webb's interviews with Blades and McCabe and following their final statements to the police, Webb met with his boss, Tom Martin, and Sandeson's legal team to present the results of his interviews. The defence lawyers were not yet aware the witnesses had gone to the police with statements that would sink their case. Webb didn't tell them.

"Do you recall a telephone call with Mr. Tan a couple of days later on November 10, 2016?"

"I don't recall that."

"So if I were to suggest to you that you had a telephone call with Mr. Tan wherein he outlined to you that he had received new statements from the police, one from Mr. Blades, one from Mr. McCabe, and he questioned you about what you had said to them, does that assist you in recalling whether you had a telephone call with Mr. Tan?"

Webb cut him off. "I don't remember any phone call with Mr. Tan. I'm sorry."

"Do you recall Mr. Tan at any point in time asking you whether or not you had told Mr. McCabe or Mr. Blades to contact the police?"

"I don't recall that; I don't recall speaking with Mr. Tan on the phone."

"Do you recall having a conversation with Mr. Martin or Mr. Martin confronting you with what you might have done or said to have led Mr. Blades and Mr. McCabe to the police?"

"No, I do not."

"So you're saying that you never were put in a position where you had to lie to either Mr. Martin or Mr. Tan with respect to your actions as far as going to the police or encouraging Mr. Blades or Mr. McCabe to go to the police," Sarson said.

"I didn't volunteer the information and I wasn't asked."

"So if I were to suggest to you that you were confronted and you had lied and said that in fact you weren't sure why they had gone to the police—there must have been a coincidence or you leaned too hard on them or something to that effect—you would disagree with that or you don't remember that?"

"I don't remember that."

On cross-examination, Crown attorney Susan MacKay asked Bruce Webb only a couple of questions: whether he had communicated to Blades and McCabe any of the information he had gleaned from defence meetings, and whether he had communicated the same information to the police. In both cases, he said he had not.

Bruce Webb was free to go, but before the defence called its own lawyer Justice Arnold wanted an explanation for this highly unusual move. Sarson explained that, since the Crown was proposing to argue the defence had an obligation to pursue disclosure—meaning they should have asked about Bruce Webb's involvement when they became suspicious—the defence should have an opportunity to show they did their due diligence. That seemed to satisfy the judge, and Sandeson's lead lawyer was sworn in as a witness to be questioned by Mark Knox, another Halifax defence lawyer. The testimony was brief.

Tan said he received the new video statements from Blades and McCabe the same day his team met with Webb for an update on his interviews with them—but not until later that day, after the meeting. It was a few weeks after the statements were obtained by the police, and five months before the trial began. Tan said he didn't have a chance to review the statements until the following day, at which point he called Webb.

"Okay, so you actually spoke to him on this occasion, true?"

"I did, yes," confirmed Tan.

It was the complete opposite testimony provided by Bruce Webb just moments earlier.

"Okay, and what was the essence of the conversation?" Knox continued.

"The essence of the conversation was that I had been surprised that police statements had been taken, particularly in such relative close proximity to the time that he had met with two of those witnesses.... I said to him, 'Bruce, what happened here? What's going on? Why would they have gone to the police?' His response to me was, 'You had told me to lean on them and I guess I leaned too hard.'"

"Okay, thank you, Mr. Tan. Those are the questions that I have."

The cross-examination went a little longer—a rare opportunity for a prosecutor to question her legal opponent.

Susan MacKay wanted to know if Tan had listened to the new statement Blades gave to police in its entirety before speaking with Webb. He said he had.

"Okay, and so in there you saw that toward the end of the statement he said, 'I think you guys have that number maybe. I gave it to Bruce.' And then the answer to that being, 'Yeah.' And then he said some other things and that he made reference three times to 'Bruce' in there."

"Correct."

"And in fact, how good it had felt to speak with Bruce," MacKay persisted.

"Right," agreed Tan.

"Did it not make you think that there was a link there between Bruce Webb and the police having his phone number and contacting Mr. Blades?"

"No, not at all."

"Why not?" MacKay asked.

Tan said that he had been assured that confidentiality would be a top priority and he was satisfied there would not be any breach of protocols.

"When I heard 'Bruce' I certainly said, 'That is a little bit of a concern,' but frankly it was also consistent with him having leaned on them, and Mr. Blades having made a decision to go forward. So I didn't question that he would have broken his confidentiality."

"And you did not ask the Crown about whether there was any connection either, did you?"

"No, I had no reason to. I understood the Crown had an obligation to disclose that."

That concluded the evidence the judge would hear in the application for a mistrial. The lawyers got set to argue their cases. The defence was up first.

Over the course of several hours, with the judge interjecting to ask questions every step of the way, Brad Sarson argued the mistrial application was based on three grounds: late disclosure by the Crown; an alleged breach of solicitor–client privilege by Bruce Webb; and William Sandeson's right to a fair trial.

"The defence takes the position that it should be uncontested that the Crown had an obligation to disclose this," Sarson declared, referring to the fact the Crown didn't inform the defence of the existence of a tipster, and further about what it knew about Bruce Webb's role in facilitating the statements Blades and McCabe gave to the police.

The Crown argued it didn't disclose the information because it believed the defence already knew. "The Crown's position is that the statement itself discloses Mr. Webb's involvement," MacKay argued, referencing the several times Justin Blades referred to "Bruce" in the statement.

Sarson said that it was easy to see the connection in hindsight.

Justice Arnold pointed out that while the name "Bruce" is mentioned in the statement, the extent of his involvement and the actions he took are not. But the Crown said it couldn't share that, because it learned when everyone else did—when the witnesses were on the stand.

Sarson reminded the judge that the defence did confront both Bruce Webb and his employer, Tom Martin, to inquire about the strange coincidence, and argued it had therefore taken appropriate steps.

"Why wouldn't the defence write to the Crown and say, 'Is there something that I should know about here?'" Justice Arnold asked Sarson.

Sarson maintained it never occurred to the defence to do so because it never occurred to the lawyers that Webb would act in this fashion.

"Having done research on this issue, I can say that I haven't encountered a case where a private investigator retained by the defence decided to actively work for the police, which is essentially what Mr. Webb did, and assist in the creation of evidence and lead that evidence to the police. Couldn't find a single case where that had happened."

"Well, did anybody call Mr. Blades, who was clearly co-operating with everybody who had spoken to him at that point, to ask him why he was mentioning 'Bruce' throughout this statement?" Arnold asked.

"No."

"Why not? He wanted to speak to everybody. He spoke to Mr. Webb, he spoke to the police, he wanted to apologize to Mr. Samson's mother. I mean, why didn't the defence just pick up the phone and call him, and say, 'Why are you mentioning Bruce all over this statement?'"

Sarson responded that the defence simply assumed that after Blades told the story once (to Webb), he decided to go to the police of his own volition. He also said that if the defence had been made aware of the information in a timely fashion it would have requested that the statements of Blades and McCabe be ruled inadmissible before the trial began.

But it was too late for that. The witnesses had already testified in front of the jury.

Sarson went on to say that giving the defence another chance to question some of the witnesses was also not an appropriate remedy for the problem because it would give the jury the impression that the defence was desperate, or that something had gone wrong.

"The clumsy sequence of events in this case cannot help but result in confusion in the community as well as skepticism about the efficacy of the jury system," he explained. "The importance of the public's confidence in the Canadian jury system and in the administration of justice simply cannot be overstated."

The defence also argued that Bruce Webb was subject to solicitor-client privilege, and that he not only alerted the police but essentially created the evidence now before the jury in the form of testimony from Blades and McCabe.

The judge asked the defence whether Webb would have been obstructing justice, as he feared, if he had not told the police what Blades and McCabe had shared with him. "What were his legal obligations?" he asked.

"He had no legal obligations, I would suggest," Sarson responded, saying there was no difference between information being given to a lawyer or a private investigator.

The Crown argued Webb was not subject to solicitor–client privilege at all, as that privilege protects only communication between a client and his lawyer.

The defence further argued that the police would never have located Blades and McCabe if not for the actions of Bruce Webb.

"What we're dealing with here are the Halifax Regional Police and the RCMP," said Justice Arnold. "We have Mr. Blades, who has testified that he was working."

"Mmhmm," said Sarson.

"At the hospital."

"Yep."

"In the emergency department."

"Yes."

"And that he was fighting sporadically, professionally, in public." (Justin Blades testified that he was an avid mixed martial arts competitor before he got involved with track and field.)

"Yes."

"Are you really suggesting to me that this would have been a stretch for the police to have located Mr. Blades?"

"There had been no contact with him since—" Sarson began.

"I understand that he hadn't raised the flag and said, 'Here I am,'" Arnold interjected.

"Right."

"Or that he hadn't given them forwarding information. So is it your position that the police are only able to locate individuals who have given them forwarding information?"

"No."

"I just have a tough time with this, Mr. Sarson, that the police wouldn't have been able to locate these guys."

"Ability to locate and motivation to locate are two different things, I would suggest," said Sarson.

"Sure, yes," Arnold conceded.

The Crown countered that while the police had no plans to re-interview Blades and McCabe, they never believed they hadn't seen anything, and both men were always on the Crown's witness list and would have been subpoenaed to testify eventually.

"The Crown submits that the information he provided was discoverable to the Crown in that it very likely would have eventually come to light to the police, but probably just closer to the actual start of the trial," MacKay said.

Finally, the defence argued there was simply no way forward because Sandeson's right to a fair trial had been jeopardized, pointing out the police were aware Webb was working for the defence but still made efforts to seek out information from him.

"What are they supposed to do?" questioned Arnold. "Are they supposed to say, 'Hey I can't talk to you?'"

Sarson said that, at the very least, the police had an obligation to consult the Crown, which they did not do.

The Crown argued that, while the defence may have no legal duty to get to the truth of the matter, the police do have a duty to investigate and reinvestigate until they find out what actually happened. Susan MacKay acknowledged that while it was certainly unfortunate for the defence that the private investigator decided to tip off the police, it wasn't unfair.

"Bottom line is, the right to a fair trial does not equate to a right to the most favourable trial possible," MacKay proclaimed.

The defence persisted in its request for a new trial.

"And then what?" asked the judge.

"As in any mistrial, the Crown has the right to elect to retry," Sarson said.

He said the defence would then seek to exclude Blades and McCabe from testifying if there was a new trial.

Arnold asked Sarson if there was any other case where a witness had not been allowed to testify under similar circumstances.

"No," he said, "not that I've encountered." He paused before forging ahead with more. "But this is part of the problem. Because of the way disclosure has unfolded, defence, mid-trial, is scrambling to address a number of issues. The entire order of the trial has been thrown out of whack.... I think all parties would agree that this trial has been anything but smooth in the way it's unfolded."

On that, everyone did seem to agree.

Still, five days later, Justice Joshua Arnold denied Sandeson's request for a new trial. "I do not think that it's necessary. I don't think that there will be a miscarriage of justice if a mistrial is not declared."

Later, in a written decision, Arnold stated the Crown was obliged to disclose the specific fact of Webb's contact with the police, and failed to do so in a timely fashion, but that the defence also did not diligently pursue disclosure of the identity or involvement of "Bruce" in the statements. Arnold felt any infringement of Sandeson's right to a fair trial as a result of the late disclosure was at the lower end of the scale. Further, Arnold ruled Webb's communications with the police did not amount to a breach of solicitor–client privilege.

Justice Arnold did offer a remedy for the late disclosure "in these very unusual circumstances." He offered to adjourn the trial in order to allow Sandeson time to consider whom he may wish to re-cross-examine and then to conduct that additional questioning prior to the Crown closing its case.

Sandeson refused the offer.

And so, the trial continued.

CHAPTER 10
THE CROWN'S CASE: FRIEND OR FOE

The next witness is Chantale Comeau," said Susan MacKay.

A number of people who knew William Sandeson, perhaps even considered him a friend, were dragged into the trial to tell the jury what they knew about his whereabouts in the days following the murder.

Chantale Comeau was a twenty-three-year-old Dalhousie student, poised to graduate the following week with a bachelor of arts. In the summer of 2015, she was working at Starbucks in downtown Halifax with Sandeson's girlfriend, Sonja Gashus. Gashus regularly drove her to work. She didn't know Sandeson very well but said she had met him. On the morning of Sunday, August 16, she thought it was odd that Sandeson was driving and Gashus was in the passenger's seat.

Comeau testified Sandeson was wearing a hunter-orange hat and what she thought was a big jacket or hoodie with sweatpants.

"Hey, Will, why do you have a hat on? It's like fifteen degrees or so outside," Comeau said she said to Sandeson when he picked her up. She said Sandeson just kind of shrugged off her comment. On cross-examination by the defence, Comeau retracted that statement, saying she didn't believe she made a comment about the weather after all.

She said the only conversation on the short drive to the Starbucks on Queen Street was about what Sandeson and Gashus had eaten at the Stubborn Goat the night before and what Comeau had had when she had gone there previously.

Comeau said the car was the same car Gashus always drove, but that there were a bunch of things in the back seat that weren't usually there. She couldn't recall what.

Comeau's testimony was brief.

Dylan Zinck-Selig, twenty-four, testified he was Sandeson's roommate in August 2015. They had been living together since September 2014, but Zinck-Selig testified he wasn't spending much time at the Henry Street apartment because he was with his girlfriend. He went back a couple of times a week to let his cat out. Sandeson also had a cat and Zinck-Selig testified he let both cats out through his bedroom window—the same window through which Sandeson told police Morphsuited intruders had entered the apartment and killed Taylor Samson.

"I'm going to take you back to Friday, August 14th," Kim McOnie told Zinck-Selig. "Can you tell us what, if any, contact you had with Will Sandeson on that day?"

"I believe he told me not to come home past eight o'clock the following day," said Zinck-Selig, telling the court he was confident in the information, just not entirely clear through which method he had received that message.

"And was it usual or unusual to get that sort of request from Mr. Sandeson?"

"For a whole night it was unusual. Usually it would be an hour, twenty minutes, tops."

Zinck-Selig did not question Sandeson about the odd request.

He was at the apartment he shared with Sandeson around 7:30 P.M. on Saturday, August 15. No one else was home at that time and he didn't notice anything about the window in his bedroom.

Zinck-Selig said the next time he was at his apartment was at 11:30 P.M. on Sunday, August 16. Zinck-Selig said when he first arrived back at the Henry Street apartment, no one was there. Sandeson arrived about twenty minutes later; Sandeson's girlfriend arrived shortly after.

"Do you recall what you talked about?"

"Just about how the apartment was clean, and he mentioned he threw out the shower curtain," Zinck-Selig testified, somewhat hesitantly.

He said Sandeson and Gashus went to bed. He left around 1:30 A.M., picked up his girlfriend, and went back to her apartment. He didn't return to Henry Street until Tuesday or Wednesday and at that point police officers wouldn't let him in. He didn't know why at the time.

He told the court he believed he messaged Will Sandeson on Monday to ask if he was home. There was no response, and he had had no contact with him since then.

On cross-examination, Zinck-Selig confirmed he and Sandeson used the window in his bedroom to access a barbecue on the roof. He also confirmed that, while there was no stair access to the roof, there were stairs on the adjacent building, and it was fairly easy to climb over the handrail to get to the roof outside his bedroom window. He said he had done it himself. (Sarson was trying to show the jury that the story Sandeson had told police about intruders entering that way was possible.)

Sarson also asked Zinck-Selig if it had surprised him when Sandeson told him he threw out the shower curtain.

"No, it didn't," Zinck-Selig replied.

"And that was because there was some mould on the shower curtain?"

"Yes, there was."

Dylan Zinck-Selig was free to go.

"Next witness is Nick Rotta-Loria," said Kim McOnie.

Rotta-Loria was twenty-five years old and in the midst of finishing his PhD in chemistry at Dal. He told the jury he lived upstairs in the same building as Adam Sandeson, William Sandeson's brother. On the morning of Monday, August 17, Rotta-Loria said he was at work at a lab at Dal when he got a call from Adam to move his car because Sandeson had his motorcycle parked at the back of the house.

"I just walked over to the house, moved my car, had a quick chat with Will about his schedule for med school, just kind of chit-chatting about this and that, and then I went back to work."

Two days later, Rotta-Loria testified he ran into a girl he had tutored who was really upset.

"I asked her what happened. She told me she'd found out that Taylor had been killed," he said. He drove her home and then went home himself. Adam Sandeson and his girlfriend were there.

"I told them. I said I'd run into a girl, she told me Taylor had been killed, and Adam said, 'Yeah, I just got off the phone with my dad a few minutes ago and Will's up on first-degree murder charges.'" That's when Adam's other roommate, Matt Donovan, came into the living room. It was around midnight on Wednesday.

"We were chatting about it and then Matt kind of said, 'Should we tell him what's in the basement?' to which I said, 'What is in the basement?'"

The group headed downstairs where they found three items: a Dal Track and Field backpack, a KitchenAid box, and a plastic bag.

"I put on a pair of gloves, and I opened the backpack and in it were what looked like freezer bags of weed," Rotta-Loria testified.

Rotta-Loria said, not knowing what to do, he and his friends went back upstairs and agreed they would sleep on it. The next day Rotta-Loria and Donovan decided they needed to take action. "We figured this had something to do with the case," Rotta-Loria told the jury.

He decided to call a lawyer who advised the group on how to give statements to the police. When they went home, they found the drug squad going through the house.

Detective Constable Illya Nielsen, with HRP's forensic identification unit, told the jury he executed the drug search warrant. He did a walkthrough of the entire residence, photographing each room as it was before police began their search. He went through those photos for the jury, identifying each room. One of the photos was of a Morphsuit, which was considered an item of interest and found hanging in a closet in the apartment. No one ever explained why it was there.

Nielsen testified he found a backpack, a green grocery bag, and a taped-up box inside a closet in the basement. Inside the box, he found two vacuum-sealed bags with markings in black marker on them; he found what appeared to be marijuana inside the bags. He said there were similar bags in the backpack and the green grocery bag. He found fingerprints on the box and the bags, but they didn't match Sandeson's or Samson's. The fingerprints were also run nationally against anyone who had a criminal record in Canada. There were no matches.

Nielsen also said a small red stain, less than half a centimetre in diameter, was located on a bag found in the KitchenAid box.

As the items were entered into evidence, Nielsen unwrapped a very large bag of weed, telling the court it contained the 14.63 pounds of marijuana that was in the box. That was followed by another 5.24 pounds of weed he said was found in the backpack and 1.03 pounds of marijuana found in the grocery bags.

On cross-examination, the defence asked Rotta-Loria why he wore nitrile gloves, the same gloves police wear to process crime scenes, when he looked at those items. (Rotta-Loria had taken a box from the lab for cleaning around the house.)

"I watched a lot of crime shows," came the response. The PhD student surely never imagined he'd end up in the middle of a real-life crime scene.

Matthew Donovan testified he was Adam Sandeson's room-mate. The twenty-one-year-old had just finished his fourth year of engineering at Dal. He told the court he and Adam Sandeson were also teammates on the Dal men's volleyball team. He had met Will Sandeson a few times.

He recounted the same story as Rotta-Loria, telling the court about discovering the weed and Adam getting a call from his dad that his brother had been arrested for murder.

"Adam was obviously very upset," he told the jury. "I spent most of the night consoling him; spending time with him."

Adam Sandeson also testified at his brother's murder trial. He told the jury he got some texts from Sandeson on August 17 between 7:00 and 8:00 A.M. saying he was coming by to drop off laundry, as he often did. Adam said he went to work, and Sandeson came by that evening. He told the court they just talked about "general stuff, nothing out of the ordinary."

Sandeson was there for less than an hour. Adam didn't see him bring any laundry.

"He said something about something might smell a little in the basement," the younger Sandeson told the court.

When Sandeson left, Adam went downstairs to see what he meant. That's when he saw an Adidas backpack with marijuana in it. He opened it but left it where it was and brought it up with Sandeson the next day.

"I asked him about it, and he said it wasn't his, I think, and that there was more."

Adam Sandeson said he and his roommates went downstairs to confirm what Sandeson had said and discovered the KitchenAid box.

"I think after we saw that down there, I learned a little more about what was going on."

As his brother testified, William Sandeson was sitting in the courtroom, writing notes.

When the Crown completed its questioning, the defence team conferred with Sandeson for a few minutes before deciding not to cross-examine his brother.

CHAPTER 11

THE CROWN'S CASE: SEARCHING THE FARM

D on Calpito, a Toronto-based senior security investigator with TELUS, told the court he's used primarily as a witness by TELUS in criminal trials and helps police interpret phone records they obtain from his company.

Calpito testified there was an outgoing call from Sandeson's phone on the morning of August 18 using a tower near Truro and Brookfield. The call lasted 189 seconds.

By 12:38 P.M. that day, Sandeson's phone was back in Halifax, pinging off a tower at Dalhousie University.

At 12:53, there was an outgoing call from Sandeson's phone on Gottingen Street, near Halifax Police Headquarters. That call was 27 seconds long. Sergeant Charla Keddy previously testified Sandeson arrived to speak with her just before 1:00 P.M. on the 18th.

Calpito also had information from Taylor Samson's phone records. Just in case there was still any doubt about whether Samson was dead or alive, Calpito testified there were no text messages to or from Samson's phone after August 15, 2015, at 10:40 P.M. His phone last pinged in Halifax, from a tower at Dal, when he sent a text message at 10:25 P.M. to William Sandeson. Calpito testified that no incoming messages meant the phone was off or in a no-service area.

The cellphone records showed Sandeson had been in the area near his parents' farm in Lower Truro at 10:05 A.M. and 10:16 A.M. on August 18. A couple of days earlier—the morning after Taylor Samson had been last seen entering Sandeson's apartment—Sandeson had texted his dad, "Think I will be home Tuesday to drop off junk from Halifax. Just not sorted yet."

That evidence led to an expansive six-day search of the family farm and surrounding areas. I was there in my role as a local news reporter, expecting to go live on the six o'clock broadcast each day with the news Taylor Samson's body had been found. It didn't happen.

Detective Constable Jonathan Jefferies was a member of the homicide unit and the scene coordinator for the search of the farm; he was tasked with liaising between the investigative team and the search team.

He arrived on August 25 around 11:00 A.M.

"Michael Sandeson was home, along with his son, and at that point I executed the warrant on him," Jefferies later told the jury.

Approximately fifteen minutes after arriving, he executed the warrant on Michael's mother, Ruth Sandeson, who also has a home on the property. Jefferies advised the family where officers would be and what they could expect over the coming days.

There were also farms on either side of the Sandeson farm, and Jefferies sent other officers to speak with those owners to obtain their consent to search their properties. They agreed.

Police erected a command bus behind the main home. Ground Search and Rescue had its own command site, down the road at the fire hall. Depending on the day, there would be between twenty-five and eighty people searching the property.

Larry Corbin had been a volunteer with Ground Search and Rescue for ten years. When it came to the Sandeson case, he didn't exactly know what he was looking for.

"They told us we could possibly find human remains and then just to search the area and look for anything that doesn't look like it's supposed to be there," he later told the court.

Combing through thick brush on the very large property, Corbin found a rusty-coloured pair of gloves, balled up, one folded inside the other.

"We were given the area to search right behind a farmhouse. There was a brook that ran up, and basically when we come out of one little spot in the treeline, they were laying right there at the edge," he testified, detailing the difficult terrain.

The gloves looked like the ones Sandeson was seen wearing in surveillance video outside his Halifax apartment.

Corbin notified the command post, flagged the area with orange tape, and continued on.

Corporal Shawn Reynolds was the Ground Search and Rescue incident commander. After trying to locate the site with the help of a GPS twice, he called on Corbin to lead him to the gloves. It was early afternoon.

Reynolds later told the court: "He led me down a little tiny trail where there's a bit of a valley, a bit of a depression in the ground, with a number of old trucks, and there was a small footpath. Down the footpath and to the left...he showed me a red pair of gloves that were in a ball."

They seized the gloves and turned them over to the investigative triangle.

Later the same day, there was another find.

Wayne Burns had been a volunteer with Ground Search and Rescue for fifteen years. He said he got a call on August 27 that a member of his team had found some garbage bags and an Adidas bag in the bed of an old, abandoned truck. He was the team leader, so he called the command post and stayed until the RCMP arrived around forty-five minutes later.

The searchers would not have been aware, but William Sandeson had been seen on video loading garbage bags and a blue Adidas bag into the trunk of his car the same morning his phone had pinged in the Truro area.

Corporal Reynolds walked down the footpath with Wayne Burns amongst those old trucks, which Reynolds later described to the jury by saying, "It looks like a former ice-cream box on a five-tonne truck." Burns showed Reynolds the bags his team had found inside. They held the scene and seized the evidence.

Detective Constable Illya Nielsen of the Ident unit, who had been at the farm earlier in the day to test the gloves for blood—it came back negative—was called back to the farm when the items were found inside the so-called ice-cream truck. The blue Adidas bag and the three garbage bags would give the police even more evidence against Sandeson.

There was some staining on the floor under the Adidas bag, so Nielsen did a swab. He said the items were brought back to police headquarters in Halifax that night, where the contents were photographed.

Later in court, he showed the jury a booklet of photos he'd taken at the farm, including those of the blue Adidas bag and its contents. "There was a strong decomposing rotting smell coming from this bag," Nielsen testified.

There was a large black duffle bag located inside that bag, and inside the duffle bag were towels, soaking wet. Nielsen explained the best way to preserve DNA is to dry items as quickly as possible, so the items were hung in drying cabinets.

He said there was a blue tarp inside the first garbage bag. Inside the second garbage bag, two yellow fibre cloths, an empty box for garbage bags, a grey microfibre cloth, an orange-and-black–stained towel, a blue microfibre stained towel, a shower curtain, a shower curtain ring, a stack of unused black garbage bags, and a soaked roll of paper towel.

"All these items were wet; soaking wet," Nielsen added.

"Were you able to tell with what?" Kim McOnie asked.

"These orange-stained cloths had a strong smell of cleaner that came from them, but the rest seemed to be soaked with water," he said.

Inside the third garbage bag, Nielsen found a roll of tinfoil, a plastic bag with a strange reddish-rusty-coloured substance inside, an empty blueberry container, a balled-up piece of dry paper towel, an empty bag of cat litter, a can of Lysol disinfectant spray, peanut butter, and other packaging and household waste.

Nielsen had returned to the farm at 10:00 a.m. the next day to take more photos in daylight. Eleven and a half metres from the truck where the other items had been located, police found some garbage at the base of a tree. It included an envelope with the name "William" and a partial address "12 something" in Halifax, Nielsen testified, a Bank of Montréal letter addressed to "William Sandeson," and a Dalhousie student planner.

Sergeant André Habib, also in the forensic unit, also visited the farm that day to help with the search and had been primarily tasked with sifting through cow manure.

"There's a lot of cow manure on a farm and one of the cadaver dogs had indicated earlier that there was something there. They're trained to sit when they believe there's human remains there," he testified.

The next day, August 29, the cadaver dog indicated there was something near a body of water, a small pond, near the family farm. Habib was part of the team that drained that pond so they could see the bottom.

"We enlisted the help of a local company that brought in pumps and that went on into the next day until finally that pond was cleared."

"What was it you were looking for?" Susan MacKay later asked.

"I was looking for a body," Habib said. It was blunt.

He never found what he was looking for.

Nearly a month later, on September 23, Jefferies went to the correctional centre to make a plea to Sandeson regarding the whereabouts of Samson's body. Jefferies testified Sandeson told him he didn't wish to speak to him about that.

CHAPTER 12
THE CROWN'S CASE: FORENSICS

Throughout the trial, the jury had heard a great deal about staining that looked like blood or that officers believed was blood. Now they would get to find out whether it actually was blood.

Detective Constable James Wasson was in his thirtieth year of service with Halifax Police. It was his job to decide which evidence would be sent to the RCMP's National Forensic Lab in Ottawa. Wasson testified he was on a day off on August 19, 2015, when he got a call asking him to coordinate this file. He arrived at work at noon and had a look at the evidence that had been gathered so far. He did a walkthrough of the scene later that day, at 6:09 P.M.

Wasson also seized Sandeson's clothes and photographed an injury on his right shoulder. He testified there were areas of staining on the inner soles of both of his shoes. They reacted positively when officers used the presumptive test for blood. He sent one of the swabs to the lab but there wasn't enough for a DNA profile.

He also marked some areas on pants seized from Sandeson's apartment. They tested positive with the presumptive test for blood and were sent to the lab for further testing, but those tests did not confirm that the substance on the pants was blood.

Wasson swabbed the handgun seized from a locked safe at 1210 Henry Street and treated it with cyanoacrylate, or Krazy Glue, fumes.

"What happens is, the Krazy Glue fumes will stick to the oils that are deposited from the hands to the gun, in search for fingerprints," he told the jury.

But he said he couldn't get any usable fingerprints from Sandeson's gun.

While he was processing the gun for fingerprints, he noticed various red stains on it.

He swabbed multiple areas of the gun and sent them off to the lab. He also swabbed the mouth of Taylor Samson's water bottle and his razor, looking for Samson's DNA. Those swabs, along with DNA samples from Samson's mother and father, were also sent to the lab in an effort to create a DNA profile for him.

On cross-examination, Eugene Tan asked Wasson whether he had checked the knives, an axe, and a sword found in Sandeson's apartment for blood. Wasson said that he had.

"Why would you have done that?" Tan probed.

"In the event the body had been cut up," Wasson replied, before explaining the results were all negative.

No one could understand how Sandeson, significantly smaller than Samson, could have disposed of a body by himself, and there was no evidence anyone else had been involved.

Florence Célestin, a forensic DNA specialist from the RCMP's forensic lab in Ottawa, was accepted by the court as a qualified expert to provide opinion evidence in the forensic interpretation of DNA profiles. (Witnesses in Canadian courts are not permitted to give their opinions unless it is determined they are unbiased and have special knowledge that is reasonably necessary to help the jury understand complex or technical matters beyond the understanding of the average person.) Célestin said she'd worked on approximately 740 different cases and testified as an expert witness twelve times in various courts across Canada.

"Do you acknowledge and accept that you have a duty, even though you work for the RCMP, to give fair, objective, and non-partisan opinion evidence?" asked Susan MacKay.

"That is correct," Célestin agreed.

She explained how her team tests exhibits when they arrive at the lab in Ottawa. She said DNA technologists go through a four-step process to obtain a DNA profile, the first of which is extraction of the DNA.

"The DNA is in most of the cells of our body. For example, if you have a peach, and you have a pit of a peach, the cell is like the peach, the pit of the peach would be the nucleus of the cell, and inside it would be where the DNA is," she explained. "So part of that extraction process is to break that nucleus open to get the DNA."

The second step is quantification, which is to determine how much DNA is present. Célestin told the court the ideal amount to obtain a quality DNA profile is one nanogram, but it can be done with less.

The third step is amplification, making copies of the very specific regions of the DNA that they use in forensic science.

"Ninety-nine percent of our DNA, or even 99.9, is the same," she said. "There's this .01 percent of the DNA that varies among individuals, and that's what we use in forensic science to help differentiate between two individuals."

The fourth and final step is to visualize the DNA profile using specialized software. That's when a specialist like Célestin gets involved to do the interpretation.

Susan MacKay asked if any of the DNA samples from the different scenes and objects submitted in relation to this case matched the DNA of Taylor Samson.

Célestin said yes.

She further explained to the jury that generally she works with known DNA samples from alleged complainants or victims. In this case that was not possible, as Taylor Samson's remains still hadn't been located, so Célestin told the jury police provided the "next best thing"—a "quasi known" or a "putative known" sample. Those samples come from personal effects. In this case, the lab received the swabs from Samson's water bottle and razor and the lab was able to obtain a profile. To have more assurance that it was correct, they compared the profile against the DNA of Samson's parents, since DNA is inherited.

From that point on, the lab proceeded on the belief they were working with Samson's DNA.

Célestin testified that swabs from the bathroom and the table at the Henry Street apartment matched Taylor Samson's DNA. Samson's DNA was also found on three pieces of flooring from the kitchen, on the frame of the entry door, on the chair in the kitchen, the heater in the kitchen, and the bullet found in the window casing.

Célestin told the jury Samson's DNA was also found on the swath of carpet torn from the trunk of Sandeson's car, on the tarp seized from the Sandeson farm, on the shower curtain also found on the farm, and inside the duffle bag Sandeson told police was the biggest bag he'd ever seen.

She testified there were two DNA matches on the gun seized from the Henry Street apartment: Taylor Samson's and William Sandeson's.

Célestin explained that sometimes the confirmatory test for blood is positive, so then they know it is blood, but at that point they still don't know whether it is human or animal blood; once they obtain a human DNA profile they know it is human blood.

She said the sample from money found in Sandeson's apartment tested positive for blood but did not meet the minimum requirement of 0.25 nanograms required for DNA processing. (Today, that minimum threshold is 0.15.)

The Crown completed its questioning by asking if there were any concerns about contamination at the lab in Ottawa. The witness said not that she was aware of.

And that's exactly where Eugene Tan picked up his cross-examination.

"In fact, at least one exhibit arrived at the lab in a plastic bag that had been perforated, is that correct?"

"I don't recall. I would have to check the file."

Tan allowed her to do so.

"Yes, one of the exhibits had some minor damage, described as small tears," Célestin finally agreed, noting it was the pieces of flooring.

"So does that raise any issues of contamination or cross-contamination?" Tan continued.

Célestin replied that it would depend on what other exhibits it was packaged with, but if the bag was placed inside a box on its own, there would be no contamination.

"In fact, there was another occasion in which there was a spill by one of the technicians," Tan pressed on.

The witness looked up the page in the file once again, telling the court the technologist reported the edge of the plate she was using got caught on her lab coat. But Célestin said there are procedures in place to deal with this kind of thing, and there was no contamination.

And as much as Susan MacKay highlighted the areas in the lab's reports where blood was found, Tan wanted to know more about the areas where blood was not found, pointing out the confirmatory tests for blood on Sandeson's pants were negative. Célestin explained that blood may still be present even if it can't be confirmed.

The Crown's next witness was RCMP sergeant Adrian Butler, one of seven bloodstain pattern analysts for the RCMP in Canada, and also qualified as an expert in this trial.

Butler began by reading from a presentation he'd prepared to help the jury understand his role. "It's the examination of the size, shape, location, distribution, and number of bloodstains in order to provide an interpretation of the physical events that gave rise to their origin," he said.

"Basically, I go to the scene or look at exhibits and try to determine what happened."

Butler said bloodstain patterns are predictable. "When blood leaves the body, its behaviour will follow the laws of the physical sciences. It is not affected by age, sex, body temperature, alcohol content, or disease process."

He told the court he can determine the distance between where the blood is and where it originated, whether the mechanism used was a baseball bat or a gun, the position of the victim and the assailant during the blood-shedding, and perhaps the minimum number of blows.

"We might be able to confirm or refute statements of witnesses or the accused," he testified. He said he was asked to look at photos of the gun, in this case, and prepared a report.

"Perhaps you could just cut to the chase and tell us about that," said MacKay. "What did you find in regard to the gun you examined?"

"There was a minimum of forty-four spatter stains less than one millimetre in size located on the left side of the handgun slide," Butler replied, showing the jury photographs.

"The higher the energy or force, the smaller the stains you'll find," he testified, explaining that a foot landing in a pool of blood would create larger stains than a baseball bat.

"What about in the example of a gun being shot?" MacKay asked.

"A gun being shot you would have misting stains, which would be more like a paint spray can."

Butler also testified there were a minimum of four spatter stains, also less than one millimetre in size, located on the muzzle of the pistol. He said the fact that there were spatter stains on the muzzle meant that it was close to the blood source and said there were a minimum of seven spatter stains, also tiny, on the right side of the handgun slide.

Butler said he would categorize the stains on the gun as "back spatter"—when a high energy force is applied to a form of blood and the blood comes back to the source of the energy—mostly because the stains were all very small and on three sides of the gun. He told the jury that means the gun was between two and four feet from the source. ("Forward spatter" is the projection of the blood in the same direction as the application of force.)

It was time for cross-examination.

"Sergeant, in preparing your report there are a number of assumptions that you have made, is that correct?" Eugene Tan began.

"That's correct," agreed the officer.

Tan pointed out that Butler had assumed the gun had tested positive for blood. Butler agreed that he had, based on the DNA analysis already before the court. Tan produced the report and pointed out that, for some of the areas Butler had assumed to be blood, the report stated "blood not confirmed."

"'Blood not confirmed' doesn't mean there wasn't a presumptive test done for blood," Butler said.

"Right, but you have not been qualified in the area of DNA analysis, have you?"

"No, but it's not saying that it's not blood," Butler persisted.

Tan's questions were coming fast and furious; he said he doubted whether Butler could really tell if it was back- or forward-spatter on the gun.

"If you're going to have forward spatter, you would have a lot more. You could have possible biological material, pieces of bone, skull. You wouldn't just have fine spatter."

"What if I were to say to you that this weapon was not seized until the afternoon or evening of August nineteenth?" Tan asked, pointing out that was three and a half to four days after it was allegedly fired.

"I can't see how it would have any relevance."

Tan pointed out that it wasn't in an evidence bag during that time and no one knows who may have handled it.

"I just looked at the photographs of the gun," Butler said.

The Crown's next witness would have much more to say about the gun.

Laura Knowles, the firearms section team leader at the RCMP's National Forensic Laboratory, was qualified to testify at this trial as a firearms expert; she attended via video link from Ottawa.

Knowles told the court she received three exhibits in relation to the firearms and toolmark evidence (toolmark identification is a discipline of forensic science that aims to determine whether a mark was produced by a particular tool). The exhibits were a Smith & Wesson pistol, one fired bullet, and one cartridge. Knowles said the gun was a restricted weapon but not a prohibited weapon; she found it was capable of discharge and had a trigger pull weight of seven pounds, which she said was pretty typical.

"To give you an idea of what seven pounds feels like, if you've ever opened a Coke can, pulling that tab with your finger, that feels like about five pounds."

She testified the gun was tested to see whether it was capable of discharge without pulling the trigger, and it was not.

Somebody had pulled the trigger.

Knowles said she fired bullets from Sandeson's gun so she could compare them to the fired bullet she was provided. She found the fired bullet had similar class characteristics, including the calibre, to the firearm in question, but she could not definitively say whether it was fired from that gun because of the condition of the bullet.

"To the naked eye it looked very pristine, but from a microscopic level, it had a lot of damage on its surface," she said. "Often we find that this is the case if a bullet goes through something post-discharge, like a window or a wall." The bullet she examined was found in the window frame in Sandeson's apartment.

When it came to the cartridge, which is a full round of unfired ammunition, she concluded that it had been chambered, cycled through, or otherwise in contact with the pistol, meaning someone had loaded the cartridge in that gun and fired one round.

On cross-examination Eugene Tan asked Knowles if it were true that the only thing she could confidently say about the bullet was that it could have been fired from any gun with similar characteristics. She agreed.

CHAPTER 13
THE CROWN'S CASE: MOTIVE FOR MURDER

rown Attorney Kim McOnie was quick to tell the jury that the Crown did not have to prove motive, that she and her colleague had no responsibility to prove *why* William Sandeson killed Taylor Samson. But that didn't stop her from arguing there was motive and laying out the evidence to show that motive was greed and financial gain.

It had already been established that there was to be a drug deal for $40,000, but the Crown told the jury the actual street value of the drugs was $90,000. The jury was later told to disregard the street value because the Crown failed to present evidence on that fact, but the seed had been planted.

The Crown then set about establishing just how badly Sandeson needed that cash. Kim McOnie called Adam Hayden, the branch manager for the CIBC in Truro, to the stand. He told the court William Sandeson had a $200,000 professional-student line of credit with his bank that was opened in July 2013. A letter from Saba University, where Sandeson completed a semester of medical school, was attached to the file.

"We used that to verify that the individual would be attending medical school," Hayden explained. During his first statement to police, when he was still a witness, Sandeson told the officer he had hated his time at Saba and that it had "soared his debt." However, on cross-examination, Hayden conceded that while the account was opened as a professional-student line of credit there was no requirement for Sandeson to confirm what the money was going to be used for upon withdrawal.

He said that meant Sandeson had $200,000 at his fingertips. His mother co-signed for the loan and had authority to deal with the account. The statements were sent to the Sandeson family farm in Lower Truro.

The recent statements were read into the record and copies provided for the jury. On July 9, 2015, the balance was $73,723.85, meaning that's how much Sandeson already owed on the account. During that month, some payments were made, including a $1,000 e-transfer from his girlfriend, Sonja. On July 14, there was an internet transfer withdrawing $3,000 from the account, and on July 17, $500 was withdrawn from a bank machine in Lower Sackville. On July 20, another $500 was withdrawn, this time from a bank machine on Girouard Street in Saint-Hyacinthe, Quebec. A couple of payments were credited to the account, but they were always less than the withdrawals. On July 29 there was an e-transfer withdrawal of another $3,000, followed by another two withdrawals on August 10 of $800 and $1,500. As of the end of the statement period on September 9, William Sandeson owed $78,518.59 and he hadn't even started Dal medical school yet.

The jury was also provided with a series of text messages between Sandeson and three different people, which the Crown argued illustrated he was under financial stress.

RCMP forensic analyst Gilles Marchand, whose job it was to recover and preserve data from electronic devices associated with the case, testified he analyzed three cellphones, all of which were iPhones. It was unclear whether Sandeson owned all three; Taylor

Samson's phone was never found. Marchand told the jury he was able to extract call logs, contacts, text messages, chat information, photos, and videos, all of which he provided to investigators.

Marchand created a series of reports based on Sandeson's text history. They were all provided to the jury; however only selections were read aloud in court.

On May 3, 2015, at 8:40 P.M., Sandeson texted his mother, Laurie Sandeson, asking, "How much money is left in the RESP?"

She didn't respond until 11:38 the next morning: "I'd have to check William."

He responded the day after that, on May 5 at 1:45 P.M., "Could you please check."

Right away his mom said, "Should have a statement at home. I'll check this evening."

Sandeson continued the conversation ten minutes after that, "Thank you! I made stock investments today though CIBC as well." And before she could respond, "Using a TFSA."

"I just had a call from James, CIBC, and he said that he met you," Laurie Sandeson texted back. "'What a fine young gentleman' he told me." And then she addressed her son's other message, "Stocks eh? I was never quite brave enough to invest in those. Did you go with local ones such as NS Power, Emera Group, (Sobeys)?"

"I went mostly with international corporations, Canadian banks, and United States business like apple [sic] and Microsoft," her son responded. "Very diversified with some money dedicated to bonds as well," he continued.

"Sounds fairly safe," his mom texted. "Apple is now the largest company in the world with billions of dollars in profit last year alone."

"I'm not surprised by that. They've developed so many products which dominate their respective markets," Sandeson said, and that was the end of the conversation between mother and son for now.

The next day at 2:16 P.M. Laurie Sandeson got in touch again. "I have a call in to Gerry Rau at CIBC regarding our RESP account.

Will let you know status when I hear back. Sounds like you are looking for some financial assistance??"

In between idle chatter about whether he'd be home soon because his younger brother wanted to borrow his leather jacket for his high school's production of the musical, *Grease*, Will said, "I was expecting a much larger tax return."

A while later, his mom said, "Just heard back from Gerry at CIBC, and yes, there's a few dollars there which you can access—how much were you hoping for?"

"I was just expecting a tax return of $1,000," Sandeson replied fifteen minutes later.

It was not until the following morning that the sporadic texting about money continued. "I believe you need to provide proof of enrollment to CIBC in order to enable withdrawal of funds from RESP," Laurie told her son. "How about a $2–3000 withdrawal?"

"How is there that much left?" Will texted back.

"We have just one RESP account, but we tried to divvy the amount up per child," his mom explained. "You didn't draw much from it during your 3 year degree program and Adam has dipped in twice now. Matthew has his own Knowledge First Fund, and we want to save something for David. We can talk more when you come home later this week."

"Save it, I'm fine without it," said William.

But his mother wasn't quite ready to let it go, "We'll chat."

If they did chat, they didn't do it over text. Sandeson did, however, text his father, Michael Sandeson, about his money woes more than two months later. On July 17 at 1:41 P.M., Sandeson received a text from his dad: "Laurie got mail today. She is mad over credit line."

"Well she has no need to be," Sandeson replied, and before his father could respond, "Will be paid this September."

On Monday, August 17, at 6:16 in the evening, William Sandeson texted his father, "Just approved for student grant of 7000!"

"Weehooo!" his dad exclaimed. Clearly, he had no idea what his son had been up to.

In her closing argument Crown Attorney Kim McOnie also referred to messages between William Sandeson and Jordan MacEwan, an associate of both Sandeson and Samson. He had been the subject of a break-in two nights before Samson was killed.

In the midst of a conversation about Taylor's disappearance, Sandeson wrote to MacEwan, "Splitting debt with him and said I'd have the money by Christmas. So I need 20k by Christmas. Fuck," and later, "I think I can make good on my other product. Can get keys for 19. Worse comes to worse, I take out a loan."

"So in the Crown's submission, there's certainly evidence that's before you that Mr. Sandeson was strapped for cash," argued Kim McOnie to the court. "He's asking his mother about making withdrawals from the RESP account, he's telling his father that he will pay the line of credit off by September, and he's telling Jordan that he owes some guy twenty thousand by December."

She went on to point out Sandeson was about to start medical school, was maintaining an apartment in the city, and maintaining three vehicles: a motorcycle, a truck, and a car. "So in the Crown's submission he's under a significant amount of financial pressure," she continued, reminding the jury Sandeson had told people he was planning to get out of the drug-dealing business with the transaction with Samson that night. "So we say, to clear off some or all of that debt, the deal had to be a big one, and it was," McOnie underlined.

While the defence argued at length about how incoherent and panicked Sandeson was the night of August 15, 2015, the Crown argued he was actually "giddy," as evidenced by text messages with his friend from high school, Amanda Clarke.

On August 16 at 1:42 A.M., only hours after Samson was seen walking into Sandeson's apartment, Sandeson texted Clarke, "Have a little catch-up tomorrow?"

At 4:53 A.M., she responded, "Potentially! I have to get a medical done tomorrow morning for my Aussie visa, then I'll message you! If not, then Tuesday morning works for me."

At 4:59 Sandeson asked, "Have a chance to [Snapchat]?" but three minutes later, before Clarke could respond, he texted again, "Student loan paid off and I'm completely squeaky clean now! Sold market share away."

It was six and a half hours after Taylor Samson was last seen alive.

"Do those text messages to Amanda give the impression of someone who was in a panic? Of someone who's incoherent?" Kim McOnie asked rhetorically, declaring the messages actually portrayed a tone of excitement. "He paid off his student loan!" she parroted. "He's squeaky clean. That is what we say this was all about," she paused for emphasis. "Money."

McOnie argued the big black duffle bag Taylor Samson was seen on video carrying into Sandeson's apartment was taken out during the time the DVR system was turned off and that it contained Samson's body—or parts of it.

"This is not a Hollywood film where masked invaders or Morphsuited intruders bust in through a window, shoot someone, and take the money with them," she said. "This is reality; a reality where every shred of physical evidence [...] points to one person as being responsible for the death of Mr. Samson."

She asked the jury to find William Sandeson guilty.

CHAPTER 14

IN HIS OWN DEFENCE

I t was June 5, 2017. By now speculation was swirling in Halifax about whether William Sandeson would take the stand in his own defence. People wanted to hear what he had to say, but they would have to wait a little longer to find out whether they would get that opportunity.

The defence decided to forgo its opportunity to present an opening address, proceeding straight to the evidence.

Jordan MacEwan, twenty-four, told the court he was employed by a temp agency, usually working at Scotiabank Centre setting up events, though he had only been doing that for a few months.

"Do you know William Sandeson?" Tan asked.

"Yes, I do."

"And how is it that you know William Sandeson?"

"I met him through selling weed."

MacEwan testified he had met Sandeson about three years earlier. "Somebody told him that I sold weed, and he needed some."

Tan asked if MacEwan also knew Taylor Samson. MacEwan said that he met him in the beginning of the summer of 2015, the same way he had met William Sandeson.

Tan asked MacEwan what he remembered about August 13, 2015.

"Are you talking about the night I got house-invaded?" MacEwan asked.

He was.

MacEwan said he was in contact with Taylor Samson that day because Samson owed him money, mostly for mushrooms and a little bit of weed. It was around $1,500 and Samson had owed him the money for a couple of weeks. "He was just going to come by and drop money off, around ten probably, I would say."

MacEwan told the court Samson said he was going to throw the money through the window of his apartment. He thought he received around $700, roughly half of what he was owed, but couldn't remember the timing or whether he had received the money at all. He testified he waited around for Samson until around 2:00 A.M.—smoking weed the whole time—but got tired of waiting and went to sleep.

He only slept for thirty minutes.

"I was woken up to a light being turned on to an unfamiliar face and that guy jumping on top of me and [he] started to beat me."

MacEwan said there were three guys in total. "Two guys were running around looking for stuff in the house and one guy was on top of me, fighting me."

MacEwan said he was in bed, but he tried to get up on his knees.

"They were just sitting there just punching me in the face, and I was kind of like, what do I do? ...Then one guy yells, 'Tie him up. We know you have more stuff here.'"

MacEwan said the men found a pound of weed and half a pound of mushrooms, and he also had about $10,000 hidden in his apartment. He tried to fight back, he testified, but it was no use; he was being beaten with police batons. He managed to grab a baton and hit one of the guys two or three times, getting away and running for the door, but one of the guys caught up to him and tackled him down the stairs outside.

"I was yelling, 'Help!' as soon as I got outside, like screaming it. And then when I went to turn around, they were running up my driveway. Gone."

But MacEwan's dramatic tale wasn't over.

"I was naked the whole fight, too, covered in blood," he continued. "I was pretty much blacking out at this point, from, I assume, lack of blood."

He said he never called the police. "Because I wanted to continue selling. I didn't want them involved with it."

MacEwan also testified he had borrowed $15,000 from Sandeson near the end of 2014, only a month or so after the two had met. It took him almost a year to pay it back, and he ended up paying more than five thousand in interest.

"Did you feel pressure to make payments?" Tan asked.

"Not at all. He didn't really give me any deadline," MacEwan replied. Tan was trying to make the point that Sandeson didn't need money, as the Crown had alleged.

MacEwan added that he faced three trafficking charges, and that he was no longer in the drug trade.

"Why not?"

"Because I'm already in trouble," he said.

MacEwan said he did eventually tell police this story when he was brought in by detectives regarding the Samson case. He said he had marks on him from the fight for about two weeks afterward, so the police would have seen them.

On cross-examination, Kim McOnie asked Jordan MacEwan whether he'd told the police he didn't think Samson had anything to do with the home invasion.

MacEwan replied he had indeed told the police Samson had nothing to do with attacking him. (This would become a critical point in Sandeson's second trial.)

The defence called Detective Constable Josh Underwood, who told the court he was detailed by Major Crime to find Jordan MacEwan and talk to him on the evening of August 18.

He said MacEwan had a black eye, and the door of his apartment looked like it had been forced open. Underwood said he told MacEwan he was investigating the disappearance of Taylor Samson. MacEwan told him about people breaking into his apartment and giving him the black eye and agreed to go to police headquarters to give a statement.

"And what, if any, information did Mr. MacEwan give you with respect to the timing as to when Mr. Samson gave him money versus when Mr. MacEwan's residence was broken into."

"It was the same night."

"Was there any more degree of specificity given than that?"

"If I recall correctly, it was about an hour after Taylor had delivered the money that Mr. MacEwan's apartment was broken into."

Sarson took a moment to confer with his client and co-counsel before finishing with Detective Constable Underwood. (Notably, the Sandeson trial did not reveal who attacked Jordan MacEwan; investigators said only that they determined it wasn't related to their case. It was investigated separately but no charges were ever laid.)

The defence called its final witness, Sonja Gashus, who had been Sandeson's girlfriend when Samson disappeared. Gashus, now twenty-three, told the jury she had just graduated with a bachelor of commerce from Dalhousie University. She now audited hedge funds.

"If we weren't at work or at track or at school, we were together, usually," she said of her relationship with Sandeson.

Sandeson sat, taking notes, as he did throughout the trial, while Gashus testified, looking up at her from time to time.

Gashus said on August 15, 2015, she was at the beach with her friends. She went back to Sandeson's apartment on Henry Street around late afternoon. They later went to the Stubborn Goat together for dinner.

"Did you notice anything in particular about the state of the apartment on August fifteenth?" Tan asked.

"It was cleaner than normal. I didn't notice it was messy and I usually would," she said.

While the couple was at dinner, Gashus testified, Sandeson asked her not to be home (at his apartment) later that evening. She said he had never asked her not to be there before.

Gashus told the court she did go back to the apartment for around an hour first. She testified Sandeson was organizing the apartment, trying to remove certificates and anything that had his name on it. She couldn't recall what time she left the apartment, but said it was dark outside when she went to her friend's place nearby. She said there was no clear time frame as to when she should return, but Sandeson told her he hoped it wouldn't be too long.

"You were sort of respecting Mr. Sandeson, saying that you would stay out of the apartment for a period of time. Is it possible that you could have returned at any time?"

"Yes," she agreed.

Tan was making sure the jury knew Sandeson would have been taking a risk to plot a murder when his girlfriend could walk in the door at any moment.

As it was, she got the go-ahead to go back to Sandeson's apartment around 12:30 A.M. and said she left to head back there within five minutes.

Tan asked if she had any observations about the apartment itself when she returned.

"It smelled like cleaning products," Gashus replied.

She testified she went to bed as soon as she got there. She had to work at Starbucks at 6:00 A.M. so Sandeson drove her to work; they left around 5:45 and picked up her co-worker along the way.

"Do you remember if Mr. Sandeson was dressed unusually?" (Gashus's co-worker had previously testified he was dressed warmly for the weather.)

"I didn't think so."

Gashus testified he was wearing a toque and a sweater.

"He would wear weird sweaters a lot," she laughed. "And he really liked that hat too."

Tan asked Gashus about the shower curtain in the bathroom at Sandeson's place.

"It was grimy, mildew," she testified, adding she didn't know how long it had been there.

Tan asked if she was aware of Sandeson being involved in any illegal activity. She said she knew he sold marijuana.

"Was it ever done in your presence?"

"Yes."

"Okay, how frequently?"

"Maybe a total of twenty times."

She told the court she didn't like his involvement in the drug trade and regularly told him that, especially after he was accepted to med school in March 2015.

Gashus told the court she had ended her relationship with Sandeson and had been in a new relationship for the past ten months.

It was the Crown's turn to question Sandeson's girlfriend.

"What was it that Will Sandeson told you about what had happened that night at the apartment?" Susan MacKay asked.

"He said that someone was beat up and they walked out and he was left to clean up the blood that was left."

"And what had he told you about what was going on at the apartment that night?"

"He had said to me that he was making a deal so that he could get out of the whole drug-dealing situation."

"Let's start with the guy who got beat up. What did he say about what happened to him?"

"That he got sucker-punched, for lack of a better word. That was about it."

She said she was concerned. "I asked, 'Was he okay? Like, what happened?' And he said that 'Yeah, he walked out, but there was a lot of blood.'"

She testified she didn't know who any of these people were—who got punched, who did the punching, or who was paying whom with what.

She said she later saw a link on Facebook about a missing person and sent it to Sandeson.

"I said, 'This isn't the person that got beat up?' I was concerned about that. And he responded and said that it wasn't the same person."

She testified he had not given her any indication at all that anyone had been shot in the apartment that night.

She told the court she had had contact with Sandeson since his arrest and that he had told her Chantale Comeau's statement to the police had made him look bad, but she said she didn't think he was in any way trying to influence her testimony.

The defence lawyers looked at each other, then at Sandeson, as though they were still trying to decide whether to put him on the stand. The courtroom was silent, many desperately wanting to hear what Sandeson would have to say for himself now. Would he—could he—continue to concoct stories about Morphsuited intruders after all that evidence?

It seemed he and his legal team thought his testimony could do more harm than good.

The defence closed its case. William Sandeson did not take the stand in his own defence.

"You've heard a lot of things throughout this trial that perhaps are going to leave a poor impression with you," Eugene Tan said in his closing argument to the jury. "What is important, though, is that there are going to be some things that you consider to be distasteful, perhaps his participation in the drug trade, perhaps the fact that he loaned money at what may be considered a fairly high rate to somebody. Distasteful, yes, but is that consistent with guilt?"

Tan told the jury that, while they hadn't actually said the words, from the testimony of Detective Constable Roger Sayer and from the words of the Crown, they seemed to believe William Sandeson to be a criminal mastermind. Tan argued the opposite was true, that Sandeson didn't think things through. He also argued Sandeson was not in financial need, that he had a $200,000 line of credit on which there were no limitations, and so that could not be his motive for murder.

"You've got to reject that. There's just no evidence whatsoever to support that," he contended.

Tan also addressed the damning evidence provided by Justin Blades and Pookiel McCabe, pointing out Sandeson knew they were home, and because of that, the elements of planning and deliberation required to convict a person of first-degree murder could not be present.

"Who would think to carry out this type of act in this type of apartment, knowing full well that there were people right next door?"

Tan was just getting started.

"The police, the Crown have invited you to believe that Mr. Sandeson is a cold, calculated murderer who mapped out every detail and every move in advance—but look for yourself." On the contrary, he said, Sandeson panicked and had no idea what was going to happen next.

Tan acknowledged that the surveillance video had become a major point in the trial, pointing out it was Sandeson himself who had installed the system.

"If Mr. Sandeson is this criminal mastermind...why on earth would he continue to let that tape roll?" Tan asked, going so far as to say that if the circumstances weren't so serious, the Crown's theory would border on "ridiculous."

He pointed out Sandeson had the opportunity to get rid of his gun and other evidence after his first statement to police during which he was still a witness, but he didn't.

Tan was adamant police chose to follow the evidence that supported their theory, accusing the Crown of shoehorning the facts to fit its case.

Finally, he argued that the police investigation was inadequate; that they failed to investigate information that was before them; that they had no right to enter Sandeson's apartment when they did; that they weren't wearing protective clothing when they should have been; that they failed to take appropriate notes; and that they did a poor job of managing the evidence.

Tan claimed there was reasonable doubt on all elements of the Crown's theory, especially the element that the murder was planned and premeditated.

He asked the jury to acquit William Sandeson.

CHAPTER 15
VERDICT

O n June 15, 2017, almost exactly two months after William Sandeson's murder trial began, Justice Joshua Arnold began his final instructions to the jury. He began by telling them he would explain the law and how they should use it to make a decision, not make a decision for them.

"Deciding the facts is your job, not mine," he declared.

He also explained that it wasn't up to them to answer all of the questions in this case, only to decide whether a crime was proven beyond a reasonable doubt. They were given the choice of four possible verdicts: guilty as charged of first-degree murder, guilty of second-degree murder, guilty of manslaughter, or not guilty.

Arnold told the jury they must not be influenced by fear, sympathy, or prejudice and that the verdict must be unanimous.

"Keep an open mind but not an empty head," he urged. "Don't just talk. Listen, too."

The jury headed to the jury room to begin deliberating.

The city of Halifax began its countdown. Hour after hour ticked by. Thursday turned into Friday. Friday turned into Saturday.

No one had anticipated it would take this long.

People began to speculate. Family and friends who had been hanging around the courthouse began to worry. What if the lengthy deliberation meant they weren't convinced beyond a reasonable doubt? What if they convicted him of second-degree murder instead of first? The wait was so long, people didn't know what to do with themselves. One of Samson's friends walked into the courthouse wearing a Morphsuit. It was a search for levity that fell flat, upsetting some of the others.

Finally on Sunday, June 18—Father's Day—after three weeks of pretrial motions, eight weeks of trial, and twenty-two hours of deliberation, the verdict was in. Taylor Samson's friends and family crowded into the courtroom, sobbing before the jury had even entered. Some had been there every day. Others had travelled from outside of Halifax to hear this moment of truth. William Sandeson's family was not present. His lawyer said Sandeson had asked them not to be.

The jury entered the room, the foreperson stood and announced the verdict: "Guilty as charged of first-degree murder."

There was sobbing and clapping in the courtroom. "Thank you!" exclaimed one of Samson's family members.

One of the jurors was also weeping; another had tears in her eyes.

William Sandeson sat at the defence table with his lawyers, his hands clasped, showing no emotion.

As Sandeson was brought out of the courtroom, one Samson family member shouted, "Tell us where he is!"

"Turn around and take a bow, Billy!" Samson's mother yelled. Linda Boutilier had been in the courtroom every day. Outside, Boutilier sobbed with relief. "I can actually sleep for a change. It's been hell for twenty-two months."

❖

In Canada, a conviction of first-degree murder comes with an automatic life sentence and no chance of parole for twenty-five years. William Sandeson was formally sentenced on July 11, 2017.

Two of the jurors, whose civic duty was already complete, showed up to court anyway.

"I felt that that showed a level of engagement above and beyond what was even required or expected of them," said Rhodes.

The sentencing hearing also gave Taylor Samson's friends and family a chance to provide victim-impact statements. Eighteen of them did, although not all were presented in court.

"He was the first person outside of my family to make me feel loved," said Samson's childhood friend Ryan Wilson. "I'll never get to feel that loving friendship again. I'll never have my ribs crushed by one of his hugs again," he told the court, his voice cracking with emotion.

Samson's good friend Kaitlynne Lowe said her own sense of security and hope had been shattered by Samson's death and that the foundation of her life had crumbled.

"It is impossible to feel safe anywhere...because I now know the horrors that can exist right next door."

"I just want to be myself again, the happy-go-lucky guy, not the one who has to wear a mask to hide his true feeling," sobbed Samson's younger brother, Connor.

Missing was a victim-impact statement from Linda Boutilier.

"I wrote it probably six months after Taylor went missing," she said, and began to cry. "And I ripped it up. I thought, why bother? He doesn't care. He doesn't care [about] the hell that we've gone through. If I stood there and let him see my pain, it's like I'm empowering him. It's like he'd get enjoyment out of seeing it, and I wasn't going to do it."

Justice Joshua Arnold told the court Sandeson had already spent 693 days in custody.

"In accordance with what I am mandated to do by the Criminal Code, I sentence William Sandeson to life in prison," said Arnold.

Lawyers on both sides admitted the workload from this case had been overwhelming.

"It was basically months of going to court every day, coming home, working every evening, working every weekend, without a break," said Brad Sarson in an interview after the trial had concluded.

"There was more than one night where I didn't get any sleep at all and then went to court the next day," said Susan MacKay. "I'd never done that before in my career and I don't want to ever do it again."

Right away, Sandeson appealed his conviction, citing ten grounds, including that his right to be secure against unreasonable search or seizure under the Canadian Charter of Rights and Freedoms was breached when police entered his apartment without a warrant, that Justice Arnold erred by not granting a mistrial, and that the jury came to an unreasonable verdict.

Brad Sarson said the jury's verdict on first-degree murder was "arguable." I asked him if that meant he thought the jury reached the wrong verdict.

"Correct," he said, "based on the evidence and the law that they were instructed on."

Eugene Tan said he did not believe his client was guilty.

"So what is that based on?" I asked. "Is that based on a personal relationship with him? Is it based on that you know his family or just the evidence?"

"It's based on all of that. It's based on perhaps, things that I know that either would not be admissible, that we didn't bring forward, or that we didn't want to bring forward," he said.

I asked if there was anything he thought I should know; anything he could tell me that didn't come up in court.

"I would love to have that conversation with you, and Will is still thinking about that, and that may be a conversation, if you have the time, if you're willing, that we may have."

It did not happen.

Sandeson did not respond to my letters, and his parents declined to participate in this work, saying, "This story is not over."

CHAPTER 16
THE APPEAL... AND OTHER LEGAL MATTERS

William Sandeson's parents were right when they said this story was not over. It was not even close to being over. On June 17, 2020, the Nova Scotia Court of Appeal overturned their son's conviction and ordered a new trial.

"'Here we go again,' that's all I thought," said Linda Boutilier, as she reflected on the moment the Crown called her with the news. "I couldn't believe that he won [the appeal]. I really couldn't."

The Court of Appeal ruled that the trial judge, Justice Joshua Arnold, had made a mistake when he opted not to grant a mistrial when Sandeson's lawyers asked for one midway through the first trial when they learned their own private investigator, Bruce Webb, had effectively switched sides and assisted the police in their case against Sandeson.

Arnold had decided an adjournment and giving the defence an opportunity to recall any witnesses for further questioning was a fair way to address the unfortunate circumstances.

But the Court of Appeal ruled that the defence had not had time during the trial to properly investigate and decide how to deal with the issue. "They were coming up with submissions on the fly. They were reading cases over the lunch break. They needed time; time that was unavailable in the middle of a jury trial where lengthy adjournments are not appropriate," wrote Justice David P. S. Farrar in his decision, which was also signed by the other two judges on the appeal court panel.

He said it was exactly the type of "extreme" situation the Supreme Court of Canada had previously decided required a more "drastic" remedy than an adjournment.

But Farrar wrote that he did not want to be overly critical of Arnold. "The startling revelation of Webb's relationship with the police, and how to deal with it in the middle of a murder trial before a jury, caught everyone by surprise," he wrote. "There were no precedents for guidance."

He wrote that Arnold had made two key errors.

The first was deciding that, because Webb didn't witness the events of August 15, 2015, and because his involvement with the police wasn't itself material evidence against Sandeson, the matter didn't have any impact on the main issues at trial.

But because the information about what Webb had done came about so late—and while the trial was already underway— the Appeal Court ruled that it "significantly infringed" Sandeson's right to fully defend himself. For example, it deprived him of the opportunity to try to get that evidence—the testimony of Blades and McCabe—excluded, which he may well have done had he known about the whole affair prior to the start of the trial.

The second mistake, Farrar wrote, was that Arnold had decided the police were "mere passive recipients of information." Farrar wrote, "The police did not passively receive information: they successfully encouraged Webb to help them in their investigations and ensured their collaboration remained secret."

The Appeal Court ruled that the matter with the private investigator was justification to grant Sandeson a new trial.

"In my view, it is not necessary to decide the other three issues identified by the appellant, and further, it would be unwise to do so," wrote Farrar in the decision.

In his appeal, Sandeson had also argued the trial judge erred by finding that the police did not violate his rights when they searched his apartment without a warrant, that the judge erred by finding Sandeson's rights were not violated during his police interrogation interviews, and that the jury's conviction of first-degree murder was unreasonable.

The appeal judges decided all of those issues would likely be the subject of evidence and argument at the second trial, and if they were to say anything about them, it would compromise the ability of the Crown, the defence, and the next trial judge to properly consider those issues.

However, Farrar wrote that it would be "entirely possible" for a judge to find that the police conduct in this matter "could amount to an abuse of process."

The Canadian Charter of Rights and Freedoms provides courts with the ability to stop proceedings if prosecutorial conduct affects the fairness of the trial or "undermines the integrity of the judicial process."

"My comments here are only to illustrate a viable argument can be made. Whether it will be successful is not for me to decide," he wrote. Indeed, prosecutorial conduct would be considered at Sandeson's next trial, but that wouldn't happen for another three years.

In fact, some still wondered whether it would happen at all.

"I can honestly say I really didn't know," said Crown Attorney Kim McOnie when I interviewed her at the end of September 2023.

Sandeson had decided to get a new lawyer to continue his defence: Alison Craig, who was based in Toronto. Craig admitted she did not think the case would proceed to another trial. "Very often, at least around here, if there's a conviction like that overturned, it usually ends up resolving, because by that point they've been in custody for so long the Crown doesn't want to put the family or the witnesses through another trial. 'Let's all agree to manslaughter and go home,'" said Craig.

"I was fifty-fifty on that," said CBC court reporter Blair Rhodes, explaining he thought Sandeson might continue to push the matter. "But the other side of that was that I still harboured the possibility that he would trade the location of the body for a plea bargain."

There were resolution discussions between the Crown and defence.

In an interview, Crown Attorney Carla Ball—new to the case—said Crown Attorneys are not able to discuss what goes into those conversations, but that generally, they have a responsibility to balance different perspectives.

"We always would resolve something if we thought that it was an appropriate resolution, given the circumstances of the evidence," she said.

Craig was more direct.

"The Crown wasn't willing to accept anything less than a murder conviction," she said, "and we weren't willing to resolve to murder."

And so, there would be a second trial.

But in the years in between, the bizarre twists in the Sandeson case would continue.

Sandeson had already successfully sued Dylan Zinck-Selig, his roommate at the time of his arrest, over sneakers and homemade wine. Sandeson took Zinck-Selig to small claims court in Halifax, claiming he had stolen from him after his arrest.

Court documents state Sandeson's apartment contained twenty-eight pairs of brand-name sneakers at the time police were searching it in August 2015. According to the documents, eighteen pairs of shoes were missing when Sandeson's family went to collect them after the forensic work on the apartment was complete. Additionally, forty bottles of homemade wine and five to ten bottles of hard liquor were unaccounted for.

Sandeson believed Zinck-Selig owed him $2,500 for the items. Zinck-Selig claimed he took only two pairs of sneakers and four bottles of wine, which he felt entitled to because some of his own things were destroyed during the police search.

In April 2018, an adjudicator ruled Zinck-Selig was a victim of systems beyond anyone's control but did not have the right to take anything that was not his. He was ordered to pay William Sandeson $500, the value of the items he had admitted to taking, plus process-serving costs, bringing the total to $700.

Perhaps this motivated Sandeson to continue his legal pursuits.

Four months later, he filed a notice of action to sue his private investigator and the firm for which the investigator worked at the time.

The investigator and the firm then indicated their intent to sue each other.

In his notice of action, Sandeson alleged he would have had a "reasonable prospect of success at trial of being acquitted" if not for Webb's involvement.

Tom Martin filed a statement of defence, denying the allegations, saying Webb was never his employee, but rather an independent contractor, and that any dealings between Webb and the police were done "without the knowledge, consent, authority, or involvement" of Martin.

In a statement of crossclaim against Webb, Martin alleged that if Sandeson suffered any injury, loss, or damage, it was not as a result of Martin & Associates, but rather the result of negligence, breach of confidence, breach of privilege, or breach of contract by Bruce Webb.

Webb filed a notice of defence, denying that his conduct breached any confidentiality. He went on to say if there were any breach of legal duty—which he expressly denies—it would not be actionable by Sandeson because his conduct was "protected by his duty to serve the public interest," and his "duty to promote public safety."

Webb also filed a notice of crossclaim against Tom Martin, alleging if Sandeson suffered any actionable injury, loss, or damage—which he again denies—Martin is obliged to indemnify him per the terms of their contractual relationship, something Martin denies.

Such crossclaims are common where there are co-defendants.

The matter has been dormant for a few years, and at the time of writing was more than five years old, so it is eligible to be dismissed for delay.

Martin declined to be interviewed for this work. Webb did not respond to a request to participate.

Sandeson's litigious activities continued.

In 2020, just over five months after he won his appeal, he began legal action against the Attorney General of the Province of Nova Scotia and the Superintendent of the Central Nova Scotia Correctional Facility over his right to vote.

In a three-page handwritten affidavit, he wrote that he began inquiring about the jail's preparedness for the 2020 October municipal elections sometime in late August that year. He wrote that his inquiries were made verbally during the scheduled daily inspections of inmate cells, and that he was "dissatisfied with the lack of positive response" so he began to record exactly when he made these inquiries and to whom he made them.

He also asked his mother, Laurie Sandeson—who was running in the election in the Municipality of Colchester—to print the voter proxy form and send it to him. He filled it out and sent it back to her, but upon receiving it, she noticed his voter ID number was missing, and thus the form was useless. According to his affidavit, he didn't have a voter ID and used the inmate telephone system to call Elections Halifax on three separate occasions, but his calls were not returned. His mother emailed and called Elections Halifax and was told that he could not vote because he was an inmate.

Inmates do have the right to vote under the Charter of Rights & Freedoms, and Sandeson noted that he had been able to vote in both the 2015 and 2019 federal elections; however, the Nova Scotia Municipal Elections Act states that "a person serving a sentence in a penal or reform institution" shall not be entitled to vote.

Sandeson acknowledged this wording could have contributed to some confusion, but asserted, "prison officials should know the difference between sentenced inmates and those simply remanded awaiting trial." He also said he discussed this distinction with staff while trying to secure his vote.

Sandeson was on remand at the time, since his conviction had been overturned.

He called on the court to find that part of the act of "no force or effect," and to compel the Central Nova Scotia Correctional Facility to provide inmates with a reasonable opportunity to vote in future municipal elections.

Ten months later, in October 2021, the Supreme Court of Nova Scotia issued a Consent Dismissal Order stating the parties had come to a mutually agreed-upon resolution, dismissing the application without costs to any party.

A spokesperson for the Nova Scotia Department of Municipal Affairs later confirmed inmates on remand awaiting trial are entitled to vote in municipal elections. "In the coming months, we will be working with the department of justice and returning officers to ensure that everyone understands the applicable rules," she said in a statement in October 2023.

At least in part, Sandeson had won again.

❖

Preparations for Sandeson's new trial were now underway, although they were delayed by the COVID-19 pandemic. The pandemic also created a highly unusual interaction, which could never have happened otherwise.

On September 23, 2020, during a court appearance to try to schedule delayed jury trials, Sandeson and another man accused of first-degree murder, Kaz Cox, appeared via video link.

Under normal circumstances, court matters are dealt with one at a time and the two would not have had occasion to interact—certainly not in such a public way. As it was, they sat chatting for more than ten minutes while they waited for court to get underway.

"At least you got to go to Pictou, right? I hear it's a little better," Sandeson, who was at the Burnside jail at the time, said.

"I tell ya man, I'd rather be down there," Cox replied. "This is kindergarten. Really personal employees. Feel like they know ya, right?" he said of the Northeast Nova Scotia Correctional Facility, going on to say it was annoying.

"I prefer that everybody there got their own life. They're just there to punch in the shift and leave right?"

Sandeson said that was typical of a small town.

"They got a bunch of Yarmouth staff up here now, and that surprised me, about how warm and fuzzy they are," he said, as the two continued chatting and laughing.

At the time, Cox was accused of fatally shooting nineteen-year-old Triston Reece in Halifax in 2019.

"They gonna give you your disclosure yet?" Sandeson asked. (This showed that they must have encountered one another previously on the inside.)

Cox said he'd been getting it in bits and pieces after making multiple requests.

"They're just taking advantage that I don't have counsel right now," Cox said. "And until I get all my disclosure, I'm not getting any. Doesn't make sense. So far, they've given me nothing; a theory."

"I really recommend you don't hire a private investigator," Sandeson said, and the two burst out laughing.

"They're beyond questionable. I feel for ya," Cox said.

"You had a nice picture in the paper about a month and a half ago," Sandeson chuckled, illustrating he was paying attention to the news.

The court session soon began, after what was extraordinary insight into how the judicial process was unfolding in the minds of two since-convicted killers.

(In June 2022, Cox would be convicted of first-degree murder.)

In the years between his two trials, Sandeson made three more attempts to get released on bail.

The January 2021 hearing was significantly impacted by COVID-19.

Sandeson was not in the room, but rather joining via video link, sitting with a phone receiver pressed against his ear, rubbing his now-bald head as he waited.

His lawyer joined the proceeding from her home in Toronto due to a stay-at-home order, but before long her screen went black.

"She appears to have disappeared," said the clerk.

"I'm sure she's not going anywhere. After all, she's in Toronto," quipped Justice James Chipman, in what appeared to be a jab at the fact Nova Scotia was faring far better in the pandemic than Ontario.

People in the gallery chuckled.

Taylor Samson's mother was present—as she continued to be at every single court appearance—sitting in the back corner by herself, as directed by sheriffs to ensure social distancing, occasionally taking notes.

Michael Sandeson was called as a witness; he swore an oath on a Bible wrapped in a plastic bag, his arm outstretched to maintain his distance from the clerk. He smiled and waved at his son on the screen—an indication that he still supported his son after all this time.

The entire Sandeson family was present—William's parents and three brothers—all pledging to be sureties this time, not just his parents. Sandeson's mother had retired from her job with the provincial government. She had won in the municipal elections Sandeson had been trying to vote in and was now a county councillor, but that required less time—meaning she would have more time to be her son's jailer.

The family pledged $500,000 this time—most of the value of their property—knowing they could lose it all.

"Yep, we'd be out on the street," testified his father.

He told the court he and his wife were speaking to their son daily. He said they had remortgaged their house to put a major sum against their son's line of credit and were still making payments on it. At this point, he said, the balance was about $26,000—down from the $78,000 it had been when Michael Sandeson had testified at his son's first bail hearing just over five years earlier.

The family also said Sandeson would be subjected to electronic monitoring this time.

"If we suspected anything, we would call the police," Laurie Sandeson testified.

David Sandeson, William's youngest brother, who had been fourteen at the time of his brother's arrest, was now twenty. He wore black dress pants, a light blue shirt, a dark tie with a tie clip, and a black mask. He was a student at Acadia University in Wolfville, NS, in the second year of his undergrad in kinesiology.

He told the court he'd always looked up to his brother and had been trying to get closer to him, but that it had been tough. He was only eight years old when his brother had moved out to go to university, but testified he still believed William would listen to him if necessary.

"'Cause if he doesn't, I have a phone that's gonna send him back to where he is," he chuckled.

Lawyer Alison Craig, who would become a central character in determining Sandeson's future, at this point asked what time court usually ends for the day here, noting it was 3:20 P.M.

"We go to all hours here in the outpost," said Justice Chipman, who seemed to be getting a kick out of this big-city lawyer in his courtroom.

Craig called Matthew Sandeson to the stand.

Matthew Sandeson, twenty-one, told the court he was also studying kinesiology and just three months away from completing his degree. He also told the court he would not hesitate to call the police if his brother didn't listen to him upon release and pledged $4,800—the grand total of his savings.

"You're willing to pledge your life savings to get him out of jail?" questioned Kim McOnie.

"Without a doubt," he replied.

Adam Sandeson arrived next, wearing a light grey suit with black shoes, and a black-and-white checkered shirt with a blue medical mask.

He said hello to his brother on the screen.

He was twenty-five, had an undergrad and a master's degree in environmental science, and was working as a consultant at an environmental firm. He told the court he "idolized" his brother because he was a good student and a good athlete, and he was always there for him while they were growing up.

When asked why he thought his brother would listen to him, he said, "I think he understands the impact that it's had on everyone around him, and he wouldn't want to jeopardize our futures."

The judge asked the defence about a disciplinary report from August 2020 that said Sandeson stated he was homicidal and would kill another inmate if he was placed on a living unit. Sandeson had said he had no particular person he was angry with, but he would choose a victim or multiple victims until stopped.

Craig said there was only one sheet of paper in the disciplinary report for five and a half years of incarceration, and there was no violence. She argued that's what should be looked at instead of an "off the cuff" remark made while upset.

She pointed out Sandeson once again had the presumption of innocence behind him; that the Crown might have a strong case for manslaughter, but "definitely not murder"; that there was a third set of DNA on the gun; and that there was a "very strong case" to have the whole case dropped once they got to the new trial.

She said if the case did go to trial, she'd be arguing Justin Blades and Pookiel McCabe—the first trial's star witnesses—shouldn't even get to testify.

The judge argued the first bail judge hadn't even had that evidence when he'd denied bail and called it a "strong case." (Blades and McCabe still hadn't come forward at the time of the first bail hearing.)

"I'll say it this way," said Craig. "It's messier than it was in 2015."

That much was definitely true. It was nothing if not "messy."

The Crown acknowledged the plan was good but said it still didn't satisfy the need to maintain public confidence in the administration of justice.

The judge interjected.

"If this plan isn't good enough, what is?"

The Crown said Sandeson was exceptional for a number of reasons: that often people before the court are on a certain trajectory and their lives have involved drugs, poverty, and childhood abuse, whereas "he had a life, really, that others would dream of."

She argued the evidence was overwhelming with respect to first-degree murder "with or without Pookiel McCabe and Justin Blades."

Justice Chipman said Sandeson had met his onus on the primary ground, agreeing it was not necessary to detain him to ensure he would show up for court.

He said Sandeson had not met his onus on the secondary ground, and that his detention was necessary for public safety. He found that the plan to increase the sureties from two to five didn't strengthen the plan, but rather weakened it, because Sandeson's brothers were not only not living at the property where it was proposed Sandeson would live, but they were all now living at least an hour's drive away.

The judge was also concerned that Adam Sandeson had known about his brother's involvement in the drug trade back in 2015 and had not reported it to his parents or the authorities. Furthermore, Chipman said, there was nothing to indicate either of Sandeson's parents appreciated what was behind their son leading a "double life" back in 2015.

He noted cell service could be poor in rural Nova Scotia and the electronic monitoring system relies on it. He expressed concerns about the homicidal threats made in prison, calling them "impulsive and dangerous," as well as the previous details about his threat to kill his girlfriend and dissolve her body in lye on his family farm.

"I have significant concerns that Mr. Sandeson could again exhibit such thoughts and, absent a jail setting, act on them to the extreme detriment of those around him," Chipman wrote in his written decision, on January 22, 2021. "In my view, this amounts to a very disturbing window into Mr. Sandeson's mind," he wrote.

He went on to say Sandeson had also not met his onus on the tertiary ground: public confidence. "Public confidence in our justice system would not be maintained if this person accused of a drug-trade related first-degree murder were granted bail," he wrote.

He denied Sandeson freedom.

Outside the courtroom, Taylor Samson's mother spoke with journalists. She sobbed as she said she was pleased with the decision and just wished the process could be over. She said she had tried not to let the three-day bail hearing get to her—but it had, and she was tired.

"I wish his parents would actually make him accountable for what he did and stop being naive—and realize that my son is still missing and he's out there somewhere, and I want to put him to rest."

Sandeson made his third attempt at obtaining bail just nine months later, in October 2021.

He was present in the courtroom this time, wearing a black V-neck T-shirt, black jeans, and burgundy loafer-style sneakers, with a blue medical mask. His defence lawyers, Alison Craig and her colleague, were both on-screen from Toronto.

Linda Boutilier and Kaitlynne Lowe were there, too. Sandeson sat directly in front of Boutilier, four rows ahead, flanked by a sheriff on either side. She averted her eyes.

The Sandesons were dialling in from another location.

This bail review application had been permitted because Sandeson's team said there had been a "material change in circumstances" since the last one.

This time Sandeson took the stand to try to explain why he'd made those homicidal comments about wanting to kill other inmates.

He said he had been feeling anxious and asked to be placed in segregation, where he felt safer. He was initially placed in health segregation, but he said staff were firm in their desire to have him placed back in the general population. He was equally firm in his desire to remain in segregation. He testified he didn't want to get involved in any disciplinary action where he couldn't control the environment. He said his disciplinary report is related to situations where he was present but not involved, but the jail disciplined everyone.

"People are not in jail for being upstanding citizens," he said.

He said he was in an interview with three "white shirts" or captains, where he spent thirty to forty minutes trying to explain why he didn't feel comfortable "on the range," and he suggested that they deem him a risk to the safety of others if they needed a reason to justify keeping him in segregation.

This time only Sandeson's father, Michael, and two of his brothers testified. Despite Chipman's comments in the last hearing that having the brothers as sureties weakened the plan, they were once again pledging to be their brother's jailers.

Sandeson's father, Michael, still had the feed delivery job but planned to retire in the spring when he turned sixty-five and had told his manager that, depending on the decision, he may retire early, starting immediately. The family also planned to install security cameras that would cover all entrances and exits to their home.

The Crown's position was that the defence had not met the requirement of a material change in circumstance. But Alison Craig said three things had changed: trial dates had been set for 2023, the release plan had been enhanced, and Sandeson had explained the offender incident report.

The Crown's position was that the defence could have addressed that back in January. The defence said they were rather taken aback by how much of a role that had played in the previous bail hearing.

Craig pointed to a letter from Sandeson's case management officer at the Northeast Nova Scotia Correctional Facility in Pictou County, NS, dated October 4, 2021, just three weeks prior to the hearing.

The letter stated that Sandeson had been at the facility for nearly eight months, that he was currently living on a privileged living unit that grants inmates access to a kitchenette with a microwave and toaster, laundry, and in-cell television access. The case management officer wrote that Sandeson was actively engaged with education and had been given materials to tutor other inmates, and that he had a passion for fitness. Since his transfer to the facility on February 26, 2021, she wrote, he had been incident-free and respectful of staff and other inmates.

Craig argued that because his trial was still more than a year away the standard should be relaxed, and that the trial dates alone represented a material change.

The Crown argued the trial dates were not a material change because the judge had considered that in his previous decision, and that the home security system didn't change anything. As for the positive report from the case management officer, the Crown argued it had never suggested Sandeson wasn't doing anything positive in prison, but that it was not a change in circumstances.

Justice Chipman agreed. He denied Sandeson's third attempt at bail.

Sandeson did not react.

Kaitlynne Lowe threw her head back in relief and clutched her notebook to her chest.

Linda Boutilier muttered, "Oh farm boy, still can't win. Never will."

In November 2022, Sandeson made a fourth attempt, applying to the Nova Scotia Court of Appeal to overturn Chipman's third denial. The Court of Appeal dismissed that application, meaning Chipman's decisions were upheld.

That was Sandeson's last attempt—at least before his new trial. But the Crown was mounting an appeal of its own.

It tried to stop the second trial by taking the case to the Supreme Court of Canada, appealing the Nova Scotia court's decision to overturn Sandeson's conviction on first-degree murder.

It didn't work. The Supreme Court of Canada dismissed the application in February 2021, refusing to hear the appeal. As is typical, there was no explanation, but Canada's highest court clearly agreed that the issue with the private investigator was significant.

There was now nothing standing in the way of that new trial.

Nothing, that is, except Alison Craig.

On March 28, 2022, Alison Craig was set to argue for a stay of proceedings—the first of a list of matters to be negotiated before a trial could start. She wanted the whole case thrown out over the Bruce Webb affair.

I arrived at the courthouse and a sheriff greeted me with, "I bet you're here for Sandeson!"

I'd gotten a new job in national news since this case began and rarely made it to court anymore. It's not often that local court matters make national headlines. I had been at the courthouse regularly in my last job as a local news reporter, often focused on crime, but it occurred to me that I was now connected with this case alone.

A short time later, Boutilier arrived, Kaitlynne Lowe at her side as usual. Boutilier was wearing flat sneakers, black with white laces, and a rose-coloured sweater with a scarf, white with pink flowers. She looked nice, I thought, somehow less stressed. I wondered if maybe time was doing its job. This was not the emotionally raw Linda Boutilier of the early days. She was composed, almost professional. She had been through this process so many times she now knew how to handle herself. It was difficult to think about all that she had been through; all that she had yet to go through.

Was it another sign I was connected to this case? Maybe. Journalists aren't supposed to get attached to the people they write about. But we are human after all, and I'd had ample opportunity to observe her pain for six and a half years. She'd invited me in.

The Crowns approached to speak with Boutilier outside the courtroom. Kim McOnie introduced her colleague, Carla Ball, whom Boutilier had not yet met. Susan MacKay had taken a management job. Ball apologized for meeting under these circumstances. Boutilier thanked them for their hard work.

We went into the courtroom, and Sandeson was brought in.

I wouldn't have recognized him if he hadn't been flanked by sheriffs. I had been rummaging in my bag and looked up to see him looking right back at me. I nearly mistook him for a lawyer. It occurred to me that in all these years I'd been covering him, this was the first time we'd ever made eye contact.

He was wearing glasses and a full suit, a baby blue shirt, and a blue striped tie. His pants seemed a bit too big. I could see some stubble on the sides beneath his blue medical mask. He looked older, distinguished somehow.

The court dealt with the matter involving the private investigator first. There was no one in the courtroom other than Boutilier, Lowe, and me. It was similar to the first time they had dealt with the matter, with largely the same people testifying about the same things.

Justin Blades was emotional as he testified—yet again—how he came into contact with Bruce Webb and explained to the court how it had affected his life.

Craig argued anything less than a stay of proceedings would not suffice, and said she felt as though she was in "an alternate universe." She further argued that it was "gobsmacking" and "beyond the realm of comprehension" to suggest the previous defence team should have inquired further or been expected to figure out what was going on, as had been suggested in the past.

She also argued the Crown's conduct in the matter was not "trivial" given they'd admitted to a breach of their duty to provide disclosure. "I am by no means suggesting that the Crown was nefarious or saying, 'Oh goody-goody gumdrops,'" she said in court. "But even negligence is a breach."

After arguing her case for two hours, Craig concluded.

"I think confidence in the justice system would be undermined by allowing this prosecution to continue," she said.

Carla Ball, arguing for the Crown, said they hadn't disclosed the information about Webb because they thought it was obvious since his first name appeared in the statements five times, but she acknowledged that didn't displace the Crown's duty to disclose.

She argued—as the Crown had in the past—that Blades and McCabe would have wound up testifying at the trial, and that it was clear they were ready to talk, with or without Bruce Webb. She said what had occurred was "nowhere near" outrageous enough to trigger a stay of proceedings.

The judge asked what sort of remedy Ball would propose to fix this situation if the case proceeded to trial.

"The remedy has already been achieved. We're in a retrial," Ball said.

In a fifty-seven-page decision released three weeks later, Justice James Chipman wrote that, ideally, as soon as Staff Sergeant Richard Lane was approached by Webb in 2015, it should have been disclosed to the Crown and in turn to the defence, and that would have "nipped in the bud" the problems that escalated.

Chipman wrote that the actions of the police were regrettable and must be discouraged but they did not warrant a stay of proceedings. He ruled that Blades and McCabe must be able to testify at a new trial and that excluding them would "shock the community and be an affront to the truth-seeking function of the Court."

He went on to write that the new trial would provide Sandeson the right to make full answer and defence, and that the concerns about late disclosure that left both sides scrambling in the midst of the first trial had subsided over the passage of nearly five years.

"Irreparable damage has not been done to the Sandeson defence and the trial must proceed on its merits," he concluded.

As the pretrial hearings continued, the defence would set about arguing which evidence would be admitted into said trial. For five days they argued over the police search of Sandeson's apartment, specifically the fact that officers did so without a warrant.

Fifteen police officers were required to testify. They maintained they had entered Sandeson's apartment because they believed Taylor Samson might still be alive and imprisoned in the apartment—and that his life was at risk without his medication.

They didn't find Samson, but they did find a large mushroom grow-op and an empty gun box, which were in plain sight. They also disconnected the surveillance system, worried Sandeson could delete it remotely. They held the scene and went back to search it thoroughly when they did get a warrant, which was not until nine and a half hours after their initial entry.

Craig argued the searches breached Sandeson's Charter right to be free from unreasonable search and seizure and that, as a result, all evidence obtained during the exigent search of his apartment should be excluded.

Furthermore, she argued the warrant authorizing a further search of Sandeson's apartment was predicated on information obtained directly as a result of the first search. So, she said, all of the evidence discovered during these later judicially authorized searches were "fruit of the poisonous tree" and should also be excluded.

But Chipman found the police entry into the apartment was necessary in an effort to save Taylor Samson's life, and as such it was "authorized in law."

As had the first trial judge, Chipman found that Sandeson's Charter rights had not been violated by the search of the apartment; all of the related evidence would be admitted at trial.

On April 19, 2022, another pretrial hearing began that saw the court set about trying to determine whether the videos of police questioning Sandeson would be seen by the second jury.

Linda Boutilier and I were the only people in the gallery.

The defence argued the statements Sandeson gave to police were not voluntary, and that the way in which they were obtained violated his Charter rights and as such should be excluded from the trial.

Justice Chipman ruled that all of Sandeson's statements were voluntary but took issue with the lengthy interrogations that took place late on August 18 and throughout the day on August 19 for another reason.

The Charter guarantees an individual both the right to be informed of the reason for their detention, as well as the right to speak to a lawyer without delay. Chipman acknowledged that although generally an initial warning is enough, in some situations the police are obliged to provide an accused with an additional opportunity to consult with a lawyer.

If the investigation takes a new and more serious turn as events unfold, as the Sandeson case did, the initial advice may no longer be adequate to the actual situation.

William Sandeson had a private phone call with a lawyer around an hour and twenty minutes after he was arrested. He asked to speak with a lawyer again on several occasions throughout his lengthy interrogation but was told he had already had that opportunity. He did ultimately get a second chance to speak with his lawyer, this time in person, but the judge ruled that meeting had happened far too late.

The police knew they had to give him a second opportunity to speak with a lawyer when his jeopardy changed—when he went from being arrested for kidnapping, trafficking, and misleading police to being formally arrested for murder. This happened when he said Samson had been shot in the back of the neck or the head. That wasn't until the early evening of August 19, at which point the interrogation was nearly over.

But the judge noted that long before that, during the interrogation, the officers had been using words to indicate they believed Samson was dead and Sandeson was responsible.

For example, Sayer had asked, "Is that what you want your story to be? Someone who led a man to his death over a bag of marijuana?"

When they testified during these pretrial hearings, the officers maintained they did not believe Samson had been murdered and rather that they were referring to his liver disease, but the judge outright rejected that.

Chipman concluded Sandeson should have been rearrested for murder at the beginning of the interrogation because the police already had reasonable grounds to suspect it.

"As the words of the officers demonstrate, this situation was that Mr. Sandeson was a murder suspect. He was not told this until he had provided self-incriminating information to Cst. Allison," Chipman wrote.

In a later interview, Allison told me he was disappointed the interrogation was deemed inadmissible and has lost sleep thinking about it. He said he now makes a point of impressing upon new officers the value of interviewing as a skill and the importance of knowing the law well. "Trying to figure it out after the fact doesn't work, as you can tell," he said.

Sayer said it was also a lesson in the importance of gathering as much evidence as possible as soon as an alleged crime occurs. "You get as many pieces of the puzzle as you can, because you don't know what you're going to lose," he said.

The retrial was going ahead, but due to those police improprieties the jury would never see those incriminating videos of William Sandeson telling police multiple versions of events.

CHAPTER 17

THE BITCOIN FACTOR

A s Sandeson's second criminal trial was inching closer, yet another dramatic twist was about to unfold—this one outside the crime itself, but no less mysterious. It involved hidden cryptocurrency—Bitcoin, at one point believed to be worth almost a million dollars—and a court yet again grappling with how to move forward in another murky area involving William Sandeson. (Note that all of these proceedings were under a publication ban until the conclusion of Sandeson's criminal trial.)

On July 6, 2022, Sandeson wrote a letter to Justice James Chipman. "I recognize that this is quite like [sic] an unconventional manner of conducting court business and am eager to express my apologies for what blunders I'm sure to produce," he began. He said he was writing to express his desire to have certain belongings—namely his personal computer and wallet, which had been seized by the police—returned to his family. He outlined a history of his various efforts to get those things back, dating back to 2016. He said his new lawyer, Alison Craig, had contacted the Crown numerous times since 2021 "seeking the return of most specifically my laptop computer."

Since her efforts outside of court had been unsuccessful and he lacked the financial means to get a lawyer to pursue this matter for him, he indicated his intention to pursue it himself. "I readily admit my ignorance of criminal procedure and the law most generally," he wrote, going on to highlight the section of the Criminal Code under which he believed he could make a "strong case" for the return of his property.

The letter outlined that he wished to have the contents of his vehicle, which were not seized by police but were still in the custody of police, returned, as well as sixty-six dollars in Canadian cash that was in a backpack, his wallet, and that seemingly important Dell laptop.

Why was that laptop so important? No one knew, and Sandeson didn't say. He apologized for the nature of the request, saying he had hoped to come to an agreement without wasting the court's time.

It was not to be. Just over three months later, in a letter to Justice Chipman, dated October 13, 2022, Kim McOnie outlined the Crown's position on the matter. According to the Criminal Code, a person whose property has been seized may apply to have the items returned when the periods of detention have expired or when the court is satisfied that hardship would result if the items were not returned.

With respect to the laptop specifically, the letter acknowledged it had not been used as evidence in the first trial, but the Crown was reluctant to return it until the criminal matter was concluded. The letter also noted Sandeson had previously been provided with a copy of the computer's hard drive.

"Mr. Sandeson is charged with an extremely serious offence," McOnie wrote in her three-page letter to Chipman. She noted the laptop contained "a plethora of information," including text messages, internet searches, and information about websites that were accessed up to and including the day Taylor Samson disappeared.

She pointed out Sandeson's new trial was scheduled to begin in approximately three months. "In the Crown's submission it would be wholly inappropriate to return the laptop to Mr. Sandeson at this point in time," she wrote.

The next day, the key players gathered for yet another hearing in Sandeson's years-long battle to get his computer back. McOnie argued Sandeson would have to demonstrate that not having his wallet and laptop returned would create hardship.

Sandeson, appearing remotely, said the laptop was his main concern, both because of the value of the machine itself—more than $3,000 when it was purchased before he left the country for med school in 2013—and the value of the contents, "namely cryptocurrency stored in the laptop itself."

It was the first time anyone understood why getting that laptop back might be so important to Sandeson.

"Bitcoin is the cryptocurrency of concern," he pronounced.

He said he had made multiple purchases in the six-to-eight–month period prior to his arrest, and that his family had the receipts to prove it.

He said the Bitcoin was valued at $8,000 to $10,000 in Canadian currency at the time. "Without getting into too many specifics, the value of that has significantly appreciated over the past seven years," Sandeson told the court.

That would turn out to be an understatement.

Sandeson said that without physical possession of the laptop he could not access those funds and, further, that he was worried the laptop could become inoperable in storage and then the money would be "lost forever."

Sandeson argued he'd been in prison for more than seven years and had had no income during that time.

"I and my family have incurred quite large expenses in trying to fund my defence in this criminal matter. I'm quite indebted to my family for how they've assisted me throughout this, and that money could go a long way towards helping them," he argued.

The Crowns could be heard whispering to one another.

Sandeson pointed out he was a co-signer on a line of credit with his mother and there was still a significant amount owing on that.

"These are my significant assets at this point in time; all of my other assets I've already rendered to my family," he said.

He said he should get his wallet back because his identity had never been questioned, nor had his address, and the wallet had no other evidentiary value. Plus, he said, it would be a hardship if he couldn't access his loyalty points from Air Miles and Shoppers Optimum, as well as his Canadian Tire money.

Kim McOnie wanted to know why he couldn't access the funds with the copy of the hard drive the court had already provided him.

He fumbled a little, saying he's not an expert in the matter, but ultimately reiterated that it just wasn't possible the way he had it set up.

Andreas Park *is* an expert in the matter. He's an economist, a professor of finance at the University of Toronto, and co-founder of LedgerHub, the university's blockchain research lab. (Blockchain is a key piece of cryptocurrency infrastructure in which a record of transactions is maintained across computers linked in a peer-to-peer network.) Park also co-authored a design proposal for a central bank–issued digital currency, commissioned by the Bank of Canada.

He said crypto assets can be moved around if you have access to what's called a private key. You use the private key to create a public key, and from the public key you derive an account. Assets are attributed to the account on the blockchain. If you have the private key, that allows you to make transactions in Bitcoin.

"It's a little bit like a password, except that it is a very long password that nobody can actually keep in their mind," said Park, in an interview.

He said the private keys are usually kept in a piece of software, which is called a wallet, and that wallet then allows the user to use the private key to sign transactions.

Park suggested Sandeson likely wanted access to his laptop because it has a wallet that allows him to use the private key to transfer bitcoins around. "Nobody can prevent him from doing that as long as he has access to the internet."

The bitcoins are not sitting on the laptop itself, but on the blockchain, and the key to accessing the coins is in the wallet, which is on the laptop.

Park said Bitcoin could "go to zero from one day to the next," and that there had been an increased demand in the years between 2015 and 2023. "I have no good explanation for you other than people want to buy it, people are willing to pay a lot for it—that's it," he said. "People are willing to pay a lot of money for Pokémon cards too, right?"

The Crown argued that Sandeson had not met the threshold for demonstrating hardship. McOnie also said not being able to access loyalty points was not a hardship.

"Two hundred dollars may not be very much to someone who earns that every day, but for me to earn $200 in prison, I have to work as a cleaner for a full year," Sandeson fired back. The hearing was adjourned.

On November 23, 2022, Justice Chipman released a decision. Chipman ruled that the laptop could not be returned to Sandeson because it might be required at the upcoming trial. He later agreed to hear more evidence under a different section of the Criminal Code.

As she'd sat in the courtroom during the discussions about the laptop, Linda Boutilier had decided she needed a lawyer, too. "I called five or six places here in Halifax and they said, 'We don't have time,'" she said. Others said they couldn't represent her because they had a conflict of interest. (By this point, many Halifax lawyers had had their hands in the case in one way or another.)

Boutilier gave up on Halifax lawyers and called James Goodwin, who practises civil litigation at Hicks LeMoine Law in Amherst, NS. "She told me I was somewhere around the twelfth to fifteenth lawyer she called," Goodwin said in an interview. "But I was the first one who understood the words that she was saying."

Goodwin, who had only moved to Amherst two years earlier—and five years after Taylor Samson was murdered—had never met Boutilier but immediately knew who she was. "It was such a big story when it happened here that I'd heard the story a few times," he said.

He also knew a bit about Bitcoin, having been involved in some investments himself.

"It's not as complicated or scary as people think," he said.

He got that call from Boutilier on December 6, two days before Chipman was set to hear more evidence on whether Sandeson could have the laptop back. Goodwin dropped everything, drafted up some documents, filed them, and asked for an emergency court appearance as soon as possible.

"My practice is not normally that exciting," he said.

On December 7, Linda Boutilier and her son, Connor Samson, with the help of James Goodwin, filed a claim against William Sandeson.

Totally separate from the criminal trial that was still to come, they wanted to sue him under the Fatal Injuries Act for all he was worth—whatever that may turn out to be.

"The Plaintiffs claim exemplary and punitive damages for wrongful death," reads the statement of claim.

They claimed special and general damages, including "the loss of guidance, care, and companionship of Taylor Samson."

The next day, on December 8, 2022, everything collided—court appearances were taking place in both Halifax and Amherst. In the morning, Sandeson appeared before Justice Chipman in Halifax via video link. Boutilier was in the courtroom.

The judge noted Goodwin's colleague, Joshua Cormier, was on the line listening in, as his firm was representing Boutilier with respect to a civil matter. Cormier said that he knew the civil case had no bearing on what was being decided that day, but he wanted to make the court aware that the laptop "forms a key part" of the civil case.

Then—for the first time—the court got a sense of what that Bitcoin might be worth. McOnie told the court she'd learned Sandeson had 8.67 Bitcoin (BTC), and that as of November 4, 2022, it was valued at $241,000 Canadian.

The value dropped slightly after that but has since been climbing more or less continuously.

McOnie said a possible resolution to the laptop matter would be to give Sandeson a "forensic image" of the laptop, which would enable him to access the Bitcoin, unlike the copy of the computer's hard drive that had previously been provided.

Sandeson agreed with the proposal and McOnie said he'd have the forensic image in about a week. "As I understand it, it's a simple copy/paste. I'm not sure why the week timeline is necessary," Sandeson argued.

He had to have known a week would give Linda Boutilier and her new lawyer more time to stop him from getting access.

And that's exactly what they did.

That same afternoon, James Goodwin appeared via teleconference before a judge in Amherst.

"What are you attempting to do here?" asked Justice Jeffrey Hunt, referring to the paperwork in front of him.

Goodwin, sounding somewhat frantic, said the matter had just landed on his desk at close of business two days earlier. "I didn't have all the opportunity in the world to kind of plan this out," he told the judge. He said he had just learned that morning that Sandeson would be getting access to the laptop within one week, and that it was now worth $241,000 in Canadian funds.

(In November 2021, it was valued at more than $722,000 Canadian.)

He pointed out Sandeson had made a number of applications to get his laptop back and the most recent one was the only one where he "disclosed the actual true reason."

"Ms. Boutilier has been attending all these hearings going back to 2015 and this may be her best shot at justice," he said.

After an eight-minute court appearance, they agreed to set a hearing four days later.

In our interview, Goodwin insisted Boutilier and her son, Connor, are entitled to Sandeson's money. "No one can bring Taylor back. No one can make an injured victim in a car accident immediately healthy again. In our system the next best thing is lump-sum damages," he said. "It's not going to get rid of all the pain, it's not going to make everything better, but it will make things a little better for her."

He also noted that whether the asset is Bitcoin, mutual funds, or cash in a bag, it's pretty rare in Canada for people to success-fully sue the convicted person after a murder. "Because murderers basically never have money," Goodwin said. "And this appears to be the exception."

On December 12, Goodwin appeared before Justice Timothy Gabriel asking him to grant an interim injunction blocking William Sandeson from receiving the "forensic image" of his laptop that another judge had ruled he could have.

"Thank you for hearing this on an emergency basis," Goodwin began. "We've moved as quickly as humanly possible to try to stop what is about to happen."

He told the judge Sandeson was due to receive the data off his laptop sometime later that week, and that if he was given access to the cryptocurrency, it could "disappear"—be transferred out of the jurisdiction—and his clients would lose an opportunity to get justice. He said Sandeson had been "deceptive" about the existence of the cryptocurrency, "hiding his assets," and that he was even getting help from Nova Scotia Legal Aid to fund his defence.

"He's allowed this asset to fall from $700,000 to $200,000, robbing my clients of the funds they will be getting from him when they're successful," he emphasized.

He said that once Sandeson had access to that private key, he could give it to someone on the outside, and they would move the coins. He said a number of major exchanges operate in Singapore and the Bahamas, and he "will have no trouble finding someone who will take his money."

In response, Sandeson argued he had no duty to disclose the existence of the Bitcoin. Furthermore, he said that the application on which the Bitcoin wallet was stored was on the desktop of the laptop that was seized so "the police must have or should have known about the existence of this Bitcoin because the application was plain as day for them to see."

He also noted the plaintiffs filed their action under the Fatal Injuries Act, which says they must file their action within twelve months. The act states that the action "shall be commenced within twelve months after the death of the deceased person."

But Goodwin snapped back, declaring that under civil law Taylor Samson wasn't even dead. Goodwin said he would eventually make a motion under the Presumption of Death Act, but until he did so, the clock on that one-year limitation hadn't even started running.

"We have no final order from a court declaring him dead; we have no death certificate," he said.

"I'd also note that it kind of sounds like Mr. Sandeson knows that he's dead, which is an interesting thing for him to..."

The judge cut him off. "Mr. Goodwin, just make your argument, okay?"

This was dangerous territory given the criminal trial was now only four weeks away. Goodwin wrapped his arguments. Justice

Gabriel granted the emergency injunction, blocking Sandeson from accessing the Bitcoin, at least for the time being.

In February 2023, five days after the conclusion of Sandeson's trial, Gabriel granted an extension of the injunction.

At that time, Goodwin told the court he would be looking to have the Bitcoin liquidated if successful, meaning he'd have it cashed in for Canadian currency and paid into the court.

"As the price of that stuff has fluctuated, I don't know how practically that gets achieved," said Justice Hunt. Goodwin admitted he didn't know how to make it happen either but said he would look into it.

They set a date for a hearing—but before that could take place, the parties settled the motion.

Sandeson was now being represented in the civil matter by Jessica Rose of Weldon McInnis, who agreed to a "consent preservation order," issued by Justice Hunt in June 2023. (Rose declined to be interviewed for this work.)

The order directed Goodwin to retrieve the laptop and bring it to his office in Amherst. It ordered Sandeson to give Goodwin the private key through Rose. Goodwin was then to hand it all over to an IT company in Moncton, NB, which would then get $100,000 worth of the cryptocurrency converted to Canadian currency and transferred to Rose's law firm, where it would be held in trust.

Beginning as early as practicable after January 1, 2024, the order states, another $100,000 Canadian would be liquidated and held by Weldon McInnis in trust, and this would continue once a year until the entirety of the cryptocurrency had been depleted.

In an interview, Goodwin said they came up with this arrangement to liquidate the coins over a period of years for tax purposes.

Cryptocurrency expert Andreas Park explained that selling the stock over a number of years could reduce the tax burden because the amount would be taxed at a lower rate. But he noted that, from the point of view of the victims, the Bitcoin could depreciate as the years ticked by, although it could also be worth even more. "I'm not sure if this is a gamble I would take," Park said.

Sandeson is also entitled to some of the money to help fund his defence and the order says some of the money was to be used to pay the IT company for seeing to the liquidation.

According to court documents, as of February 23, 2024, $198,000 worth of Bitcoin had been liquidated. As of March 27, 2024, the approximate value of the remaining Bitcoin was $468,270.

Goodwin said the next step would be for the parties to sit down and see if they could come to an agreement as to who gets what. If they couldn't, there would be a civil trial on damages. He declined to speculate on how much Boutilier might end up walking away with.

"She will recover something from this for sure; something that will certainly make it worth her time," he said.

"Whatever he has, I want it," Boutilier said. "That's where it's gonna hurt him."

TOP: A William Sandeson mugshot taken by a Halifax Regional Police officer shortly after the Dalhousie medical student was charged with murder. (*COURT EXHIBIT*)

BOTTOM: William Sandeson (foreground) and Taylor Samson in the hallway of Sandeson's building. The surveillance tape is dated 08/15/2015, 22:26.00, and Samson is carrying a black duffle bag. Samson was never seen on camera leaving the building. (*COURT EXHIBIT*)

TOP: A surveillance tape shows Sandeson and his girlfriend, Sonja Gashus, dated 08/15/2015, 20:49.25, heading to his apartment. Sandeson appears to be carrying a pizza box. Gashus testified that she left the apartment and then received a text from Will at 12:30 A.M., telling her she could return. (*COURT EXHIBIT*)

BOTTOM: Recovered bags of weed. The court was told that on August 15, 2015, Taylor Samson went to Will Sandeson's downtown Halifax apartment to sell nine kilograms of marijuana for $40,000 as part of a prearranged deal. (*COURT EXHIBIT*)

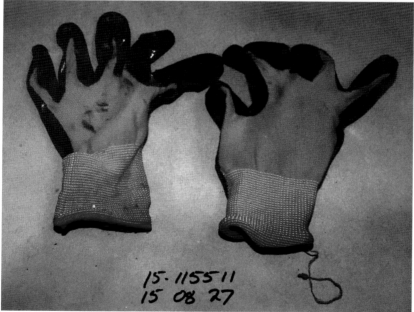

TOP: A Smith & Wesson SD9, an exhibit at the murder trial. The jury was shown a gun, bullets, and cash seized from Sandeson's apartment. (COURT EXHIBIT)

BOTTOM: Gloves entered into the trial as evidence. (COURT EXHIBIT)

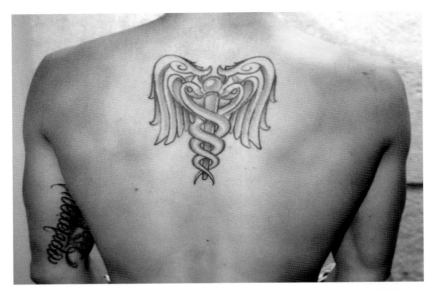

TOP: William Sandeson's back tattoo depicts a caduceus, which is often used as a symbol for medicine. Before he was accepted at Dalhousie, Sandeson briefly attended a med school in the Caribbean. (*COURT EXHIBIT*)

BOTTOM: The site on the Salmon River where William Sandeson claims to have dumped Taylor Samson's body. (*AUTHOR PHOTO*)

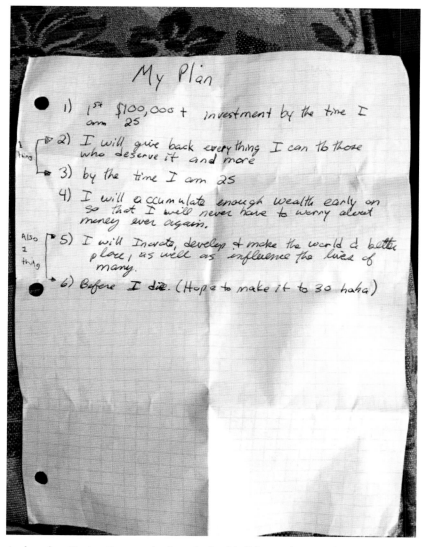

A plan that Taylor Samson had made for his life. By the time he was twenty-five he wanted "to accumulate enough wealth early on so that I will never have to worry about money ever again." Ominously, he also wrote, "Hope to make it to 30 haha." (*COURT EXHIBIT*)

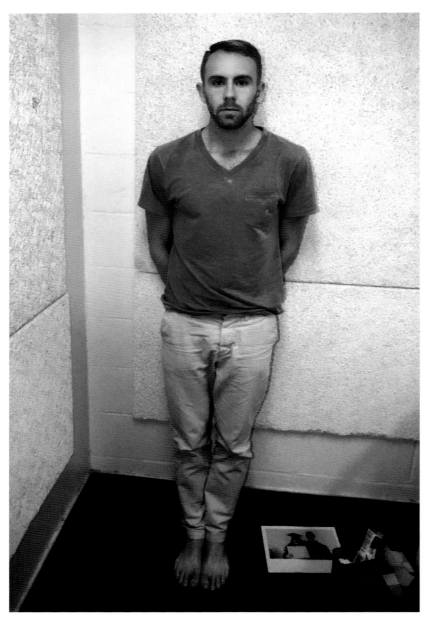

William Sandeson photographed by police. On the floor is a photograph of Taylor Samson and his brother, Connor, used by police during their interrogation. (*COURT EXHIBIT*)

The exterior of the South End Halifax building where Sandeson lived, not far from the Dalhousie Medical School, where he was scheduled to start classes. (*COURT EXHIBIT*)

The crime scene. In the trial's most shocking twist, two of Sandeson's track teammates testified that they went to Sandeson's apartment after hearing a gunshot. There they saw a body slumped over in a chair, bleeding. They would become the trial's star witnesses. (*COURT EXHIBIT*)

TOP: Taylor Samson and his girlfriend, Mackenzie Ruthven. She testified she was in a relationship with Samson for about six months before he disappeared. (*COURTESY LINDA BOUTILIER*)

BOTTOM LEFT: Samson's grade two school photo. (*COURTESY LINDA BOUTILIER*)

BOTTOM RIGHT: Samson in a Halloween costume. (*COURTESY LINDA BOUTILIER*)

TOP: William Sandeson's car, a black Mazda Protegé. He was seen on video loading garbage bags and a blue Adidas bag into the trunk the day his phone pinged in the Truro area. (*COURT EXHIBIT*)

BOTTOM: William Sandeson being escorted by guards to the courtroom for his bail review hearing on October 26, 2023. (*AUTHOR PHOTO*)

Taylor Samson's physics classmates placed this memorial plaque outside the Dunn building on the Dalhousie University campus. (*NIMBUS PHOTO*)

The author and Taylor Samson's mother, Linda Boutilier, after the first trial.
(*AUTHOR PHOTO*)

CHAPTER 18
NEW LAWYER IN TOWN

The first time I met Alison Craig was in the winter of 2022. Pretrial negotiations for Sandeson's second trial had just begun.

Court had been in recess for lunch, and as we gathered outside waiting to go back in, I approached her and introduced myself as a journalist who had written a book about the case.

"Oh wow! A whole book!" she exclaimed.

Odd, I thought. Was she being disingenuous? Condescending? I couldn't tell. But I found it difficult to believe she hadn't *read* the book, let alone not heard there *was* a book.

I welcomed her to Halifax. She thanked me and said it was only her fourth time in the city. I asked if her visits had been for business or pleasure. She said it had been a little of both, and that her friends had just bought a beach house near Lunenburg, a small fishing town often featured in Nova Scotia tourism ads.

Then it was time to head back into court, so I told Craig I'd see her around. I'd already seen enough to know she'd be well worth writing about.

She graduated from the University of Guelph in 2002 and from Queen's Law School in 2005. She was called to the bar in 2006 and made partner in just five years.

Alison Craig was unlike any lawyer I'd ever seen in Nova Scotia courts.

When Sandeson was brought into court that morning, she walked over to him and said loudly, for all in the courtroom to hear, "What do you think Justice Chipman would think of my mask? Huh? How inappropriate is that?" She laughed uproariously.

She was wearing a cream-coloured face mask with the words NOT GUILTY written across it in big block letters.

She returned to her seat and said out loud to no one in particular, "Over/under on how many times I say Your Honour instead of My Lord."

The clerk asked if there was an active wager on that and Craig laughed.

Crown Attorney Carla Ball asked if they say "Your Honour" in Supreme Court in Ontario. Craig confirmed they say "Your Honour" at every level.

That was all before 9:40 A.M. when the judge entered the courtroom.

When she called for her first witness, Craig said she wasn't sure of the process to bring them in, and asked if they should be paged. The judge seemed mildly amused as he explained that there is no paging system; the sheriffs would just go get the witnesses. It was already clear that things were a little different in Nova Scotia than this big-city lawyer was used to.

But court reporter Blair Rhodes said Craig wasn't like other lawyers he'd seen come down from Toronto. "She was respectful of the people and the process here...and sort of folksy, in a way."

The Sandeson case was her first time practising outside Ontario. She loved Nova Scotia, but she wasn't charmed by all of it, once tweeting, "Seriously Nova Scotia? Cash only tolls? In 2022?!?" She was referring to the $1.25 charged each time drivers crossed one of the two bridges spanning Halifax Harbour; while electronic passes were available, debit and credit cards were not accepted at the booths.

She begrudged the weather. Fair enough, who doesn't?

And the hills.

"Heading home for a couple of weeks to allow my butt to recover before returning to the Halifax Hill from Hell," she also tweeted.

During breaks, Craig chatted away in what would otherwise be a silent courtroom.

One day, she brought up the 2022 Oscars, which had aired the night before, telling the other lawyers about how Will Smith had punched host Chris Rock after he had made a joke about his wife, Jada Pinkett Smith.

"As a defence lawyer I would strongly advise you not to punch someone on live TV!" she quipped.

It was a direct quote from Craig's Twitter feed, @lawandchocolate, the night before. She tweeted actively—extremely actively—and continues to do so. By her own admission, she's "addicted" to the social media platform, now known as X, and says it's her community.

On the day the pretrial motions in the Sandeson case began, she posted, "I have to wear robes—and pants—ALL WEEK. Pray for me."

What she *really* loves wearing are what she calls her "court socks."

She has a whole dresser full, an estimated two hundred pairs. They're wild and wacky, some pure nonsense, others making a statement. And of course, she shares photos of them on Twitter.

One morning, while seated in court directly behind Craig, I noticed she'd tweeted, "I miss my cat, so I'm wearing her to court," with a photo of her legs, black dress pants hauled up to reveal white tights with pictures of a cat's head all over them. I looked up to see if she was joking. She was not.

Another post said, "Today's court socks. Need I say more," along with a photo of socks covered in the poop emoji.

She even scrolled through Twitter during court, including when a witness was on the stand being questioned by the Crown, regularly checking her mentions page to see who had commented on or "liked" her posts.

"She's a different creature in that regard," said Rhodes, noting he'd never before seen a lawyer actively tweeting during court.

When I asked her about it, she said, "I'm very particular about not tweeting about cases when I'm in the middle of them."

I pointed out that in fact I had sat behind her one day in court in pretrial hearings, watching her in person and online, and saw her tweet, "Listening to an officer testify about my client's burping habits and why they're indicative of guilt and God give me the strength to get through this day."

(Roger Sayer had been making the point that people often get watery eyes and burp while they're being interrogated due to being nervous.)

She rephrased.

"When a jury is involved, I'm very careful, because you don't want to ever be seen as influencing in any way, shape, or form."

At one point, Craig asked whether the Crown could complete their questioning of a witness within an hour and fifteen minutes. "I would love you forever!" she exclaimed. Ball offered a weak laugh.

It seemed the Crowns didn't know what to make of this new lawyer in town.

But after the second trial was complete, both Ball and McOnie agreed they enjoyed working with Craig, noting her efficiency and ability to focus on the legal issues that mattered, and her willingness to make concessions when appropriate without interfering with the flow of the trial.

"She's a very smart, bright person who was collegial to work with. I really appreciated her," said Ball, acknowledging Craig had unique ways of practice in the courtroom.

"Her personality was unique, maybe, to other people we know, but her legal skills were top notch."

As I sat watching Craig in court, I texted a friend I knew to be a fan of the American legal and political drama *The Good Wife*.

"Remember Elsbeth Tascioni?" I messaged. "I think I'm watching her in real life right now." (Tascioni is a fictional lawyer on the show, played by Carrie Preston. She's friendly, loveable, extremely eccentric, and uses unorthodox methods in court, often surprising—shocking—opposing counsel when she wins. There's also now a spinoff series simply called *Elsbeth*.)

Like Tascioni, it seemed Craig was who she was, whether in court or on Twitter.

I sat down for an interview with Craig in Toronto in the summer of 2023. She enthusiastically agreed to talk, and invited me to her office, located in Toronto's Cabbagetown district. Craig's office at Posner, Craig, Stein is in an old Victorian home, a tall, grey building with black trim with a black wrought iron fence around it encasing overgrown shrubbery.

I arrived early and the receptionist told me Craig wasn't there yet, so I sat in the waiting area until she arrived, fifteen minutes late, muttering about the heat.

"Hi! Come on in!" she greeted me, inviting me to follow her up the stairs. Out of breath, she explained she'd already done two guilty pleas and a bail review that day. I accepted her offer of coffee and we continued to her office, which she said probably looked like a bomb went off.

It didn't, but there were things all over the desk—papers, a tube of gum, boxes of documents, some electronics, a highlighter, and a couple of boxes of nice chocolates. Law and chocolate, after all. The walls were adorned with art and her various diplomas, and in the corner of the desk there was a plaque that said, "No Bullshit Allowed" beside a flowchart explaining how you should know whether to call your lawyer on a Saturday. Spoiler alert: you should only call your lawyer on a Saturday if you're under arrest, or if you do not want them to be your lawyer come Monday.

We settled in and I finally began to understand what makes Alison Craig tick.

Born and raised in Mississauga, or "in the burbs" as she said, her father was a lawyer, but she said she never grew up planning to be one herself. "When I was in high school, let's just say, I hung out with the less-than-studious crowd," she began, going on to explain that many of her friends dropped out of school and got involved in the justice system. She recalled thinking how unfair it was.

"They were no different than I was other than privilege, honestly, so it made me mad that they were all kind of labelled criminals. Anyway, that's why I did defence law," she said, as though there was nothing remarkable about it.

Her phone started buzzing—one of five times this would happen during the seventy minutes I was in her office. "When I retire, I'm going to rent an eighteen-wheeler and drive overtop of my phone, back up, and drive over it again," she said.

I laughed. She didn't.

"Maybe people think I'm just this loon who cracks jokes and doesn't work all that hard until I walk into court!" Craig told me.

"But do you care?" I asked.

"No!" she said immediately; confident, but not arrogant. I learned she considers that friendly approach both part of who she is and part of her strategy. "It's an adversarial system, but everybody should just get along and be professional and keep things light," she told me. "It's a hard job no matter which side you're on."

She said that approach also serves her clients. "If you're known as somebody that's reasonable and easy to get along with, your client tends to benefit from that. If you're the one who's always grumpy and calling the Crown names and accusing them of, you know, bad conduct, which is very rarely true, you're not going to get any favours for your clients—ever."

Like most defence lawyers, she doesn't see her work as helping the "bad guys," though she knows that's how many outside her profession view it. "Half the time, I don't know whether my client's guilty or innocent," she said. "We're protecting everybody's rights by enforcing them in court."

She said her goal is to make a difference in people's lives, but also to protect the Charter of Rights and Freedoms and to ensure the justice system functions as it should. If the evidence doesn't exist to properly convict someone, she said, they shouldn't be convicted. "That's how wrongful convictions happen."

Injustice in the system infuriates her. "I would rather have one hundred guilty people go free than one innocent person go to jail," she said.

For fifteen years, she worked with prominent Canadian lawyer James Lockyer. A criminal lawyer for fifty years and a Member of the Order of Canada, Lockyer is perhaps best known for his role as the founding director of Innocence Canada, formerly known as the Association in Defence of the Wrongly Convicted, a national organization that advocates for the wrongly convicted. He's been involved in many high-profile cases, including, in Nova Scotia, those of Clayton Johnson, who was wrongly convicted of the first-degree murder of his wife and spent five years in prison, and Glen Assoun, who was wrongly convicted of murdering his former girlfriend and spent sixteen years in prison.

As pretrial hearings were getting underway in the Sandeson case, there was a buzz in Halifax—James Lockyer was getting involved.

But it wasn't Lockyer who showed up; it was Craig.

She had never heard of William Sandeson when Lockyer put this file on her desk. "But it was fascinating from the outset. Like, a med student, a physics student, like, what the hell?" she said, going on to say that from the beginning she found the matter with the private investigator "intriguing and a little bit horrifying."

She left Lockyer's firm and started her own about a year before Sandeson's retrial began.

I asked Craig who inspired her legally. I thought she might say former American Supreme Court Justice Ruth Bader Ginsberg, since Craig had once showed up in court in Nova Scotia with a woolen RBG finger puppet.

She didn't.

"God help me if he ever finds this out, but probably James," she said.

We both laughed.

Undeterred, I called James Lockyer and told him what she had said.

"I think she's a first-rate lawyer, so if she thinks that in any way I helped her become such a thing, then God bless," he said from his Toronto office. He said her clients are very fond of her, and that "flamboyant" is the best word to describe her.

"She brings her humour and her talent into the courtroom," he said. "Her results are excellent. And I'd trust her with any case."

Her work ethic was also clear. In court one day, as the Crowns mused about someone in their office sending emails while on vacation, Craig told them she'd be emailing them if she was on vacation.

"I have, like, severe anxiety if I go an hour without answering an email," she said in court that day.

She later told me, "I have no life. Honestly, all I do is work."

Even those on the other side had to admit Craig was good at her job, including Taylor Samson's mother. "Some of the things she'd be saying in court, I used to just snicker, thinking, 'Okay, I'd like her representing me if I ever got in trouble,'" laughed Boutilier. She said she did ultimately lose respect for Craig throughout the trial due to some of the comments she made on social media that she perceived as jokes.

One in particular "crossed the line," Boutilier said, when Craig tweeted a photo of a large garbage bag in her Halifax hotel room saying, "It could hold a body. Dear Hilton: I'm afraid you've made a mistake. I am here to defend a homicide, not commit one."

Kaitlynne Lowe took issue with the same tweet.

"I don't begrudge her because she's doing a job. And clearly, she's good at it and passionate about it. But there was a lot of times when I felt that she was very disrespectful about Taylor and his memory," she said.

She commended Craig for the work she's done to call out police brutality, and the work she's done defending the rights of people of colour.

I asked Craig about the tweet. She said she posted it long before she had any idea a large bag played any significant role in the case.

"It was early in my involvement in the case when I was focussed only on the material relevant to the pretrial motions," she said in an email. "One had absolutely nothing to do with the other. Had I realized, I certainly never would have tweeted it."

Rhodes said Craig was efficient. "There was not a lot of wasted drama or effort. She did what was needed. She conceded points that weren't worth fighting," he said, noting the retrial was smooth, unlike the first one, which he said was "chaotic."

He also pointed out it was Craig who had persuaded the judge to exclude the video of the police interrogating Sandeson from the pending retrial, meaning the jury would be completely unaware Sandeson had already told police multiple versions of what happened that night.

"That's what opened the door to the very different trial," said Rhodes.

CHAPTER 19
IN HIS OWN WORDS

The courtroom was packed. It was early February 2023, William Sandeson's retrial was now in its fifth week, and the defence was about to open its case.

There were so many people the sheriff asked everyone to keep their face masks on, though the mask mandate in Nova Scotia had long ago been dropped and the trial was taking place at a new, spacious courthouse, purpose-built to handle jury trials during the COVID-19 pandemic.

"I want to impress upon everyone that this is a criminal jury trial, not a spectator sport," said Justice Chipman, "and the court will not tolerate any overt reactions to anything that takes place here—and this includes any attendees making verbal remarks and or physical gestures such as head shaking, eye rolling, or the like, and should any such infractions occur, the sheriffs are at the ready to eject anyone who behaves in this manner."

No one knew for sure whether Sandeson would take the stand and testify in his own defence. He hadn't in his last trial.

Alison Craig had already asked for a directed verdict on first-degree murder at the conclusion of the Crown's case. That means she asked the judge to rule that Sandeson could not be found guilty of first-degree murder because the elements of the offence had not been met.

Craig argued there was "no evidence" upon which a jury could convict of first-degree murder. The test for the judge to consider was whether a jury, properly instructed, could reasonably convict.

It was under a publication ban at the time, but Chipman immediately dismissed that application. "The totality of the evidence led by the Crown buttresses the reasonable inference that Mr. Sandeson deliberated on his plan to kill Mr. Samson and then cleaned up afterwards," Chipman stated in his written decision two weeks later.

So, with all other options exhausted, Alison Craig stood and addressed the jury.

"You may have noticed that I haven't asked many questions so far during this trial, and that's because most of what happened in this case is not in dispute," she said.

Not in dispute? That was surprising to those of us who had been listening to the facts being disputed for the better part of eight years. But Craig said there was no disputing that Sandeson shot and killed Samson on August 15, 2015.

"He only fired once, but unfortunately that resulted in Mr. Samson's death," she said. "However, I expect that what you will hear is that he didn't fire that shot with the intent of killing Mr. Samson, but rather that he fired it in self-defence."

She spoke for two minutes and eight seconds, saying the jury was about to hear that Samson had tried to get a hold of Sandeson's gun not once, but twice, and that Sandeson feared for his life.

"With that, I'm prepared to call Mr. Sandeson," she said.

When I sat down with Craig after the trial, I asked her what she thought of the case the first defence team had put forth. "I think it's next to impossible to win a case like that without your client taking the box," she said. "The jury wants to hear from them."

So there we were, nearly six years later, with a totally different defence.

❖

William Sandeson was thirty years old when he testified, wearing a suit and tie. He told the court he'd had an "idyllic" childhood, with two loving, supportive parents, acres of land and woods to play in, and a farm where he could look after animals, drive tractors, and play sports.

He had a piece of land plotted out on that same property where he intended to live someday and run a sports medicine clinic along with a family practice.

In August 2015, he was doing very well financially, he said, earning $8,000 a month between drugs and his legal occupation, with his expenses roughly $450 dollars in rent, about $50 on a shared internet connection with his roommate, and a $250 monthly payment on his line of credit.

This testimony was an attempt to dispute the Crown's argument that his motive to kill Taylor Samson was greed and financial gain.

Sandeson estimated that his four years at Dal med school would cost him $80,000. He intended to use the student line of credit to pay for it, but he was also going to apply for government student loans, and he expected half of the tuition amount would be in the form of a grant that would be forgiven upon graduation.

He said he decided to get a gun licence sometime in the late winter or early spring of 2015 because the people he was dealing drugs with in Montréal were uncomfortable with the idea of him driving back and forth with drugs and money without protection.

"I didn't know where to go to get a gun or who to talk to to get a gun, so I think I just googled it and went about doing the courses to allow me to buy one," he said.

He ultimately purchased one around June 2015 at Hnatiuk's Hunting & Fishing in Lantz, NS.

He said he took it to the gun range twice—once by himself and once with his girlfriend—and once to Montréal, but otherwise it didn't leave his safe.

That is, until August 15, 2015.

He said he was looking for twenty pounds of weed in Halifax because he was "tired of driving back and forth to Montréal" and he was also looking to wrap up his drug dealing and thought it would be easier to pass off to someone else if all of his product was in one location.

In a series of text messages read in court, it seemed as though Sandeson was looking for the weed for another person, not himself.

"I'm talking as if there's another person," he testified. "There was no other person. I often did that in almost all my dealings. I acted as an intermediary to protect myself."

He said he met Taylor Samson on three occasions.

The first time they met was August 5, and that was "just a quick hello," where Sandeson said he explained what he was looking for in terms of quality and quantity of marijuana.

The second time was on August 13 at Samson's apartment, where he said Samson showed him a small duffle bag with two bags of weed inside and let him look at the two different strains. They discussed how a deal would work in terms of what would make them both feel safe, including not having any other people around and packaging up the deal into smaller amounts of around five to ten pounds at a time. He said that meeting lasted no more than ten minutes, and when he left there was no confirmation a deal would even happen.

"I was pretending to represent someone else so I had to consult that other person before I could go ahead with anything," Sandeson said on the stand.

He said he next communicated with Samson via text on the evening of Friday, August 14.

In the texts, Sandeson told Samson that he could go ahead and get the weed Samson had shown him. Samson didn't reply until the next day.

Sandeson said he did not wake up on the morning of August 15, 2015, planning to do a drug deal with Taylor Samson later that day.

He went to work at 8:30 A.M. and was there until 4:30 P.M.

At noon, Samson texted, "Can you meet right for 9?"

Sandeson said, "Is this to finalize everything? I've gotta go to Truro for the cash. I can meet at 9 no problem though to talk it over."

"So what's going on here?" asked Alison Craig.

"I don't expect an actual deal to be happening so soon," Sandeson said on the stand. "Generally, these things take multiple days or weeks or one week."

But Sandeson testified Samson told him he thought the deal was happening that day. Text messages show Samson had texted Sandeson: "buddy is gonna be sour."

So Sandeson said he could do it that night, just a bit later than 9:00 P.M. He testified it was the first time he'd heard Samson refer to another person being involved. "It seemed strange to me, especially the way that he was speeding things up and now introducing someone else. And also having so much ready on short notice," he testified.

Still, he agreed to meet Samson no later than ten o'clock.

"So by this point, Saturday at 4:08 P.M., had you finalized the deal with Taylor or were discussions still happening?" Craig asked.

"No. I essentially just kept kicking it off 'til later," he said.

The texts continued and Samson said that he had all twenty pounds ready to go. "I was confused by him wanting to do everything at once, when we previously, and for good reason, set up a plan to do smaller amounts at a time," Sandeson testified.

"That made us both feel safer because there'd be less money and drugs in one place at any one time, meaning there's less of an incentive for one or the other to rob the other. But he's changed that now."

Sandeson said he got off work at 4:30 and went home and watched Netflix with his girlfriend. Around 8:30 he was out for supper with his girlfriend; they discussed their plans for that night and she said she was going to a friend's house.

That's when his plan came together, he said.

"I had free time on my hands and decided that I would meet with Taylor that night," he testified.

When they got home, he said, he went around taking down everything with his name on it—even anything that said Dalhousie Tigers—and took his shoes off the shoe rack, trying to "anonymize" the apartment.

He was trying to make the point that he did not *plan* to kill Samson that night—because if he had, he wouldn't have had to worry about any of those things. He also testified he started prepping the apartment in case he might be robbed—putting away anything that might be used as a weapon. He said he emptied one of two safes in his bedroom, putting $10,000 of the cash "in a stack of backpacks that was next to the safe." He put the remaining $2,000 to $4,000 in the other safe, installed high on the left side of his bedroom closet under a bunch of blankets, and left what remained of his weed in one of the safes in case he had to hand something over.

He admitted he didn't even have the money to do the deal. He said he had somewhere between $12,000 and $14,000 in cash and about $8000 in Bitcoin. "I didn't make any efforts to go get the cash because, at that point, I'd made up my mind that I intended to confront Taylor Samson about something else that had happened earlier in the week," he said.

This was the first time he'd ever mentioned a confrontation of any kind.

He said he planned to challenge Samson about his potential involvement in a home invasion at Jordan MacEwan's place. He testified MacEwan had reached out to him asking for some debt relief on money he owed him because he'd just lost a significant amount of money and drugs when he was robbed late Thursday night into Friday morning.

"He knew that I was looking for Halifax suppliers of drugs, and that I'd been talking to Taylor. He'd warned me not to do any deals with Taylor," Sandeson said. He testified he had installed security cameras at his apartment in the late spring or early summer of 2015 to secure his home and to keep track of who was coming and going.

He admitted he turned them off shortly after 11:30 on the evening of August 15.

"Why did you not turn them off before Mr. Samson arrived?" Craig asked.

"Because I wanted to keep track of who was going to be in and out of that apartment in the event that someone tried to rob the apartment," Sandeson replied.

Craig was setting up the argument that if Sandeson had been *planning* to kill someone, he'd have turned the cameras off from the beginning.

But there was another explanation—one the jury didn't get to hear.

In the police interrogation video that was excluded as evidence in this trial, Sandeson told the officer he had put cameras in, but they didn't work properly.

"They're shitty," he said in the video, explaining that the system had been recording over itself every twenty minutes.

"That was huge," Carla Ball told me in our interview after the retrial. She said the exclusion of that evidence left the Crown in a tough spot. "We didn't have any explanation besides theories."

On the stand, Sandeson said he was uneasy, not entirely convinced it would be Samson that actually showed up that night.

Sandeson said Samson seemed uncomfortable with the cameras and said he made a lame joke to try to put him at ease, telling him, "Don't worry, nothing very interesting happens here anyway."

As they entered the apartment together, Sandeson said he offered Samson a beer.

"I was still thinking that it could be a diplomatic interaction," he testified. "He pretty quickly shot that down and in a pretty gratuitously rude way, just kind of swore and said something to the effect of, 'I just want to get this the fuck over with.'"

He said he checked the duffle bag to confirm that what was inside was actually weed, and then went to his room to get the $10,000 he intended to give Samson.

Sandeson believed Samson had stolen from MacEwan, but MacEwan owed Sandeson a "considerable amount" of money (later revealed to be $14,750) so Sandeson felt that, by not paying Samson the full amount agreed upon—and taking his weed—they would be square.

"He asked me where the rest of the money was and I told him that he already got the rest of the money from Jordan," he said.

"He stood up and said something like—again, apologies for the language, but there was swearing pretty much every exchange going forward—'If you're gonna fuckin' play around, I'm gonna take this all and leave.'"

Sandeson said he told Samson he was lucky he was getting anything at all and lifted up the baggy sweater he was wearing to show him that he had his gun in the front pocket of his pants.

He said he opened the door to his apartment and told Samson to get the fuck out, speaking loudly, hoping to attract the attention of Blades and McCabe across the hallway.

He said he'd asked them to stay home that night for exactly this sort of situation.

Sandeson said his friends didn't come over, but Samson calmed down and asked him to come back in and "talk it out," so he did. "He asked if he could have the beer that I'd previously offered him and now I said no because I was worried that he might be trying to arm himself with the beer bottle."

This was the part everyone had been waiting for.

He was finally about to say what happened in those critical minutes before Taylor Samson's death.

"The next thing I remember him saying was something to the effect of, 'When's your pretty girlfriend get home?' or 'Is your pretty girlfriend home?' and that stunned me because I didn't think he knew it was my home or much about me, and the next thing he did was—we were at opposite ends of the kitchen table, he was coming at me, trying to get his hands on where I'd shown him the gun was on my right front hip, in my pants pocket," he testified.

This is where Samson's friends and family sitting in the courtroom started to doubt Sandeson's story.

"Not only would Taylor not say the words that Sandeson was saying he did, but like, none of that made sense to who Taylor was in his character. And he's not given the ability to speak for himself," said Kaitlynne Lowe.

"That assessment of Taylor's character is now public record, and I think that that's probably what infuriated me the most of Sandeson taking the stand, because it's like—you murdered him. Do you really have to lie about what his last words were?"

Sandeson said they struggled for the gun.

"I was twisting away from him, trying to keep my body between him and the gun, and he ended up with both arms around me as we jostled for control of the gun," he testified. He said at one point one of them did pull the trigger, but no shot went off because he hadn't chambered a round.

"As we wrestled around the kitchen, eventually I ended up pinned against the kitchen table and I had the gun under the table to keep it away from him," he continued. "I was kicking back at him behind me, trying to stomp his feet and kick his shins, kick in between the legs, anything to get him off me. Then eventually he let go, and I remember him laughing and he took a seat at the chair closest to the door that led out of my apartment. I spun back away from him, pretty much as far as I could get in the kitchen from him."

Samson's mother told me in an interview that at that moment she had to put her head down. "I thought I was gonna get kicked out," she said. "He's so dramatic; the theatrics that he was going through on the stand, it's ridiculous. Taylor's arms are this long," she said, expanding her own reach wide. "And he's a tiny little guy. Like, come on—if Taylor wanted the gun, Taylor would have grabbed the gun."

The sensational testimony continued.

"At that point I racked the slide; I chambered a round in the gun and I pointed it at him with both hands and I screamed at him to get the fuck out of my apartment."

He let out a big sigh.

"He just kind of sneered and said, 'Well, what do you think's gonna happen now?' And he said, 'You're done.' And then he lunged out of the chair towards the gun again, and I pulled the trigger."

There it was: *I pulled the trigger*.

The people in the courtroom had waited nearly eight years to hear those words. For the next seven seconds, there was only silence.

"It let some of the air out of the room," said court reporter Blair Rhodes.

Sandeson said he then dropped the gun. "I tried to kick or push the gun by putting it back into the furthest corner of the kitchen away from him, back where the cat food was. And then I turned back to him. He was back in the chair, but he was slumped," he testified.

"As I went towards him, I heard this breath that didn't sound natural. And I remember thinking for a second, he must have been shot in the chest. Because the noise didn't sound natural. But when I got to him, I went to first check for a pulse. I went for his neck because it's just one of the easiest spots. And when I went to touch his head, that's when I just noticed there was blood everywhere all over his head and neck."

Six more seconds of silence.

"And the next thing I did was I ran to my neighbour's apartment to tell them they had to get out of there, because I didn't want them to get in any trouble. I asked them to stay back and now this had happened."

He said the rest was "kinda blurry."

He said his friends followed him back to his apartment, and he was telling them to leave but they wouldn't. "Justin was standing there, acting like a site manager, trying to tell me what to do. 'Oh, you need to clean this, you need to do that, you need to do this.' And it seemed insane to me at the time. I couldn't understand what he was doing. He should have just been leaving," he said, sounding exasperated.

Craig asked him why he had put the gun in his pocket before Samson came over. He said it was to deter any sort of robbery. She asked why he showed it to Samson.

"'Cause I thought it would defuse the situation," he said. "It's a show of overwhelming force. If you see a gun, then you're gonna listen to the person with the gun."

"So why did you ultimately fire it?" Craig asked.

Sandeson replied without hesitation: "To keep him from killing me."

Craig said that McCabe and Blades had described him as distraught, panicked. "How would you describe your own state of mind?" she asked.

"Terrified; in total shock," he sobbed. "I didn't know what to do or what to think. It didn't seem real."

He said he asked McCabe to call 911 if he didn't hear from him by a certain time, because he still didn't know if others would be coming behind Samson.

McCabe testified that he didn't recall Sandeson saying that.

Craig asked Sandeson why he didn't call for help himself.

"Once I saw the amount of blood and how fast it was coming, I knew there was nothing I could do for him," he said.

"Why not call the police and tell them what had happened?" asked Craig.

"Even if what I did in that moment wasn't wrong, there was so much else in there. There's drugs, money, I've got my gun out of the safe that's not supposed to be out of the safe. I was definitely going to go to jail for something."

He set about trying to clean his apartment before his girlfriend came home.

"There was no method to it," he said. "I'd go to clean something else and set something bloody on that surface again. It was a shit show."

Craig asked why he turned the cameras off from 11:30 P.M. to 1:00 A.M.

"That's when I started taking garbage out of my apartment," he said. "And I also took Taylor out of my apartment."

His testimony was direct.

"The bloody stuff, the garbage, I bagged up and I put it in a green bin that sat outside my apartment. And I put Taylor inside of the black duffle bag that he brought, and I put that in the trunk of my Mazda car."

He said when his girlfriend returned, he was "coughing bleach fumes pretty bad" and though he'd already taken a shower by then, she made him take another one because he was covered in sweat.

They went to bed, but he couldn't sleep, so he got out of bed, turned the camera system back on, and sat in the computer chair in the room, watching the surveillance "in case anyone else was coming."

He said he didn't sleep at all that night.

He started to feel bad about having the TV on in the room where his girlfriend was sleeping, so he moved to the kitchen and watched on his laptop. He texted a few people throughout the night.

He texted Samson: "This isn't cool man. Want that stuff."

He also texted Jordan MacEwan: "Man, I got fucked. Taylor took money and won't answer."

Sandeson testified it was "a pretty lame attempt to make it seem like either [Samson] hadn't shown up or he'd shown up and took off on his own."

He also texted his friend Amanda in Australia, who was awake due to the time difference. "Student loan paid off and I'm completely squeaky clean now. Sold market share away," he texted.

The two had met through mutual friends in high school. "She was my best friend. I just wanted to talk to someone," he sobbed.

Craig asked if it was true that he'd paid off a student loan. He said that it was not. He knew Amanda was concerned about her own student loans and didn't necessarily approve of his plans to leverage investments, borrowing in order to invest elsewhere. He acknowledged the "squeaky clean" comment seemed "terrible in context now."

"She knew I was involved in some sort of illegal activity, and I thought it would make her happy to know that I wasn't doing anything illegal anymore," he testified. He was referring to his involvement with illegal drugs, but Sandeson admitted he carried on doing other things that were illegal—like getting rid of a body.

The next day, Sunday, August 16, he is seen coming and going on surveillance video.

He testified he was taking anything he thought had come in contact with blood out to the garbage. He added some of it to other people's piles of garbage along the road.

Craig asked what he did with Samson's body.

It was the question Samson's family most wanted answered—indeed, the question many Nova Scotians wanted answered.

He said he dropped his girlfriend off at work—with Samson's body still in the trunk of the car—then hit the highway.

"And as I was driving, I was trying to figure out what to do. Sometime along the highway, I had thought that I should just pull over and leave him somewhere alongside the highway, inside the treeline. But I ultimately decided against that, just thinking it would look strange, someone walking on the side of the highway with a big duffle bag."

He said he turned off the highway at Stewiacke, went to a gas station, purchased two drinks, and poured one inside a garbage bag that had Samson's phone in it to "soak the phone" and left it in a garbage can at the gas station.

Police had never been able to find Samson's phone.

He looked for a place to leave Samson's remains in that area but said he couldn't find a place, so he got back on the highway and kept going toward Truro.

"I had been raised cautiously to fear the Fundy Bay," he said. "Most of our farmland butts up against it or comes near it. And then I was always told as a kid not to go near the mud, which would be tempting for kids to play in, when the tide was out because the tide could rush in at any time and I'd never be seen again. And that's what came to mind as I was driving."

According to his testimony, he had used a childhood safety lesson to try to get away with murder.

The Fundy Tides are the highest in the world. Twice a day, the bay fills and empties of a billion tonnes of water, more than the flow of all the world's freshwater rivers combined.

Sandeson said he continued driving the route he always took to go home to the farm but stopped short of that and pulled into a carpool spot just off the highway. "From there, there's a trail that leads out to the top of the dykes," he testified.

He said he carried Samson's body out to the top of the dyke and put it in the water on the opposite side of an aboiteau so it was on the side where the water flowed into the Bay of Fundy. He said the bruising on his shoulder in police photos is from the strap of the duffle bag. "I'm surprised both shoulders aren't equally bruised because the bag was so heavy it was cutting into my shoulder and I had to switch shoulders multiple times," he said.

He kept the duffle bag because he thought it would stand out; that someone might be tempted to open it. Samson was covered in garbage bags, and he didn't think someone would be as likely to dig through garbage bags.

It was probably around 8:00 A.M. or a little earlier, based on the timestamps on the video surveillance that show him leaving and returning to his apartment, and on what he said he did in between.

Boutilier doesn't believe his story. "I know that area off by heart," she said.

She went to the area that day immediately after court. "People sit there and they watch the water coming in, the tides coming in. And people are out there walking with their dogs that hour in the morning," she said.

I also decided to go there. I followed the path Sandeson said he took, headed for Truro, took the same exit he took and went through the roundabout in the direction of Lower Truro. Just after I'd passed under the overpass, past the little bridge he mentioned, there was a small dirt parking lot on the right-hand side. I pulled in and used my smartwatch to clock the distance—190 metres from the parking lot to the dyke head—the distance he'd have had to carry Samson's body before he could be concealed by the dykes themselves. It was later in the day than he'd been there, but two women were out walking and said hello as I took pictures.

The body of water where Sandeson said he dumped Samson's remains is actually the Salmon River, which flows into the Cobequid Bay, which flows into the Minas Basin, which flows into the Bay of Fundy. It is the highest point of the Fundy tides, which range from 3.5 metres along the southwest shore of Nova Scotia to 16 metres at the highest point in the Minas Basin. According to bayoffundy.com, the force created by these "mighty waters is equal to 8000 locomotives or 25 million horses at the Minas Channel."

Is it possible that this was where Sandeson actually disposed of Samson's remains? It's possible, perhaps, but if he had done it as he described, it was a fluke that no one saw him—or thought to say anything about it if they had.

When he had finished, Sandeson said, he stopped to buy an air freshener for the car because his girlfriend had complained that morning that the car smelled like weed. He said he was still in shock at that point, and he couldn't get warm despite wearing a sweater, pants, and a hat in the middle of August. He said he doesn't remember much of the drive there or back.

On August 17, he took the weed Samson had brought to his apartment to his brother's place because he couldn't think of anywhere else to put it. On August 18, he took more garbage out of his apartment—including the duffle bag—and brought it home to Truro.

"Why were you going home?" Craig asked.

He broke down again.

"Because I wanted to talk to my dad." He said he hadn't really been eating or sleeping for a few days and was scared. "I trusted him, and I wanted to tell him what happened and ask his advice on what to do," he said. But when he got home, his dad wasn't there. Instead, he dumped all the evidence on his parents' farm.

He spoke with Sgt. Charla Keddy later that day. He testified he hadn't told her the truth. "I was still scared. I didn't know who I was dealing with, really. I didn't know Taylor's last name. I didn't even know if Taylor was his real first name until I started seeing things in the news. I was worried about revenge, reprisals against myself or people close to me if I took any sort of responsibility for that; for him being missing." Sandeson was arrested later that day.

"When you met Taylor Samson that day on August 15th at your apartment, did you plan or want to hurt him?" Craig asked.

"No."

"Did you plan or want to kill him?"

"No, definitely not."

The defence closed its case.

Now it was the Crown's turn to question William Sandeson.

"It's not too often that, you know, people have the opportunity to speak to someone who is alleged to have committed a high-profile murder," Ball said later in our interview. "It's hard to get your head around, as a Crown Attorney, that that's what you're going into work for that day. But, you know, I was prepared."

She jumped in firm and fast, wanting to know about Sandeson's familiarity with the Fundy Tides.

"You knew the tides would rush in and you'd never have a chance to escape that, right? That was a common theme that ran through your house—not to go near that tide. And you knew that the water was mucky and brown like chocolate milk."

"Yes," he said.

"And you knew that there were enzymes and bacteria and seagulls that were around that location."

"I'm not certain I'd put a mind to enzymes and bacteria or seagulls," Sandeson replied.

"Now, you testified earlier that there were two rivers that you actually approached when you were contemplating what to do with that person that day."

"Yes."

"And at that time did it ever occur to you that this was someone's son?"

"Yes, it did." His voice broke, the words barely audible.

"Did it ever occur to you that this was someone's brother?"

"Yes, it did."

"Did it ever occur to you that this was someone's boyfriend, friend?"

"Ah, someone's boyfriend, yes."

"And all you were thinking about at that time was getting rid of *any* evidence that would confirm anything that you have to say today, wouldn't you agree with me?"

Sandeson regained his wits.

"You just asked me to confirm whether I was thinking about all of those things and then just asked me to say I was only thinking about *one* thing," he said. "So I was thinking about those other things and I was thinking about trying to save myself."

"You knew that there was a more likely chance that that bag would get discovered, but the body would be eaten by fish, seagulls, destroyed by tides, right?"

"It was the only place I could think of to leave him in that morning."

"That was the only place you could think of. That's exactly right, you thought of that before you killed Taylor Samson, didn't you?"

"Absolutely not," he said.

He confirmed that he had taken a mandatory course at Saba University called "Human Body Structure and Function." Ball read the course description saying it "explores basic gross human anatomy, allowing students to understand the relationship between the anatomical structure and function through lectures, regional dissections of cadavers, and evaluation of radiograph, including MRIs and CT scan."

"So you knew exactly how to dissect a body, didn't you?" Ball asked.

"Um, dissection is opening the body to look at what's inside," he said.

She suggested he was leading a double life.

"Yeah, there were different aspects," he agreed.

"You would agree with me that the purpose of a semiautomatic handgun is to kill?"

"No, you can engage in sports shooting."

They began to spar.

"You can go to a range and you can shoot a target, right?" Ball said.

"And compete in competitions," he said.

"But when you're taking it back and forth to Montréal in a vehicle, the purpose is to kill."

Sandeson disagreed. "The purpose is to intimidate," he said.

"And the purpose of taking it out when there are other people isolated in your apartment is to kill."

"No, the purpose is to intimidate," he said again.

"You planned to use that gun that night to kill."

"No, I planned to use that gun to intimidate."

He said he got the gun registered because he was required by law to do so.

"And the purpose of going to the range is to practise to use it, right?" Ball was so firm and direct here she sounded angry.

"Yes," Sandeson agreed. He acknowledged he didn't have any other experience with that handgun.

"So you wanted to be sure how to shoot that gun," Ball said.

"It was a date with my girlfriend. She had never handled a gun either."

"Romantic date with your girlfriend, shooting a 9 mm semi-automatic handgun two months before you kill someone," came Ball's retort.

Sandeson was calm. "There was no idea two months beforehand that anyone would be killed by that handgun."

She asked him why there was another bullet in the barrel of his gun—one found after he killed Samson.

Sandeson dropped another bomb.

"Because I was contemplating killing myself."

There were five seconds of silence.

"How did it get up into the barrel of the gun?"

"I loaded it in a magazine. I inserted the magazine into the gun, and I racked the slide."

He firmly denied ever having discussed the Hells Angels with anyone at any time, including Justin Blades.

Ball brought him back to the texts with his dad about his mom being mad over the line of credit, where he replied, "Well she has no need to be. Will be paid this September."

Ball was trying to bring evidence to show that Sandeson planned the murder.

He agreed with her that his plan was to pay back the line of credit by September 2015.

"About two weeks after Mr. Samson was shot and murdered," Ball underlined.

Sandeson said the text was in reference to switching the line of credit from one bank to another and removing his mother as co-signer—more about getting rid of his mother's awareness of it than actually getting rid of the debt itself.

"You put a deadline of September to pay back almost eighty. Thousand. Dollars," Ball stopped after each word as though there were periods on the page.

Sandeson reiterated that his plan was to transfer it to another bank.

Ball suggested to Sandeson that he was overstating how much money was owed to him.

"You want this jury to believe you had lots of money coming in, but, in fact, you didn't."

"No ma'am, I already answered in the negative to that question, I'm just trying to be honest."

"I thought he was a pretty good witness," said Craig in our interview. "It didn't fluster him. It was impressive. To me, that's a sign of being truthful."

"How much did you coach him?" I asked.

"Not much," she said.

She said she had walked him through what to expect because he hadn't testified in the first trial. "But in terms of the actual evidence, he knew the case better than I did," she laughed.

Sandeson recounted the story that Jordan MacEwan had told him about being beaten in his home.

"He also told you that Taylor had nothing to do with it right?" Ball asked.

"No. He said that Taylor was definitely not one of the three people that were present in the apartment but that he thought Taylor had put them onto the apartment and given them the idea to do it," he testified.

This was an important point, since he had said it was the very reason he confronted Samson the night he was killed.

"Somebody that was supposedly involved in a violent home invasion as you described, capable of pulling together three people with batons and beating up a person severely, you invited to your house?!" she sounded incredulous. "I'm going to suggest to you that that was never said to you."

"It was said to me."

Sandeson argued with her on nearly every point calmly, never raising his voice as she continually did, but he wouldn't concede any point.

She wanted to know exactly what MacEwan said about Samson.

"That he believed Taylor was behind the home invasion but was not physically taking part in it," Sandeson said.

The Crown later called MacEwan as a rebuttal witness. He testified that he did not believe Samson had anything to do with the home invasion and that he did not tell Sandeson that he did.

"We had a good relationship as far as I'm aware, and we did business together. It wouldn't make any sense for someone like that to rob me," he told the jury.

Ball directed Sandeson to text messages where MacEwan—thinking Samson had just gone missing or disappeared of his own volition at this point—offered to get some people involved who might be able to help find him and talk some sense into him to get him to come back.

"And you say, 'No man, I don't want to be involved at all.' Why's that?" Ball asked Sandeson.

"That's because I know what happened."

"That's because you murdered him," she corrected.

"No ma'am. Murder is, you're using a specific legal word." Sandeson showed his intelligence again.

Ball continued reading MacEwan's texts. "Yeah man, this is bullshit. I really hope he turns up.' What did you say back to that?"

"Me too," Sandeson said on the stand.

"Did ya really hope that he turned up?"

"A part of me did want him to turn up."

"In which way would you like him to turn up on the 17th after you shot him?"

"His body turn up, so that I didn't have to keep feeling so bad about leaving it where I did."

It was Sandeson's third full day on the stand, but Ball still had more questions.

She got to the part where he said he had flashed his gun at Samson, then Samson asked him to calm down and come back inside and asked for the beer Will had previously offered.

"I say no because I'm worried that he might try to use the beer bottle as a weapon," he testified.

"You're worried that he's gonna use a beer bottle as a weapon and you have a 9 mm loaded semi-automatic handgun on your body? That you're trained to use! That you've practised with! What are you afraid of?!"

"I'm afraid of him using the beer bottle against me as a weapon. I don't want to use my handgun."

Sandeson was calm and quiet, in stark contrast to the way she was speaking to him.

"You're six feet away from him. You have a gun in your hand. He's sitting. You *rack* the gun!" She was hurling—spitting—the words at him.

"Yes," he said, never wavering from that calm voice.

"Get the fuck out of my apartment!" Ball shouted.

"Yes," he said, his voice almost a whisper.

He confirmed Samson did not have his hands on him when he pulled the trigger. Ball wanted to know what was said in the moment before he pulled the trigger. Sandeson said there was no time to say anything.

"You didn't say, 'Stop! I have a gun!'"

"I didn't have a chance to, and I think announcing the fact I had a gun would be pretty clear when it was pointed in his face."

"Help! Pookiel!"

"No, I didn't yell that."

"Blades! Come quick!"

"No, I didn't yell that."

"Somebody help me!'

He said nothing on the stand.

"You just shot the gun!"

"As he came and tried to take it from me."

"And he magically falls back into the chair behind him at the table three feet backwards?"

"I don't know how far he was from the chair. I didn't watch him because I was looking at the gun then falling and worried about it going off again."

"You would agree with me that if you shoot someone with a semi-automatic handgun, they're probably gonna fall on the floor."

"I'm not an expert in this, ma'am, but I know people who've been shot in the head and lived."

Craig stood up. "My Lord, I think I'd like to address this in the absence of the jury," she said.

The jury was dismissed for lunch.

This next part was under a publication ban until the jury began deliberating.

"I have resisted all throughout the cross-examination rising for obvious reasons, but I am starting to get concerned," Craig said. She said she was concerned that Ball was repeatedly putting to Sandeson, "You said..." about things he'd never once said.

"And I cannot just keep rising and looking like I'm trying to fix things when things are being stated inaccurately," she said.

"Well, I'll stop you there," Justice Chipman said. "As you well know, you're free to rise at any time and I will exclude the jury forthwith, and that hadn't happened until now and the moment you asked for it, it happened."

Chipman was asserting his protection of the rights of the defence and trying to prevent another appeal.

"Of course, but the optics are terrible," said Craig. "We all have a responsibility to state the evidence accurately, My Lord."

"We do," Chipman agreed.

Craig went on to say that anybody who has practised criminal law knows that people don't just necessarily collapse when they're shot. "That is my friend making a suggestion that we all know full well is not true," she said.

Ball said that she certainly did not mean to misstate the evidence; rather, she was having some trouble following Sandeson. She promised to be careful.

"I don't understand the difficulty thus far," Chipman said, saying some of the new information Sandeson was now sharing had come as a result of questions of clarification.

"It hasn't, My Lord," Craig continued to argue.

The decision was made to caution the jury that there was no evidence to support the Crown's suggestion that if someone was shot with a 9 mm handgun they would immediately fall to the ground, and they should disregard it entirely.

With the jury back in the courtroom, Ball's tone changed dramatically. She wanted to know where Samson was injured. Sandeson said he didn't know. (In the now-excluded police interrogation video, Sandeson had told the officer Samson had been shot in the back of the neck or head. Now, he said he didn't see a wound.)

"It's just when I got to him and went to touch his neck, I noticed blood all through his hair, over his head, coming down his neck."

Ball's voice got quiet. "What did you do with Mr. Samson?" She was about to elicit information that had not been heard before in any manner.

"At some point through the night, I moved Mr. Samson from the chair to the bathroom so that he wouldn't bleed so much more in the kitchen," he said.

Ball's voice was still very gentle. "How did you do that?"

"I had two arms under his armpits and through the hallway to the bathroom and into the bathtub."

He testified he left Samson's body in the bathtub, fully clothed, his head at the end opposite the faucet, and he went to clean the kitchen.

"'Cause you were worried about *yourself*, right?" she emphasized the word.

"I was worried about myself in that moment," he admitted.

"And that's because you know you lured him in that apartment and shot him point blank!" It was the loudest she'd shouted yet.

"I didn't lure him there and I only pulled the trigger when he came at me a second time," Sandeson said calmly.

About forty minutes passed from the time Blades and McCabe left his apartment to the time he texted his girlfriend. "You write, 'See you in an hourish. Kissy face,'" said Ball.

"Yes," he said quietly.

"You've got someone's child, someone's brother, someone's boyfriend dead in your bathtub!"

Alison Craig rose and asked to take the afternoon break. Chipman agreed and the jury left the courtroom.

"I've been resisting rising, My Lord, because as I said before it's not a good look to be standing up in front of the jury all the time and interrupting. But it is getting way too inflammatory, screaming at Mr. Sandeson over and over again," she said.

"I can move on from that line," Ball said.

The judge said that should take care of it and adjourned.

People started to leave for the break, but in a sign of just how heated it had become, the lawyers continued talking amongst themselves in the courtroom.

Craig said something indecipherable. Ball responded, "I honestly don't know what you mean, like, I'm..." The conversation became indecipherable again before the court clerk interrupted with, "Oh, excuse me. Counsel, we're still on the record."

They got quiet for a few seconds.

Then Craig could be heard saying, "A little much!"

I later asked Ball about her tactics.

"He literally admits that he takes someone's life in his own hands. Whether you believe it was self-defence or not, someone died at his gun, in his apartment. So I felt that his answers were very clinical, given that there was such an emotionally charged situation that he said he was involved in," she said.

"Sometimes we raise our voices, sometimes we are very quiet, sometimes we're fast, sometimes we are slow," she continued, changing her voice to mimic each of the actions she was describing. "And those techniques are quite on purpose to be engaging—there's an audience—but also to get the information that you want to get, which is the truth...and certainly, I did not intend anything improper by it."

Sometime during the cross-examination, Alison Craig had posted to Facebook, "Grump level: extreme." When I asked her about it, she laughed heartily and said, "I would be surprised if it had anything to do with that. I'm always grumpy." She did say that, while she thinks Ball is an "excellent advocate" and she "loved" both Crowns, she thought the cross-examination of her client "crossed the line a few times."

Samson's friend Kaitlynne Lowe, not surprisingly, disagreed. "I thought Carla was brilliant. I thought that she really tried to hit as hard as she could," she said. "She went in guns blazing and I think she was unrelenting in those cross-questions."

Blair Rhodes came down somewhere in the middle. "Alison Craig did object. Justice Chipman reigned them in. And Carla didn't go as far as she could have," he said.

Ball herself warned Samson's mother that the next part might be difficult to hear.

"I said, 'You do what you have to do to keep him in there,'" Boutilier said in our interview. "'Don't worry about me.'"

So, Carla Ball set about trying to figure out how Sandeson could possibly stuff a six-foot-five, two-hundred-and-twenty–pound man into a hockey bag.

Lead investigator Roger Sayer, sitting in the gallery, brought tissues to Boutilier. "He goes, 'You're going to need these,'" she told me.

Sandeson continued to testify. He said he had put Samson in his bathtub, then wrapped him in black garbage bags and lined the black duffle bag with a towel. He took the bag out to the trunk of his car.

"Did you dismember Mr. Samson?" Ball asked.

"No," he answered without hesitation. He had to have known that question was coming.

"How did you get his body into that bag?"

"I folded his legs up toward his chest."

Ball announced she had a measuring tape. She said the length of the bag was three feet, six inches long, eighteen inches high, and sixteen inches wide. Sandeson agreed. Ball was adamant that Sandeson must have dismembered the body in order to fit it in that bag.

"I'm going to suggest to you that you put bits of it in various locations, would you agree with that?"

"No."

According to an admission of facts entered as evidence in the trial, Halifax Regional Police were able to confirm with Fisheries and Oceans that the tides were out at the relevant times in the Bay of Fundy near the Sandeson family property, and thus the police did not expect that to be a likely place to find Samson's remains.

Ball asked him to explain how he'd managed to achieve what he'd said in his testimony if the tides were not high.

"There's a stream there that runs into the Bay," Sandeson said, "and when the tide's out, the stream runs into the aboiteau."

With that, court wrapped for the day, resuming at 9:17 the next morning for Sandeson's fourth and final day on the stand.

The judge began by saying that he had thought about Craig's objection and that he was also concerned about the content of some of the Crown's questions and would give instruction to the jury about that. He stood by his comments about the Crown's tone, citing case law from Ontario in which a judge dealt with a Crown's cross-examination that was considered overzealous by some.

"This was not a tea party," he quoted. "It was a hard-fought murder trial, and both sides were entitled to press their case and put their best foot forward. Crown counsel here did just that. Her cross-examination was firm and relentless but fair," he said.

He read his instruction to the jury: "I must caution you about some of the questions posed thus far by a Crown prosecutor in her cross-examination of Mr. Sandeson. By times the Crown strayed into questions which included her personal opinion and contained rhetorical excesses. The language employed was at times inflammatory. For example, some of the questions contained the phrasing that Mr. Samson was murdered. Some other questions included content about Mr. Samson being a son, brother, and boyfriend. These were improper aspects of the questions, and this content must be banished from your minds. As I indicated on the first day of this trial, and as I will repeat in my instructions to you, as jurors you must be dispassionate and approach your job in a businesslike manner and not be swayed by appeals to the heart strings."

"I think that the Justice was doing his role quite well," Ball later said in our interview. "He was balancing what the concerns were of defence counsel with what I was doing, and it's always important to make sure that the accused person gets a fair trial."

Back at the trial, she started out the day by taking Sandeson back through it all again, from the moment he and Samson first met on August 5 until she came back to the main point.

"And you dismembered him."

"Nope, I never did."

"And I'm suggesting that those dismembered body parts were stuffed into the bag in which he had brought the marijuana."

"There was no stuffing in parts," Sandeson insisted.

Ball suggested that the following morning, after he dropped his girlfriend and her friend off at work, he returned to his apartment because he had to get one final item that was very damaging.

Sandeson said he didn't remember what he picked up then but said he had gotten rid of anything he thought was potentially damaging the night before.

Ball suggested it was an axe or a power tool.

"It was not an axe or a power tool. The one axe that was in the apartment was still there when the police arrived and I didn't have power tools," he said.

Ball brought out a photo and suggested it showed a "chunk of Taylor's hair and head stuck to the bag."

Craig was on her feet as soon as the words were out of Ball's mouth, asking to address the judge in the absence of the jury.

She started out calm, but her voice soon reached a fever pitch. "There is no evidence of *anything* she just said about that photograph. NONE! ZERO! And it is playing into speculative nonsense in the jury's head, and it has got to stop! The same thing with dismemberment and dumping body parts all over the world. Where is the evidence of that?! There is none! Suggestions to witnesses have to be based on facts as known to the Crown."

They argued for a while, but the judge ultimately decided the question was "reasonable and appropriate," given the evidence from Sandeson thus far.

The jury was called back in, and after three and a half days on the stand, Sandeson concluded his testimony.

"I believe the skeleton of it," Kaitlynne Lowe said later. "I don't believe what he filled it in with."

Linda Boutilier didn't (and still doesn't) believe Sandeson disposed of her son's remains in the Bay of Fundy. "Just another story, that's all it was," she said. "He's up on the farm. I say from day one, he's up on that farm. I still say it."

CHAPTER 20
CONVICTED...
AGAIN

On February 16, 2023, the second jury in the William Sandeson case began its deliberations. Unlike the first trial, this trial had taken place not in the middle of June at the Law Courts on the scenic Halifax waterfront, but in the dead of winter at the new custom-built courthouse in the Burnside Industrial Park in Dartmouth.

"Justice in the strip mall in an industrial park is different," said Blair Rhodes. "There's tractor-trailers rolling by; it just doesn't have the same vibe as a law court set in the urban core."

The public gallery overlooks the parking lot, and Rhodes and the others who were waiting for the verdict could see the jurors being escorted outside by the sheriffs for smoking breaks.

As Thursday turned into Friday and Friday turned into Saturday, more and more jurors were taking breaks—only a few were actually smoking; the rest were stretching in the parking lot. Rhodes said he sensed something had begun to change in the way they were interacting with one another.

"You could tell that things were getting frosty," he said. "They were joking and chatting the first couple of times. As it dragged on, they'd be in their little cliques; less interaction, less sort of humour, there was sort of a grimness about it."

These were excruciatingly difficult days for Taylor Samson's family and friends.

"The absolute most intense period of both trials is definitely those days of jury decision," said Lowe.

During the first trial, she said, she and the others would go for walks along the waterfront, but this time they were stuck in one spot with not even a coffee shop close by.

It was a long weekend—the upcoming Monday was Heritage Day in Nova Scotia (also called Family Day in much of Canada).

In Nova Scotia, jurors are usually sent to a hotel for the night if they haven't reached a verdict by 6:00 P.M.

It was now around 5:30 P.M. on Saturday.

"The sheriffs had called the hotel and said, 'Set aside the block of rooms again; we're coming,'" said Rhodes. "They'd called the limousine company to come and pick them up, and minutes after they made those two calls, a note comes out of the jury room: 'We have a verdict.'"

Everyone piled into the courtroom.

William Sandeson and Alison Craig stood.

The court clerk asked the jury foreperson for the verdict.

"Not guilty of first-degree murder, but guilty of second-degree murder," she said.

No one in the gallery made a sound.

"When they said, 'Not guilty of first-degree,' I went, 'Oh, please, don't be manslaughter or self-defence,'" said Boutilier. "That's what I was scared of."

Lowe said she was hoping for first-degree but bracing for second-degree. "I still can remember the feeling of when the [conviction] of first-degree was laid out at that first trial, and that was a true moment of, just, relief," she said.

This time, when she heard "not guilty of first-degree," she said she could barely breathe. But she said the sentencing was even more disappointing than the verdict.

As with first-degree murder, a conviction of second-degree murder in Canada also comes with an automatic life sentence. The difference is that, while first-degree comes with no chance of parole for twenty-five years, second-degree has a parole ineligibility period of ten to twenty-five years, to be decided by the judge.

Justice Chipman explained to the jurors that it was his job, not theirs, to decide what Sandeson's punishment would be, but that the law requires him to consider their opinions.

He told them they should consider Sandeson's character, the nature of the offence, and the circumstances surrounding the commission of the offence, but said they were not required to make a recommendation and they did not have to be unanimous.

All twelve jurors decided to make recommendations.

Nine recommended William Sandeson serve twenty-five years before being eligible for parole; two jurors recommended twenty-two years; and one juror recommended the minimum possible—ten years—before parole eligibility.

"That made it clear to us what was going on," said Rhodes. "There was one holdout. Everybody was prepared to go to first-degree except one."

The judge remanded Sandeson until April 20, when his sentencing hearing would take place.

Taylor Samson's family and friends set about preparing their victim impact statements. Many of them had done this before, but there were more this time—twenty-six as opposed to eighteen in the last trial. The stakes were higher now that it was possible Sandeson could get out on parole much earlier. Key among the additions was a victim impact statement from Linda Boutilier.

She had chosen not to provide one for the first sentencing, deciding it wasn't necessary and that she didn't want to show Sandeson her pain.

This time, it was different.

"I was scared. I didn't know if the judge was going to give him ten years and then he'd be out in a couple more years," she said. She spent several months trying to write something. She'd start, struggle, then put it away or throw it in the garbage.

But the day she started packing up her son's belongings, preparing to donate them—heartbroken and angry—she sat at her kitchen table and started to write.

"Today, after seven years, seven months, and ten days I have come to terms with the fact my son Taylor was murdered and I am never going to see my son again," she wrote. "The pain today is unbearable. Today, as I packed Taylor's belongings, it is the first day of my grieving process. Today, I accept the fact that my son has been taken from me. Today, I hate the world with all this evil and cruelty in it."

She described how she took a leave of absence from work and searched for her son from dawn to sunset, searching the city, walking the back roads and highway from Halifax to Truro. She walked so much, she got heel spurs, and wound up in the hospital in so much pain she could barely walk at all.

"I remember the knots in my stomach the first day we had the first snowfall. 'Taylor is out there all alone, he must be cold, he needs his coat.' The first snowfall every year since, I still get this uneasy feeling," she wrote.

She described the anger she feels because she has no resting place for her son, instead placing flowers at a memorial outside the physics building at Dal—a simple plaque mounted on a rock that reads, "In Loving Memory of Taylor Samson 1993–2015."

"Taylor isn't there, but where else do I go?" she wrote.

Connor also wrote a statement. "My brother was not perfect," he said. "He was human. He made mistakes, as we all do, but he was a very kind-hearted, loving, beautiful soul who knew how to make you feel better about yourself after you felt bad about yourself, a guy who would help you out any way he can."

In addition to the victim impact statements before the court, there were also eight letters of support for William Sandeson. I obtained all of them.

Predictably, five came from Sandeson's parents and his brothers.

His mother wrote: "His decision to enter the drug trade in 2014 was most unfortunate and is a decision he will regret for the rest of his life. I hope and pray that in the not too distant future, William will be given the opportunity to make amends and give back to a society that so desperately needs his commitment to make the world a better place."

His father wrote: "I will continue to be a shoulder for William to lean on, offering my honest stories and life experience. The path that both of us may have envisioned looks different now but I will do my best to help him explore his purpose."

But there were three more letters, far more surprising.

Karine St-Michel of Montréal, Quebec, wrote that she had known Sandeson for five years after having met him on the website Inmates Connect and said she considered him one of her closest friends.

"I reached out to three inmates on the website because I wanted to make a difference in the life of people who think they are not worth doing great things for society," she wrote. "I ended up only answering to William. His profile caught my attention because he was one of the only inmates not looking for a romantic relationship."

She helped him learn French and visited him in prison every two weeks or so until the COVID-19 pandemic put a halt to that. "William is so much more than the offence he was found to have committed. He has a strong will inside of him to help people," she wrote.

Eric Paquet of Saint-Pie, Quebec, wrote that he was incarcerated with Sandeson in December 2017 at Donnacona, a maximum security institution forty-five kilometres west of Quebec City.

Sandeson would have been in prison for nearly two and a half years by that point.

Paquet wrote that "violence was a part of everyday life at Donnacona," and said Sandeson "was always disposed to help those in difficulties and defused tensions and disputes where folks could have been hurt."

"During my incarceration, I have witnessed a calm, polite man, respectful of the rules," he wrote, saying on several occasions Sandeson "could have easily been attracted by money, but always refused categorically."

The two were eventually transferred and reunited at Cowansville Institution, a medium security prison about a hundred kilometres east of Montréal. Paquet wrote that in this institution, after three months without any disciplinary offences, offenders could be integrated into a building called "the pods," which housed "independent and responsible" men.

He wrote that he "believes sincerely" that Sandeson can be rehabilitated. He did not write about the reason he was incarcerated but did say he has since been released from prison, now works in construction, and continues to speak with Sandeson each week.

Finally, Maura Hunter wrote to the court that Sandeson was one of her volunteers on a Special Olympics swimming team in Truro. She wrote that she knew him as an "intelligent, altruistic, and kind young man" throughout his high school years and his first year of university. Though she was "horrified on learning he had been seduced into the cesspool of a lifestyle made evident upon his arrest," she has continued to correspond with him since that time and had written ninety-seven letters at the point of her letter to the court, dated March 12, 2023.

She wrote that she would trust Sandeson to be a companion to her adult son who lives with Down Syndrome and noted, "I am convinced Will is much more than a self-centered villain and, given the chance, remains extremely capable of contributing in a positive way to society."

In addition to these letters of support and victim impact statements, Justice Chipman also considered a pre-sentence report prepared for the court by a probation officer, which I also obtained. In it, Sandeson indicated, "I testified at my second trial. It has been a relief to speak publicly about it. My family has been in the dark. At least now the Sampson [*sic*] family has an answer as to what happened to his body. They can stop looking and I hope that it offers some relief."

Several of Samson's friends and family said that it did not offer them any relief.

"He's telling a version of the story that doesn't make him look as monstrous as he is," said Lowe. "I think he was so dishonest about some of the really, really key things that it took so much away from any relief that could bring."

"The only thing that's ever gonna bring me any kind of peace is having Taylor home, and I'm not going to get Taylor home," Boutilier said.

On April 20, 2023, William Sandeson's lawyer argued he should be eligible for parole upon serving ten years. The Crown argued he should not be eligible for parole until he had served twenty-two years.

"You can shoot for the stars, but let's get real here," said Justice Chipman to Ball, laying out his concern that if he gave Sandeson anything in the twenty-year range when it came to parole ineligibility, it would surely be appealed again.

Kaitlynne Lowe said she understood the judge's concerns. "But I also hate that this entire second trial was, for the vast majority of people involved, just trying to avoid appeal," she said. She certainly wanted to avoid another appeal as well, but said she felt the pursuit of justice for Samson didn't seem to be the motivating factor.

Rhodes said based on his experience, judges always aim to run smooth trials. "Chipman knew what the stakes were; there'd been a retrial already. He *was* the retrial. And I think he was determined not to have it happen again," he said.

"It goes hand in hand," said Ball. "Avoiding an appeal *is* the administration of justice, because it means you're doing it right."

In court, she acknowledged the twenty-two years she was asking for was the highest requested for a contested hearing for second-degree murder in the province's history.

She acknowledged Sandeson had no criminal record prior to being charged with murder, which is generally considered a mitigating factor, but she pointed out that, by his own admission, he had been involved in drug trafficking for more than a year and just "didn't get caught."

She asked the judge to find as fact that Sandeson dismembered Samson's body.

Chipman struggled with how he could know that beyond a reasonable doubt.

In trying to understand the root cause of what led to this crime, Ball said that Sandeson used his pro-social, supportive family life, education, and opportunities as a "mask" to manipulate people.

Chipman said twenty-two years is for the "worst kinds of cases and the worst kinds of offenders," acknowledging that every murder is brutal, but that sadly there are far worse. "I can go out on a high wire or something and get all emotional and get upset about poor Taylor. And I did find it emotional, of course I did, I'm a human being. We all are."

He pointed out McOnie was overwhelmed with emotion and couldn't finish while she was reading victim impact statements into the record.

"But I have to be dispassionate. That's our job. And so do you as the Crown. And so I'm having trouble. If I gravitated to your position, Ms. Ball, I'm sure it's a direct route to the court of appeal, that's what I'm sure about."

Ball argued there can always be a worse situation.

She gave the example of the case of Penny Boudreau—forever seared into the hearts and minds of Nova Scotians. Boudreau is serving a life sentence for the second-degree murder of her twelve-year-old daughter, Karissa, in January 2008.

She was ordered to serve twenty years before she could begin applying for parole.

Ball acknowledged those circumstances are "absolutely horrific" and not what was being considered in the Sandeson case, but she also pointed out Boudreau pleaded guilty. "We mitigate sentencing recommendations when people acknowledge and accept responsibility—sparing the family, witnesses, court time—because, at the end of the day, not only is it a public expense, it shows that there is some real recognition and insight. That is not what we have," she said.

She also noted the case of Christopher Garnier, who is also serving a sentence for second-degree murder and improperly interfering with human remains after he killed off-duty police officer Catherine Campbell in 2015—just one month after William Sandeson killed Taylor Samson. The Crown alleged Garnier put her body in a green bin and disposed of it. Garnier testified Campbell died during erotic asphyxiation gone wrong.

He was sentenced to thirteen and a half years before parole eligibility, but the Crown pointed out that in that case there was no drug-dealing, no loaded handgun, and the remains were not concealed in such a way that they could never be found.

Ball concluded by noting the high-profile nature of the Sandeson case.

"Mr. Sandeson's conduct needs to be denounced because it has impacted Nova Scotians significantly. It's harmed friends, families, medical communities—many, many, many people," she said.

Craig argued that Chipman should consider that Samson was also a drug dealer, that both he and Sandeson were doing it to get money for university, and that it was not just "greed." She added there was not enough evidence to find as fact that Sandeson dismembered the body.

"I have an awful lot of trouble with arriving at a parking lot and dragging a bag through a trail and pitching it over an aboiteau and into the Salmon River and into the ocean. I mean, I'm really struggling with that," Chipman said.

Craig said Chipman could reject Sandeson's account, but it still doesn't mean he dismembered the body.

Chipman agreed with that point.

Craig argued that sometimes a drug deal gone bad is just a drug deal gone bad and there may be no root cause for the crime. "My friend, with respect, is trying to paint a picture that simply is not there. Did he do something horrific on this one day? One hundred percent; absolutely. But to suggest that his lifetime of otherwise exemplary character is somehow all a ruse to cover up being a psychopath is unmerited and unwarranted."

She pointed, as a mitigating factor, to an incident report showing that Sandeson had gotten into trouble since he had been incarcerated. About a year after he was incarcerated, in November 2016, he was part of a group of offenders who disobeyed an order to "lock in" during regular lockdown hours and demanded to speak to a captain. Six months later, in April 2017, he was marked as a "no return" and refused to pack his belongings for court when directed to do so.

He then remained "squeaky clean," to borrow a term from Sandeson himself, until the August 2020 incident where he stated he was homicidal and would kill another inmate if he wasn't kept in segregation.

Finally, in March 2022, he received mail that contained contraband.

"If I ever saw a one-page sheet of five incidents in seven and a half years," Craig said, waving the page in front of the court, "I would do the happy dance...I have never seen somebody with so [few] problems in jail," she said.

She acknowledged the disposing of the body was an aggravating factor but said there were many mitigating factors, including that there was no history of violence, the fact that he has been educating himself and working in prison, and his history of volunteering in the community. She noted that while it was clearly of his own doing, an "obvious collateral consequence" of the offence is that Sandeson will never be able to pursue a career in medicine.

In an unrelated case, the Supreme Court had previously ruled that "a collateral consequence includes any consequence arising from the commission of an offence, the conviction for an offence, or the sentence imposed for an offence that impacts the offender."

Chipman asked Sandeson if he had anything to say.

"No, My Lord," he replied.

Chipman said he did not accept Sandeson's testimony of what led to the killing. He found as fact that Sandeson lured Samson to his apartment for the purposes of conducting a robbery of twenty pounds of marijuana, and that within three minutes of his arrival Sandeson shot Samson once.

He also found as fact that Sandeson shot Samson "point blank in the head less than four feet away while he was seated at the kitchen table"; that Sandeson performed a cleanup that lasted less than two hours; that he dragged Samson's body to the bathroom and placed the body in the tub; and that he put the body in the black duffle bag, shut off his video cameras, carried the bag containing the body outside, and placed it in the back of his Mazda hatchback for the night.

He found as fact that Sandeson dumped Samson's body off at an aboiteau leading into the Salmon River in Colchester County.

Chipman "categorically rejected" the notion that Sandeson had any reason to fear Samson.

"There was simply no credible evidence to support the theory of the defence that Mr. Samson had been involved in any way with the home invasion in the lead-up to August 15, or at any time," he said. He found Sandeson's use of a firearm, the besmirching of the victim's reputation, and the disposal of the body to be aggravating factors.

On April 20, 2023, Justice Chipman noted that William Sandeson had been incarcerated for seven years, eight months, and four days. He sentenced Sandeson to life in prison with no chance of parole for fifteen years.

Since Sandeson had essentially served half of that time already, he could begin applying for parole in seven and a half years, at which point the Parole Board of Canada will decide whether he can be released.

"With the continued passage of time, the court can only hope that William Sandeson will someday become a productive community member again," Chipman said, upon releasing his decision. "And that Taylor Samson's memory will serve to inspire the lives of those whom he touched and continues to touch through his time on earth."

Despite knocking ten years off Sandeson's sentence, Alison Craig said she was disappointed and doesn't consider the case a win. "It's one of those verdicts where everybody was unhappy. The Crown was unhappy. We were unhappy. The family was unhappy," she said.

"There's no good outcome ever, right? Two families are destroyed forever."

CHAPTER 21
WHERE ARE THEY NOW?

O n a Friday night in March 2023, Taylor Samson's family and friends got dressed up and went to a dance bar to throw him a thirtieth birthday bash like no other.

Green-and-red disco lights flashed across the dance floor, creating stripes and circles on people's bodies and faces, and a large, bright, purple screen flashed "The Mellotones" in white letters as the sound of the R & B funk band boomed through the room.

Samson's younger brother Connor, twenty-eight, sported a collared shirt and a bow tie as he danced his heart out, waving his hands in the air and shaking his long hair all around.

He was having fun. Everyone seemed to be.

Samson's mother, sixty-two, was also there, dressed in a sharp white blouse. "The last time I went to a bar like that, what was it? The Palace, years ago, before he was born!" she later exclaimed, gesturing to Connor. "I felt like I was back at The Palace again!"

There was a joy in their voices I hadn't heard before—not in the eight years I'd known them.

They'd rented out the whole top floor of Pacifico, a nightclub in downtown Halifax—the same club Samson had planned to go to the night he died—and turned the party into a fundraiser for a scholarship in his name.

Initially worried they wouldn't draw enough people to recoup the costs, Linda Boutilier said attendees included people from Amherst, Samson's hometown, some of his old friends from the fraternity, people from his physics class, and some she didn't know—and who didn't even know Samson.

"It was packed," said Boutilier, and she began to cry.

She and Connor had long ago left their home in Amherst and relocated to Halifax. "You can't walk down the street in Amherst without people looking at you, whispering, 'That's the mother,'" she had told me in 2017.

Six years later, she still wanted to know where her son was. And she desperately wanted people to know her son was more than a drug dealer.

We were sitting in her living room in the Halifax apartment she shared with her son Connor on a Saturday night in September 2023. A lamp in the corner set a warm glow over the room.

A lot had changed since the last time the three of us had met here in the summer of 2017.

Connor had returned to work at Walmart a couple of months after Taylor's death, but Boutilier could not go back to work—instead dedicating her time to searching for her son and attending court.

She went from employment insurance to being on social assistance for more than five years. She maxed out all of her credit, sold items of value including her mother's wedding set, and got seven months behind in her rent. She says if not for an understanding landlord, both she and Connor would have been living in a car. She still owes some of these debts. And as of January 2024, she had not received any of William Sandeson's Bitcoin money.

She did return to work in the fall of 2021. She's also at Walmart, a department manager in the bakery, getting up in the wee hours of the morning to be in for 5:30 A.M. to get the first round of treats out for customers.

She still manages to attend every court appearance. Her determination to be present for her son hasn't changed, but her attitude has, which is why she felt ready to go back to work. "I was tired of him controlling my life," she said. Instead, she's putting her energy into doing things Taylor would have wanted her to do, things he loved to do—starting with a trip to Montréal.

"Today is the day, going to...MONTREAL WITH MOMMA!!!" Connor posted on Facebook, along with a photo of their smiling faces holding boarding cards. "First time going to Quebec. We're so excited, we just can't hide it. We're about to lose control and I think we like it," he wrote.

They went on the trip with Boutilier's friend Darlene Sudds whose son, Matthew, was also murdered—killed by a single gunshot to the head in October 2013. Just two years after losing her own son, Sudds helped Boutilier search for Taylor in the early days of his disappearance, looking under stairways and in dumpsters. The two have become close friends, drawn together by the terrible circumstances they have in common.

"We really don't talk about that," Boutilier said. "We both know we're just there for each other. I know I can call her anytime and she knows I'll show up for court or do whatever when she needs me."

I asked Connor if he'd made the same decision—to stop worrying and go on living.

"No," he said, and laughed his big, unrestrained laugh.

"He can hide it really well," his mother said, citing her son's autism. "I don't even know if something's bothering him sometimes."

"Do you ever talk about it?" I asked.

"No," he paused for a moment and then continued, "because some people use it to their advantage too."

"How?" I asked.

"Some people like to try and manipulate with that tactic," he said.

He went on to tell a story about how he'd been trying to help an old friend struggling with substance abuse, and they'd gotten into an argument. "And he said to me...'But if I go missing just like your brother, you're gonna regret it.' And I punched him right in the mouth. The first time I've actually punched someone," he said.

He also said losing Taylor has changed the way Boutilier mothers him. "She's on my ass all the time," he said.

Boutilier acknowledged that if he stays out late or doesn't let her know if he's staying the night somewhere, she worries. "By ten o'clock, I'm on the phone. 'Where are you? Are you coming home tonight? I need to know.'"

Then there's the gossip, which was rampant during the first trial, then quieted down a bit, then reared up again during the second trial.

"It actually happened last week," Connor announced. Someone approached him while he was working. "They're like, 'I read about you.' And I'm like, 'What do you mean, you read about me?' And they're like, 'That book about the murder, I know that's you.'"

"But who was it?" his mother asked. She hadn't heard this story yet. "Some random customer," was his reply. He said sometimes he brushes it off, lets people go on, and tries to zone them out.

Boutilier said she ignores it now.

"I've gotten numb to people saying, 'You know, it's probably true, he did chop him up.' Like, who walks up to a mother and says that stuff?"

"Or walks up to you and goes, 'I know who you are,'" said Connor.

"It's like, 'Okay, good for you. But respect my privacy like I respect yours.'"

Connor is featured in another book—*Halifolks*, a compilation of photos and stories about the diverse people of Halifax, edited by Jack Scrine and published by Nimbus in 2022. In it, Connor spoke about his brother: "I looked up to him more than anything. He was like a father figure in my life."

I told him that perhaps he should tell people that book is how they recognize him.

He said sometimes he does.

Connor's father has since moved to Cape Breton.

I called Dean Samson out of the blue in September 2023. Connor had warned me his father was hard of hearing now, so the conversation might be difficult. Indeed, it took him a few minutes to understand who I was and why I was calling. I asked if he'd like me to call back, but he said there was no better time than the present.

Now seventy, Samson told me he had split from his partner, Karen Burke, and had moved to a seniors' residence in Petit-de-Grat, a small Acadian community on the southern tip of Cape Breton Island, just over three hundred kilometres from Halifax. His health was declining, he hadn't left his apartment in months, and he had begun the process of moving to a nursing home. He explained that he'd had a second stroke in 2018. He was dealing with a left-side deficit, was wearing a brace, using a wheelchair to get around, and had no peripheral vision.

Clearly, life had not gotten any easier for Dean Samson in the six years since we'd last spoken.

He told me he'd followed William Sandeson's second trial closely, mostly by monitoring the Twitter feed of my colleague, Blair Rhodes. "I look at it and I think, 'What the hell is this idiot doing?' It feels like he's torturing us," he said in that telephone interview. He said he didn't believe anything Sandeson said on the stand and that hearing from him did not help him or bring him closure in any way.

"I wish he'd just go to hell and shut the fuck up, to be perfectly honest with you. I'm tired of all his foolishness, and I hope he rots in hell," he said, not mincing words. "At least he finally admitted that he did shoot him. That was the only good thing of it all."

He said there is nothing Sandeson can do or say at this point to help him in any way. He does not believe he can be rehabilitated. "He's a scary person. There is absolutely no way he should ever be on the street again," he said.

He thanked me for calling.

Taylor Samson's girlfriend, Mackenzie Ruthven, left Nova Scotia in 2017 and moved back to Ontario—unable to remain in a province full of reminders of the young love she lost. "For years, fear of the unknown and suspicion of other people rendered me unable to participate in society in normal ways," she wrote in her victim impact statement.

She said publicly reliving that terrible week in August 2015 numerous times over the course of many years, and having to explain it to friends, professors, co-workers, and bosses, has affected her ability to form relationships. She wrote that she has had years of therapy to unlearn unhealthy coping mechanisms.

In 2023, at twenty-seven years old, she moved back to Nova Scotia and began working for Nova Scotia Health in Bridgewater as a medical device reprocessing supervisor, overseeing people who clean and re-sterilize instruments after they've been used in the operating room.

She's also working toward a graduate diploma in education and is in a new relationship.

She says she feels the "confidence, motivation, and ambition" she lost as a result of the trauma she experienced beginning to return.

"I think the trial feels a lot more final this time," she said in her first-ever interview. "I don't know if it is final. I know court never is done."

She didn't attend the first trial. "I didn't need to be there for that circus. It wasn't going to add anything to my life," she said. She did dial in to the second trial by phone from Ontario, and said it brought her some closure because it answered more questions than the first trial.

She said it's impossible to know how her life would have been different. She tries not to think about it but can't help herself.

"I know it's an idealized version, but I picture him finishing his master's and us moving to Cape Breton or something. You know—owning a house and having kids and doing all of that. I can see that life being something that would have existed," she said. "It's hard that he didn't get to do that."

She said Samson used to write her notes if he left the house before she woke up in the morning. She had a tattoo artist create a stencil from one he left her just a couple of weeks before he died, and now has "XOXO" in his handwriting tattooed under her rib-cage, near her heart.

Kaitlynne Lowe has continued to attend every court appearance, a constant presence at Samson's mother's side. In a victim impact statement, which she read aloud in court, Lowe said Samson's death shattered her own sense of "self, security, and hope." She said she has struggled with a relapsing eating disorder, anxiety, and depression.

Despite her grief, she has continued to accomplish a great deal. She had to take an additional year to finish her undergraduate degree due to all the lost time spent attending court but went on to complete a master's in public administration at Dalhousie University and plans to do a PhD. She has a full-time job as a research assistant at Dalhousie, plus a part-time position as a research manager for Mount Saint Vincent University. She's also a board member for Fusion Halifax, a non-profit organization that aims to empower young leaders to improve their communities.

When I met Lowe for an interview at her home, she sat clutching a giant mug with the words, "All of me loves all of coffee" written on it.

I asked where she found the energy—beyond coffee—to persevere through such trauma.

For her, the answer wasn't complicated—she'd done it before. She explained that her dad had died when she was fourteen, and "not even breakfast was the same anymore." She said she and her dad had been really involved in their church and when he died, she just felt she should keep doing things in his memory, stay motivated, get into a good university, make him proud, and create the life she wanted.

It worked.

At least it was working until August 2015 when "everything went on fire" and she was again faced with unimaginable grief. Still, she felt she couldn't stop then—not after she'd already worked so hard to overcome adversity. "I'd done so much to make my dad proud," she said. "Can't stop now; [I] need to make Taylor proud." She also thought she could use everything she'd learned about the grief process to help those around her.

She's become quite close with Samson's mother and brother. "I love just getting to know Connor. He's his own fabulous, incredible human that I think, even circumstances aside, I still would absolutely love and adore," she said, noting the two of them were going to a drag show together that night.

Boutilier said Lowe took Connor everywhere with her when they first moved to Halifax, following Samson's death.

"She'd take him to her apartment. They'd be playing video games and *Mario Kart*, all the guys there. They all took care of him," she said.

"He's really easy to love. And my life is blessed by having him in it," said Lowe.

She said Samson would not be surprised she's become close to his brother. He had always said the two would get along, even though they didn't meet until after his death. "I think he would kind of find it really, really funny to be perfectly honest, but I think he'd think it was a really great thing."

In his victim impact statement, Taylor Samson's friend Thomas McCrossin wrote that the years following Samson's murder saw the "complete collapse" of his mental health. He dropped out of school, lost his job, lost contact with his mother for more than two years, abused drugs, and left Nova Scotia for four years to live in Calgary.

He's returned to Nova Scotia and has mended things with his family. He finally finished his undergraduate degree in 2020 but is still paying back the student debt he incurred after failing thirteen courses following Samson's death.

He has a dog named Samson, and his son, born in July 2023, is also named after Taylor. "The reason his middle name is Taylor and not his first is because I refuse to burst into tears every time I call out to my dog after I say my son's name. 'Taylor, Samson,'" he wrote.

He attended the thirtieth birthday party held for Samson and became overwhelmed while dancing with Connor and Kaitlynne. "I excused myself, proceeded to find my girlfriend, and made the most guttural sounds I've ever made in an uncontrollable fit of crying," he wrote.

He calls Samson's death the "defining trauma" of his life.

Sonja Gashus, Sandeson's girlfriend at the time of the murder, attended law school and graduated from Dalhousie University's Schulich School of Law in 2022. She is now a practising lawyer in Toronto. She politely declined to be interviewed for this book, saying she has moved on with her life.

Laurie Sandeson retired from her job with the Nova Scotia Department of Agriculture in 2019 after thirty-two years of service. In October 2020, she became a councillor for the Municipality of Colchester, representing Lower Truro and surrounding communities. In a "Meet the Candidate" profile by Saltwire, Laurie Sandeson said she had chosen to run in the election because she was recently retired and had more time to give back to the community. She said she was focused on health services, youth employment, and becoming a greener community. She noted there were seven new medical residents in her region and said, "We need to embrace these young doctors and make them feel a part of our community early on in their training so that they will be more inclined to choose Colchester County as a place to live and work."

When asked what strengths she would bring to council, she said she was well known in the region and had a long history of volunteerism. She did not mention and was not asked about her son William.

In her 2023 letter of support to the court, she wrote, "Since William's incarceration, my family has received nothing but support from my church and local community. Many noted that this could have happened to any one of their families and that bad decisions do not make bad people."

Michael Sandeson has retired from his truck-driving job and now works full-time on the family farm.

Adam Sandeson completed his bachelor of science with a major in environmental science at Dalhousie University in 2017 and went on to obtain a master's degree in environmental science from the University of Toronto in 2018. He works full-time as an environmental science consultant in the Halifax area. According to his court testimony, he talks to his brother, Will, several times a week and has visited him several times.

Matthew Sandeson studied kinesiology at Dalhousie University and holds two jobs—one as a registered massage therapist and the other at a local tap room. In court testimony, he said he talks to his brother regularly and they remain very close.

David, the youngest Sandeson brother, has a degree in kinesiology with applied nutrition from Acadia University in Wolfville, NS. He works as a personal trainer and at a local cider company. In court testimony he said he talks to his brother once a month and they remain very close.

Through their lawyer, all of the Sandesons declined to be interviewed for this book.

Justin Blades was thirty-one when he testified during Sandeson's second trial at the end of January 2023. He was extremely emotional during his testimony, as he was every time he took the stand. He said then that he was working but didn't provide any details. He hadn't been in school in 2015 because he'd run out of money, but he'd had plans to go back to finish the bachelor of arts he'd been working on prior to the murder. He never did, saying the "turmoil" was just too much.

"I can't even do normal things, let alone go back to school," he testified.

In earlier testimony, he said he had been working in the emergency department at the QEII Health Sciences Centre for four years at the time of the murder. He said it was the "most well-paying, most stable job" he'd ever had, but he quit the day before he took the stand in the first trial in May 2017 because he knew it would be "mayhem" with everyone asking him about the trial. He was still blinking back tears as he left the courtroom.

Outside, as he sat with Sayer and Bruce Webb, I heard him say, "I'm sorry Bruce."

I didn't hear a response from Webb, but Sayer said, "You're on the right side of history, bud."

Pookiel McCabe also testified in the second trial, but police had to issue a Canada-wide warrant for his arrest to get him there. Police went to Ontario to pick him up and bring him to Halifax. He was thirty years old at the time and told the court he was "freelancing." He offered no other details.

Lead investigator Roger Sayer was promoted to Sergeant in 2019. Due to the structure of the Halifax Regional Police Department, that meant a return to general patrol. In an interview, he told me he misses working in the homicide unit and would like to get back there someday.

He was called to testify in the Sandeson case twenty-one times.

"I have been the lead in several homicides, and it wouldn't be uncommon to maybe be called back to the stand a handful of times," he told me. "But to get into the double digits, and then over twenty or something is very rare."

He estimates he's worked on fifty to sixty homicides in his career and said each one comes with a tremendous amount of pressure, but the Sandeson case created even more stress because it was so drawn out and highly publicized. It's the only homicide he's worked on that had to be retried.

It's also the only one where police couldn't find the body—which is something he still thinks of often, especially when he hears on the news that human remains have been found.

"It always piques my interest, just in case, because you just never know," he said.

He called the Sandeson case his "career file" and has twice been invited to present on the investigation at police conferences.

He also developed a bond with Samson's mother.

"I think Linda is a strong, strong woman," he said. "She's never quit. Not once. Not once has she stopped wanting to try and find her son and what happened to him. I admire her deeply for that."

He said he felt a responsibility to put the man responsible for her son's murder behind bars. "The day of the decision, this time, I found that it was hard not to be emotional around Linda, and that's not my way. And it was because I knew how heartbroken she was," he said.

After eight years, there was a connection between the two that made the trial's result more difficult to swallow. "I believe, based on the evidence, that he was responsible and should be found guilty of first-degree murder, that was my belief on the evidence we had," he said.

"I was disappointed that it was second-degree this time."

Derrick Boyd, who was the team lead and family liaison officer, has been promoted to superintendent in charge of HRP's patrol division, which is all of the uniformed officers, including Roger Sayer. Like Sayer, he misses being in the homicide unit.

He testified in the case thirteen times—by far more than he had in any other case. He also learned some lessons from the case, in particular, that speed matters.

He said he and Sayer have a similar style, which is to investigate quickly. Other homicide investigators prefer to take things more slowly, write search warrants and take weeks to arrest a suspect. He said sometimes that works, and neither approach is wrong, but in this case moving quickly was the right course of action. "I think that was a main factor in solving this case because I think had we given Will Sandeson more time to dispose of evidence and come up with a good story it would have been difficult to solve," he said, calling the case the most interesting he's ever worked on.

As family liaison officer, he was in touch with Boutilier weekly for the first year, and then every two or three weeks for another year. He said he grew attached to Samson's mother and, as he began to learn more about Samson, he came to understand that while he was selling drugs, he was doing it to help his mother and brother. "I did develop a bond with Linda. And I don't think that [will] ever be broken," he said. "If I saw Linda, it would warm my heart."

The RCMP's Jody Allison, who was in the integrated Major Crime Unit when the Sandeson case began, and who, along with Sayer, interrogated Sandeson in the video that was not seen by the second jury, has been promoted several times. In October 2023 he became a staff sergeant and is a watch commander in the Halifax area, over-seeing everything that happens on his shift.

He said interviewing Sandeson was very different from the many other interviews he's conducted throughout his career because Sandeson was a "regular person"—one who had been accepted to medical school, and yet was somehow involved in something "far out there."

He said he sometimes misses working in homicide, but he was sometimes bothered by thinking about the families left behind, the cases he couldn't solve, and the things he wished he'd done better.

In the Sandeson case, he thinks about the second jury not get-ting to see that interrogation video and what he could have done to get Sandeson to tell him more in the first place. "If I had really pressed this guy, maybe, you know, been a little bit harsher, maybe he would have told me what he did with the body," he said.

The thing that stands out to him most about this case is the "sheer senselessness" of it. "What was this for, you know? Two lives, two families ruined."

Beyond the families, he thinks about how many lives were impacted. "The people that had to sit through—not just listen to me talk for twelve or fourteen hours—but had to listen to all the gory details, the people that were in the courtroom, the jurors—it has an effect on everybody," he said.

A spokesperson for the Nova Scotia Department of Justice con-firmed Bruce Webb is no longer among the 106 licensed private investigators in Nova Scotia. She said she could not comment on the reason why a person may no longer hold a license.

She said that under the Private Investigators and Private Guards Act, the department may issue or renew a license "where the pro-posed licensing is not against the public interest."

Tom Martin still owns the firm Bruce Webb was working for at the time of his involvement in the Sandeson case. Martin & Associates was hired by the law firm representing the majority of the families who lost loved ones in the 2020 Nova Scotia mass shooting in which a gunman went on a rampage, masquerading as a police officer, killing twenty-two people, including a pregnant woman and an RCMP officer. The firm was retained to provide expertise in police command procedure, crime scene analysis, and police investigation procedures ahead of a public inquiry examining the crime and the police response.

Susan MacKay, the lead Crown in Sandeson's first trial, is now the director of policy development and education for the Nova Scotia Public Prosecution, a management position that sees her rewriting policies, sitting on committees that propose amendments to the Criminal Code, and generally supporting the work of Crowns still in the courtroom.

The Sandeson case was her last as a front-line Crown Attorney and, apart from offering emotional support to her colleagues, she didn't work on the case the second time around.

She was called as a witness during the pretrial arguments in the leadup to the retrial, which she says was "an unpleasant task" that required her to review the transcript of the first trial.

"This was a very intense trial, [...and] I had to go back into it when I had to review it. And it was stressful," she said. She noted she didn't leave courtroom work directly because of the Sandeson case, as she had already applied for the new position, but with the piles of homework she was required to do each night, it was one of the most extreme examples of what she had already come to know over the years—that Nova Scotia Crown Attorneys are not properly resourced.

She decided that in the latter part of her career she wanted to help change that. "It was a significant motivating force behind my application to become a manager," she said, "to try to address this; to help the system be sustainable."

She said sometimes she misses being in the courtroom, but she gets a lot more sleep these days. She didn't follow the retrial that closely because she wanted to "guard" her energy, but she did read about it in the news occasionally.

When she looks back at her twenty-three years in the courtroom, she says the Sandeson case was one of the most memorable—and certainly the most high-profile—she prosecuted. She recalled being in the checkout line at the grocery store and hearing people chatting about the case, knowing they had no idea who she was.

"I don't think Kim and I, when we started that case, had any idea that it would be as salacious and gather as much attention as it did," she said.

Kim McOnie is still a practising Crown Attorney. Two years after Sandeson's first trial, she received the Senior Crown Counsel designation, one of seventeen to hold this distinction among 107 Crown Attorneys in Nova Scotia. It is a title for which prosecutors must compete, and it signifies distinction in the practice of criminal law.

She said the Sandeson case was the longest, most interesting case she's ever worked on. "It was a fascinating case," she said, pointing to the very novel legal issue pertaining to the private investigator.

But it was also extremely difficult.

As the only lawyer involved in both trials, she's gotten to know Samson's family. "They're such strong people, and I think a lot of all of them," she said. She said she felt the incredible pressure of the responsibility to ensure that justice had been served for them.

"It's the immense loss, right?" she said, struggling to compose herself. "Taylor was so loved and had so much promise. And this is totally senseless; totally senseless."

❖

William Sandeson's first defence lawyer, Eugene Tan, has also received a promotion since the first trial. Now the managing lawyer at Walker Dunlop, he's responsible for the direction of the firm, including hiring and finances. "It just means that everyone around me has retired," he told me when we met at his office in August 2023.

It also means less time in the courtroom, something he laments.

He says the Sandeson case impacted his overall practice, and not in the way one might think. The high-profile case didn't bring him more business, but rather less, largely because it preoccupied so much of his time that he spent months not involved in the day-to-day dealings of Halifax's justice system. "If your face isn't in the provincial courthouse every day—you're not making deals, you're not seeing people—people move on very quickly," he said.

He said he received fewer calls in the summer of 2017 after the first Sandeson trial wrapped up than he'd received since the late 1990s, and because the case received so much attention, some people told him they assumed he was too busy or too expensive.

He said there was no discussion about whether he would defend Sandeson at the retrial, and doesn't think it would have even been possible, since, like Susan MacKay, he also became a witness during a pretrial hearing.

"It was frustrating, and honestly a little bit intimidating...and it's kind of humiliating," he said.

Unlike MacKay, Tan did follow the retrial very closely. He also happened to be in the same courthouse on another case while the trial was underway. He resisted the urge to poke his head in, thinking it might be a distraction, but did introduce himself to Alison Craig and offered her space and access to his file.

He doesn't keep in touch with William Sandeson but does, to a small degree, with the Sandeson family.

I pointed out that the version of events now on the public record is not the one he put forward at Sandeson's first trial, and asked whether the latest version is the one he's always known. He declined to comment, citing solicitor–client privilege.

I tried again, asking whether, as a defence lawyer, he cares about truth.

He pointed me to the Nova Scotia Barristers' Society's Code of Professional Conduct, which states lawyers can't put forth something they know to be untrue.

Speaking generally—and not about William Sandeson specifically—Tan said, "Before anybody tells me everything, they also need to know that I am hampered by certain ethical considerations."

Tan's co-counsel, Brad Sarson, got the biggest promotion of all the lawyers involved in the Sandeson case: he's now a provincial court judge.

Sarson declined my request to interview him, as judges usually do.

During his robing ceremony on April 21, 2023, Sarson said he was grateful for the opportunity, graciously acknowledging there were a lot of people who applied for the position who are intelligent, knowledgeable, and every bit as qualified as he.

He had actually been appointed to the bench on June 3, 2022, so he'd already been in the job for a while by the time of his robing ceremony, which was delayed due to the pandemic.

"I think it's been a good fit; I hope everyone else agrees, but I'm very, very happy to be here," he said to a standing ovation of other judges, lawyers, and his friends and family, whom he thanked for their support throughout his life.

Justice Josh Arnold, who presided over Sandeson's first trial, is still a Supreme Court judge.

❖

William Sandeson said in court that his correctional plan was to continue serving his sentence at Cowansville Institution in Quebec. He has been very busy furthering his education since he's been incarcerated.

According to a pre-sentence report, he has completed a paralegal certificate and a master's in business administration from Adams State University in Colorado, and an electrician program from the Stratford Career Institute in Mont-Royal, Quebec. He's also completed the requirements for the Canadian Securities Institute certificate and upgraded his certificate with the National Strength and Conditioning Association, a non-profit association dedicated to advancing sport science professions around the world.

He's also completed multiple programs while in custody, including anger management and Buddhism courses. He's registered for a Transition to College program for inmates and has completed three out of the four modules required. According to a letter of support from his father, he's also learned about Indigenous peoples and cultures through sessions with local elders and smudging ceremonies.

He assists other inmates with their educational goals, and at one point had a landscaping job, which required the highest level of security clearance in the prison.

According to an updated profile on the dating website Canadian Inmates Connect, Sandeson has learned French while in prison and now claims to be bilingual. According to a letter of support before the court, he is also determined to learn Russian so he can communicate with a family from Ukraine his parents are hosting.

"He's never said, 'I'm sorry' yet," said Boutilier.

She's finally packed up all of Taylor's things. For nearly eight years, half of her storage room was piled up with totes full of Taylor's clothes, shoes, and other belongings.

It was time, she said.

She donated everything to the Parker Street Food and Furniture Bank in Halifax.

She says the only thing that will ever bring her any kind of peace is having Taylor's remains. August 15 remains a difficult day. Boutilier likes to gather with Taylor's friends on his birthday, but not on that day. "I want [Connor and I] to do something together, is what I want. I don't want other people around, I just want the two of us," she said.

She visits the memorial at Dalhousie to be near Taylor. And on the eighth anniversary of his death, in 2023, Connor and Linda toured Halifax aboard the Harbour Hopper—an amphibious vehicle with the likeness of a frog.

"Ribbit, Ribbit!" Conner interjected, and they laughed.

Then they went out for pizza. "It was a good day," Boutilier said softly, thinking back. It's important to her that people know who Taylor really was. "I'm tired of hearing about Sandeson the aspiring doctor and Taylor the drug dealer, you know? There were two people doing a drug deal," she said, weeping. "I mean, Taylor was in university, doing physics."

I told her that, at least from my perspective, that didn't seem to be the general narrative in Halifax anymore thanks to her tireless efforts to let people know that Taylor had so many who loved him.

"I hope so; I do," she sobbed. "I keep thinking what life would be like with him here now—how different it would be."

EPILOGUE

Four weeks after he was sentenced to life imprisonment a second time, William Sandeson appealed his conviction again.

In his own handwriting, he outlined the grounds: that the trial judge erred in law by failing to remedy an abuse of process—not granting a stay of proceedings after his private investigator went rogue; and that the trial judge erred by not finding that the search of his apartment breached his Charter rights—issues the court has already dealt with.

Sandeson is again requesting to have the whole case thrown out. If that is—again—unsuccessful, he requests that the evidence obtained from the search of his apartment be thrown out in a third trial.

At the time of our interview, Alison Craig was unsure whether she would be involved in the second appeal because it would primarily be determined by whether Nova Scotia Legal Aid would fund out-of-town council again. But on March 27, 2024, Nova Scotia Legal Aid denied Sandeson any further funding. In a letter to Sandeson, Lee Seshagiri, managing lawyer of Nova Scotia Legal Aid's appeals office, said Sandeson did not qualify financially because his net worth was $174,000—even after he settled the civil suit with Linda Boutilier and Connor Samson, paid the taxes on the Bitcoin money, paid off what was remaining on his student loans, and paid the $19,000 he already owed Nova Scotia Legal Aid from a previous cost-contribution arrangement in 2020. (This is not the total funding provided by Legal Aid.) Seshagiri did not count as debt the $180,000 Sandeson says he owes his mother for helping with his defence.

Sandeson appealed the Legal Aid decision and was denied once again. Then, in May, 2024, he began an application for state-funded counsel under a section of the Criminal Code that says a judge may assign a lawyer to act on behalf of an accused who is party to an appeal where it is in the interest of justice. On July 18, 2024, the Nova Scotia Court of Appeal denied this application, noting that Sandeson had neither established that his debts would prevent him from obtaining counsel for his appeal, nor that he had exhausted all other sources of financial assistance.

Sandeson is still appealing his conviction. In September 2024 he told the court he intends to try again to get assistance from Legal Aid after the civil suit with Linda Boutilier and Connor Samson has been settled, at which point he expects his financial situation to have changed. The court adjourned the matter until January 2025. The supporting documentation for the case now totals more than eleven thousand pages.

A week after Sandeson filed his appeal, the Crown filed a cross-appeal—appealing Sandeson's acquittal on the charge of first-degree murder, on the grounds the judge made mistakes in his instructions to the jury. Court documents state that should the court order another new trial, the Crown would ask that the new trial be on the charge of first-degree murder.

Boutilier says she tries not to worry about whether Sandeson will win another appeal, or whether there might be a third trial. She knows she can't change any outcome and feels William Sandeson has already taken too much from her.

Dean Samson told me how difficult it's been to have to go through the court proceedings "over and over and over."

"I think it took him seven years to come up with a story and now that's what he's gonna stick with, and he's gonna drive us crazy forever," he said.

Kaitlynne Lowe agreed it feels as though the process is never-ending. She's already turning her mind to parole hearings, which could begin in August 2030. "Thinking that there's a world where he could walk the streets again, a world where I'm going to fear my children growing up, it's not that far off," she said.

Six months after he was sentenced the second time, Sandeson tried to get out of prison again—it would be his fifth attempt at bail. He showed up in court on October 26, 2023, representing himself. Standing at the table directly in front of the judge, he seemed nervous.

His parents and brother Adam were in the courtroom. Matthew and David were running late. All of them were again pledging to be sureties. The plan was similar to the ones he'd presented in the past.

He said he'd be in the presence of a surety at all times and was willing to be subjected to constant monitoring by wearing a GPS ankle bracelet. He also proposed to provide police with access to the video cameras installed at the family home.

He was not seeking access to a computer or a cellphone. "I wanted to propose the most restrictive bail plan possible," he told the court.

Then Laurie Sandeson took the stand.

After the usual questions from prosecutor Mark Scott, there was a highly unusual exchange that saw William Sandeson questioning his own mother on the stand.

"Is it possible to put a password on the computer?" he asked her.

"Yes," she replied.

"Would you be willing to?" he asked.

"Yes," she said again.

"And would you keep it away from me?

"Yes," she confirmed.

It was an extraordinary moment in a Canadian courtroom, only possible because Sandeson didn't have a lawyer and was smart enough—or bold enough—to represent himself. He thanked the court for allowing "this unprofessional application." He argued that ensuring public confidence does not equate to a popularity contest—"or in my case, an unpopularity contest."

"I'm thirty-one today and not the person who made the series of terrible decisions at age twenty-two," he concluded.

In his decision, released on October 31, 2023, Justice David Farrar denied Sandeson bail, saying he failed to establish that his detention was not necessary to ensure public safety and public confidence in the administration of justice. "His grounds of appeal, which I consider to be weak, are also relevant to consideration of the public interest," Farrar wrote.

After Sandeson's first conviction, Dalhousie University changed its medical school admissions requirements for the first time in ten years.

In an interview, Dr. Gus Grant, registrar and CEO of the College of Physicians and Surgeons of Nova Scotia, the body that regulates the province's medical profession, said the dean of the Faculty of Medicine asked him to conduct a review of the admissions process. The review committee included a member of the public as well as experts in the fields of medicine, law, diversity, university admissions, and undergraduate medical education.

Grant was quick to point out he doesn't believe the review—which was conducted in the Spring of 2016—was as a direct result of the Sandeson case, but rather to "ensure that the admissions process bolstered the Faculty of Medicine's commitment to service, excellence, and broad considerations of diversity."

But the report states that the committee undertook the review "conscious of recent cases in the public domain involving applicants accepted to Dalhousie's Medical School charged with serious crimes."

Grant confirmed the cases referenced were those of William Sandeson and Stephen Tynes. (Less than a week after Sandeson was arrested in 2015, another Dal med student was arrested after telling a psychiatrist he planned to kill twenty people, including the school's associate dean of undergraduate medical education and her daughter.)

"The publicity associated with these cases has cast a shadow for some on the admissions process," the report continued. "The question arising from the publicity is whether the admissions process takes adequate steps to screen out individuals inappropriate for a career in medicine."

"It would have been disingenuous not to mention it," Grant said in an interview. "Both those cases were very much in the public eye at the time of my generating the report. ...I'd heard a fair number of exasperated murmurings about, 'How did these people get into medical school?'"

He said the admissions process is not an exact science.

"You're making a point-in-time assessment about a young person's ability to succeed over the course of a career in a very challenging field," he said. Acknowledging that scholarly ability is important, his committee was concerned that Dal puts too much emphasis on cognitive power, placing too much weight on grade point averages and MCAT scores.

"The day-to-day success of a doctor, the day-to-day well-being of his or her patients is rarely dependent on the doctor's staggering genius," said Grant. "Success in medical practice is mostly composed of compassion, consistency, empathy, diligence, humility."

The committee also recommended that the Faculty of Medicine review its admissions process every three years. In a statement in January 2024, Janet Bryson, Dalhousie's director of strategic communications, said the Faculty of Medicine reviews its admissions process every year.

"Our admissions process continues to evolve to ensure we are following best practices and meeting the health-care needs of the region," she said.

Over the years, Amherst Regional High has awarded the Taylor Samson Memorial Scholarship—valued at $1,000 per recipient—to five students who demonstrated financial need and intended to study sciences, particularly physics. A portion of the proceeds of both this book and its first iteration, *First Degree*, have been directed to that scholarship fund.

Emma Mattinson received the scholarship in 2021. She was twelve when Samson was murdered, but says she certainly was aware of who he was by the time she graduated from his high school.

"Physics—a lot of people hate it," she laughed, adding that she was passionate about it, scoring above 95 percent in high school. She isn't entirely sure what she'll do when she finishes university, but she wants to help people. "I want to go to work knowing that what I do today is contributing to the rest of the world and that I'm helping society along in some way that's just bigger than myself," she said. She said she used the scholarship money toward her first-year tuition and can't overstate how grateful she is to Samson's family. "I'm very thankful for what they chose to do with all their grief and their emotions—to channel it into a positive light."

Breanna Taylor received the scholarship in 2019. She grew up in Amherst and was fourteen when Samson was killed. She always loved sciences, especially physics. After she got to Dalhousie University, she realized she was more interested in chemistry. Like Mattinson, she wants to work in a field where she can help people, and plans to do a PhD with the goal of working in the pharmaceutical industry. "The dream job would be working at a cancer institute finding new cancer medicines," she said.

She said receiving the scholarship was a huge help for her, but beyond the financial assistance, it was a meaningful gift from Samson's family. For years, she walked by the memorial plaque outside the physics building at Dal on her way to class.

"I'd always take a minute to stop and just think of how grateful I was that I'm able to do this and that Taylor and his family were able to help me get to where I was," she said.

Samson's father, Dean Samson, told me the scholarship in his son's name really means a lot to him. "I guess it'll end up being Taylor's legacy, other than [him] being a nice guy and a wonderful kid."

"To me, this scholarship is about keeping Taylor's memory and achievements alive," said Samson's mother, Linda Boutilier. "Taylor was always about helping others."

NOTE ABOUT SOURCES

This book was written using in-person observations from court proceedings, court audio from William Sandeson's retrial, numerous court documents obtained over a period of nearly a decade, and twenty-six original interviews conducted by the author with the following individuals: Linda Boutilier, Connor Samson, Dean Samson, Karen Burke, Kaitlynne Lowe, Mackenzie Ruthven, Ryan Wilson, Thomas McCrossin, Tanya Bilsbury, Roger Sayer, Derrick Boyd, Jody Allison, Alison Craig, Kim McOnie, Carla Ball, Susan MacKay, Eugene Tan, Brad Sarson, James Goodwin, James Lockyer, Blair Rhodes, Stephen Schneider, Andreas Park, Dr. Gus Grant, Emma Mattinson, and Breanna Taylor.

ACKNOWLEDGEMENTS

In May 2017 I was sitting in courtroom 301 at Nova Scotia Supreme Court live-tweeting William Sandeson's first trial in my role as a local news reporter when an email flashed across my screen. It was from Elaine McCluskey, whom I did not know, asking if I'd like to write a book about the case. She became my first editor.

Elaine, thank you for being the first to recognize the value in this story, and for choosing me to write *First Degree*.

To the editor of *Second Degree*, Angela Mombourquette—thank you for your attention to detail and for understanding the importance of ensuring that this book maintain a journalistic tone.

To the entire team at Nimbus Publishing, especially Whitney Moran and Terrilee Bulger, thanks for your continued support of my work and that of so many Atlantic Canadian authors.

To my employer—the Canadian Broadcasting Corporation—thank you for supporting this work. Thanks specifically to my boss, Lianne Elliott, who helped ensure it meets the rigorous journalistic standards Canadians expect, and whose management style is such that she looks for ways to say "yes" when it would almost certainly be easier to say "no."

To Jennifer Stairs at the Nova Scotia Judiciary, thank you for your patience, assistance, and commitment to facilitating the rights of journalists to access court proceedings.

To Chris Hansen at the Nova Scotia Public Prosecution Service, thanks for seeing the value in the work of journalists...and for arranging the Triple Crown!

To my colleague, Blair Rhodes, thanks for your participation in this project. But even more, thanks for all the newsroom chats and your insights on all things court and crime.

To Eric Woolliscroft, my video producer of the last seven years—thanks for always asking about this book and understanding when I had to prioritize it. I have been so grateful to learn from you. Happy retirement!

To my friend Amanda Hiscock, who is a whip-smart Newfoundland lawyer with an extraordinary passion for the administration of justice—thanks for reading early versions of this work and for always pointing me to the relevant case law.

To my childhood friend Katie Malone, thanks for your interest and for listening to me talk about this book ad nauseam. I expect you know more about journalism than any non-journalist should!

To Julie Caswell, who believed in this story, and in me, when many did not. Thanks for reading early versions, and for your continued enthusiastic support over the years.

To Steve Murphy, thanks for your notes. There has been no greater influence on my journalism and on my career than yours.

To Connor Samson—thanks for trusting me.

To Linda Boutilier—thanks for everything. I still remember when I told you there would be parts of the first book you might not like to read. "That's okay," you said. "I know if you write it, it will be fair." When I asked if you were up for a second edition, you said, "For you, anything." I have done my very best to be fair. I hope you now get a chance to live as you've told me Taylor would have wanted.

To my own mom and dad—thanks for raising Jordan and me in a way that gave me the courage to take on this project. You have always encouraged and never doubted me—even when I quit my job to write a book!